St John A. Robilli

Religion and the law

Religious liberty in modern English law

Manchester University Press

Copyright © St John Anthony Robilliard 1984

Published by
Manchester University Press,
Oxford Road, Manchester M13 9PL, UK
51 Washington Street, Dover, N.H. 03820, USA

British Library cataloguing in publication data

Robilliard, St. John A.
  Religious liberty and the law.
  1. Religious tolerance — Great Britain
  I. Title
  291.1'772   BR1610

ISBN 0-7190-0956-1

Library of Congress cataloging in publication data
applied for

Printed in Great Britain by
Butler & Tanner Ltd, Frome and London

Religion and the law

Contents

	Introduction	ix
1	General protections of religious belief	1
	Racial and religious discrimination	1
	Incitement to religious hatred (Northern Ireland)	7
	Seditious libels and utterances	8
	Defamatory libel	10
	International standards	11
	The protection of churches and ministers	15
2	Blasphemy	25
	Historical background	25
	Blasphemy in recent times	29
	Aftermath of 'Gay News' — a future for a law of blasphemy?	36
3	Sunday laws	46
	Introduction	46
	Sunday entertainment	48
	Sunday trading	50
	Sunday employment	53
	The future of Sunday legislation	53
4	Charitable status, taxation advantages and related matters	59
	Advancement of religion — the advantages	59
	Definition of religion in the law of charities	61
	Advancement of religion	63
	Religion and politics	65
	The Charity Commissioners	66
	Taxation	68
	Giving — certainty and public policy	73
	Giving and taking back — the doctrine of undue influence	75

5	The constitutional position of the Church of England	84
	Church, Parliament and Crown	85
	Figure 1: the government of the Church of England	86
	Church in Parliament	90
	The financial position	92
	The ecclesiastical courts	92
	Figure 2: courts set up under the Ecclesiastical Jurisdiction Measure 1963	96
	Principal duties owed by the Church	98
6	Freedom of movement; freedom of association	104
	(1) Freedom of movement	104
	Moral Rearmament	105
	Scientology	106
	The Unification Church	110
	(2) Freedom of association	111
7	Clashing with the criminal law	117
	Witchcraft and spiritualism	117
	False prophets and pious frauds	119
	The Senior approach	120
	Some solutions	123
	Extreme religious belief	126
8	Prisons and the armed services	132
	Prisons	132
	Military service	137
9	Religion, medicine and the law	142
	General observations	142
	Minority medical beliefs — Christian Science	144
	Abortion	145
10	Public education	150
	The duty of the local education authority	152
	The agreed syllabus	153
	The daily act of worship	157
	The right to withdraw	158
	Teachers	159
	The clergy in schools	162
	Race Relations Act 1976	162
	The future of religion as a compulsory element in schools	163

11 The workplace	169
In general	169
Northern Ireland	172
Religious objection to the closed shop	174
Clergymen and ministers of religion	178
12 Family matters	183
Parental wishes at common law	183
The favouring of Christianity	185
The change to the child's welfare	186
Judicial support of religious upbringing	186
Welfare and religion in disputes about children	187
'Christian' marriage and polygamy	190
Forms of marriage and religion	193
Religious duress and marriage	193
Divorce	194
Appendix: Principal moves towards religious toleration in the nineteenth century	199
Table of statutes	205
Table of statutory instruments	209
Table of Church of England Measures	210
Table of international covenants	211
Table of cases	212
Index	220

Introduction

'Religious liberty and religious equality are complete,' wrote Maitland[1] at the beginning of our century, but this is a statement which commented merely upon the repeal of the old penal laws[2] which had made a crime of belief, or some forms of disbelief. The early story of the struggle for religious liberty is of sects establishing an identity of their own, with their members being freed from the obligation of supporting a faith they did not hold. From the struggle for existence we pass to the struggle for equality, in many important fields, with the established Church. The traditionalists have tended to think that these two developments suffice to give us religious liberty. They would perhaps equate religious liberty with religious toleration in the sense advanced by Gladstone:

[Religious toleration requires] that civil penalty or prohibition be not employed to punish or to preclude a man's acting on his own religious opinions ... it requires that no privilege or benefit which a person is capable of receiving rightly and of using beneficially be withheld from him on account of his religious opinions as such.[3]

Gladstone supported toleration because it meant that: conscience should not be prejudiced by threat of material disadvantage; the evil of vesting absolute power in one ecclesiastical establishment was avoided and true religion would grow in strength, its foundation deriving from conviction rather than coercion. A view of religious liberty thus expressed today raises two fundamentals. There are many who whilst advocating religious liberty deny it to a particular group by not regarding that group as a religion. As religious groups are often entitled to privileges above other lawful groups, such as attitude could be considered a mark of intolerance. In England, compared with the United States of America, an attitude of that sort is more likely. This is because in the United States religion was considered to be far too important a matter for the state's attention.[4] Constitutional guarantees meant that the courts strove, and indeed strive, to achieve 'impartiality as among all religions and irreligions'. Religious liberty in Britain, having a different starting point, has suffered many constraints in the past, but how different the results are in practice today is a matter of debate. Moreover, it is arguable that what the American constitution provides as a matter of law is found in Britain as a matter of convention, in the broadest sense of that term.

The other limitations on religious liberty in its traditional sense are 'paramount social concerns' — those laws that will not give way to religious liberty.

Since the time of Maitland a new and compelling reason has developed for an examination of religious liberty, namely the human rights movement. Seeing freedom of religion as a basic human right, this movement impells us to look at religious liberty as something wider than merely being restricted to 'liberty of conscience or inner Christian liberty or liberty to worship'.[5] The movement finds a more concrete form of expression in such materials of legal importance as the European Convention on Human Rights and Fundamental Freedoms and encourages us to consider the legal position of such a right. Coupled with the human rights argument there is also a theological one — if man's understanding of the ultimate is not perfect he must have a society which allows him to get somewhat closer to that goal by passing along his own path.[6]

As law in society provides protection for those who wish peacefully to follow their chosen (lawful) life style, there can be no religious liberty in a state that refuses to act when powerful groups aim to suppress what they do not like. Law must provide good soil in which the flower of religious liberty can bloom, and so there must be some protection from verbal attacks and false propaganda. Such protection is not easy to provide, as the state must walk a tightrope between seeming to interfere with freedom of speech on the one hand and protecting its citizens' religious feelings on the other. (Indeed, religious feelings may provoke such attacks.) State protection may be quite positive, with certain facilities being provided for the advancement of religion. This may involve, for example, special fiscal laws and may even lead to the prohibition of activities which interfere with religious observances (e.g. Sunday restrictions), although it may be felt that very great justification indeed is needed for the law to travel this far.

Where the state is not actively protecting and advancing religion it has to coexist with it, and this may lead to conflict. The resolution of such conflicts depends on the importance given to religous liberty by a society and this will depend on the reasons behind its advancement. Thus in the context of whether a state, in this case that of Ontario (Canada), should consider the suppression of religious groups David N. Weisstub has written:

> There are two fundamentally divergent perspectives on religious liberty. ...in the name of 'police power' it is asserted that the state has the right to interfere with any or all of its citizens' activities even if they only endanger the individual. On the other side is the belief that the social order is founded on individual liberty. In this perspective society represents a combination of individuals who, in their individuality, possess natural and inherent rights, that precede any social organisation. From this vantage point, social organisation is provided to ensure that natural rights of freedom of belief and action will not be violated.[7]

The state may be found enforcing a course of action which is in direct opposition to the beliefs and practices of a religious group (e.g. Sikhs and crash helmets) or it may be called upon to arbitrate in such areas as family law and employment relationships.

Religious practices may be accorded great consideration, but can they ever outweigh legal duty? The conflict becomes the more likely the more religious liberty is seen as a full-blooded human right rather than merely a matter of toleration. Religious conscience is surely the father of religious observance, but how will the state react when such observance is contrary to its policy? Even a state that shouts about religious liberty from the rooftops will find itself in difficulty if it also shouts about other freedoms which conflict with religious liberty, and is moreover the advocate of many social policies. In the absence of any clear landmark for the courts, such as a Bill of Rights, it is likely that the legal results of such conflicts will be somewhat confused — a confusion which may be added to where the judge takes a restrictive view of the liberty (toleration) or an expansive one (full human right). It may be concluded that such instruments as the European Convention are changing the climate of thought in this area and even those who believe that our domestic system is not in need of such drastic surgery as a Bill of Rights will generally be seen wishing to present that system in the best possible light.

Notes

1. Quoted in the foreword to C.E. Crowther, *Religious Trusts*, 1954.
2. See the Appendix.
3. Quoted in A.R. Vidler, *The Orb and the Cross*, 1945, pp. 117–18.

4. Editorial, *Journal of Church and State*, VIII, 1967, 333, at p. 334.
5. T. Lorenzen, 'The theological basis for religious liberty: a Christian perspective', *Journal of Church and State*, XX, 1979, 415, at p. 425.
6. Lorenzen, 'Theological basis', at p. 428.
7. *The Legal Regulation of Cults: a Policy Analysis*, 1980, pp. 632–3.

1 General protections of religious belief

If the Minister of State is still prepared to argue that we do not need the word 'religious' in the Bill, what other remedy will a person have if he finds himself being persecuted, discriminated against, or otherwise maltreated on the grounds of religion? This is a matter of great importance.

[*per* David Lane, M.P., Standing Committee on the Race Relations Bill, 29 April 1976, H.C. Deb. (1975–6), s.c.A, col. 109].

Racial and religious discrimination

The orthodox view has always been that the common law should not prevent a man from discriminating in any way that he may think fit,[1] with the rather minor exception that applies to innkeepers,[2] and this principle has never been altered with regard to acts of religious discrimination within the United Kingdom[3] (Northern Ireland apart). Thus where what appears, or claims, to be a religion encounters hostility for its beliefs and practices, supposed or otherwise — for example the Scientologists who in the 1960s[4] were refused such things as motor insurance, hotel hirings, and central and local government grants[5] — they will be without legal redress. Despite this general principle there has been much discussion as to whether the Race Relations Act of 1976 can affect cases of religious discrimination through the 'indirect discrimination' provisions. Before 1976 it was clear that the previous race relations legislation did not enter into the sphere of religion — in *Ealing London Borough Council* v *Race Relations Board*[6] three members of the House of Lords expressly stated that the words, 'colour, race or ethnic or national origins' did not include discrimination on the grounds of religion,[7] Lord Kilbrandon's justification for this opinion being as follows:

Turning to section 1, we see no provision is made for the prevention of discrimination in the extremely sensitive fields of religion and politics, a refusal (at least by a private landlord) to house Roman Catholics or Communists as classes would not offend against the Act. ... The forbidden grounds are 'colour, race or ethnic or national origins'. These characteristics seem to have something in common: they have not been acquired, and they are not held by people of their own choice. They are in the nature of inherited features which cannot be changed, as religion, politics and nationality can be changed, more or less at will.

However, the new concept of indirect racial discrimination may have changed this dictum with regard to those religions that are identifiable with particular racial groups. That this would be the effect of the new provision was first foreseen by the Minister of State for the Home Office during the committee stage of the 1976 Race Relations Bill:[8]

The Bill's new concept, that of indirect discrimination, does a great deal to protect those who are discriminated against by reason of their religious observance or otherwise. As I have said, where it impinges upon race relations Clause (1(1)(b)(i) provides a great deal more protection than Hon. Members seem to think.[9] ... Let me give some practical examples of what I mean. It is perfectly possible to lay down what is in law notionally equal treatment, such as that all men who are employed as chauffeurs by a particular company should wear a peaked cap. That obviously would, by its very nature, discriminate against a proportion of persons of the Sikh religion because their chances of complying with that requirement would be considerably smaller than those persons not of that particular religious group. The onus is then thrown on the employer — and here we come back to my Hon. Friend's point about 'justifiable' or not — to say that the restriction with which the Sikhs cannot comply is justifiable.[10] ... [Take the] employer who wanted to limit Hindu workers to one shift and Muslim workers to another. He said that of course this was discrimination on religious grounds and would therefore be outside the scope of the Bill. In my view and that of the Government, this would be caught by the concept of indirect discrimination, because it would manifestly — whether one takes the Hindu[11] or the Muslim[12] side of it — constitute (unlawful) discrimination against the particular group.[13]

On the other hand, David Lane, M.P., who later became Chairman of the Commission for Racial Equality, did not think that this new concept could either assist Jews from being discriminated against on religious grounds[14] or prevent Catholics and Protestants from discriminating against each other in Liverpool or in Glasgow.[15]

The assumption that discrimination against Sikhs, with regard to the wearing of beards, is covered by this law was briefly made by the Employment Appeal Tribunal in 1979,[16] and in 1980 Lord Denning M.R., sitting in the Court of Appeal,[17] appeared to accept that racially based religions are covered by 'indirect discrimination'.[18] Although other courts have preferred to approach the problem by regarding the

Sikhs as a religious group outside the protection of the Act,[19] in *Kingstone and Richmond Area Health Authority* v *Kaur*[20] the Employment Appeal Tribunal held that where a nurse's uniform was laid down by a Statutory Instrument the Health Authority was justified in refusing to allow a Sikh girl permission to wear trousers under it. Miss Kaur was, in the end, successful, as the result of her action brought a change of heart within the Health Authority and they resolved[21] that where an applicant was unable to comply with a uniform requirement because of cultural or religious reasons the individual's request would be 'considered sympathetically'. Sensible changes by employers such as this one will be objected to by no one.[22]

The comments quoted earlier in this section occurred during a debate on an amendment to add the word 'religion' to the Bill. Most of the support for this proposal came from those who thought it was somewhat untidy to leave it out. However, the Government was not minded to include it expressly as the committee were dealing with a Race Relations Bill, and, in their view, intermixed racial–religious discrimination was in any case covered by it. Other members of the Committee objected to including 'religion' because:

(1) if there was a real problem it should be dealt with by a separate bill;[23]
(2) if 'religion' were to be included in the Bill many new exceptions would have to be enacted[24] — indeed the whole emphasis of the legislation could shift through such a move;[25] and
(3) no religious group had been consulted about such a change in the law.[26]

One may wonder why these points did not apply to the types of religious discrimination that the Minister explained would in future be outlawed.

The decision of the House of Lords in *Mandla* v *Lee*,[27] may prove one of the most important cases decided on religious liberty in the last decade. An independent school admitted pupils from all different racial groups but insisted that a school uniform be worn and that boys' hair be kept short. It did this as it did not wish to emphasise racial and cultural differences and, being a school run on Christian principles, it objected to such things as Sikh's turbans which were regarded as non-Christian symbols. In the Court of Appeal the sole question of importance was whether the 'ethnic origins' of the Sikhs meant that they were a group protected by the Race Relations Act 1976 — all three members of the Court were unanimous — they were not. Lord Denning considered that 'ethnic' meant, in effect, a sub-racial group[28] which had probably been placed in the Act to make clear that the Jews were covered by it. Oliver L.J. felt that,

'What is embraced in that expression, to my mind, is the notion of a group distinguished by some peculiarity of birth, perhaps as a result of inter-marriage within a community, but lacking any element of freewill. It seems to me entirely inappropriate to describe a group into and out of which anyone may travel as a matter of free choice; and freedom of choice — to join or not to join, to remain or to leave — is inherent in the whole philosophy of Sikhism.'[29] Kerr L.J.[30] stated that ethnic meant something 'pertaining or peculiar to race' and, like the other members of the court concluded that the history and characteristic of the Sikhs meant that they fell outside that definition. The attitude of the Court of Appeal may be sumed up as one of cautious conservatism. It is also of interest to note that the no-turban rule had been produced here not as a rule to keep those with brown skins out (as has sometimes been the case in the past with, for example, clubs) but rather to accord with the sincerely held religious views of a headmaster of an independent school. Outside the confines of a courtroom, however, an authoritative ruling that the Sikhs fell outside the race relations legislation could be seen as an invitation to practice discrimination lawfully against a group which, unlike most religious groups in the country, were likely, because of their distinguishing features, to suffer real hardship as a result.[31]

The House of Lords, seemingly not concerned with the criminal law aspects of the matter as they had been in a previous decision on the 1968 Race Relations Act,[32] were prepared to take a broader view of the term 'ethnic'. The principal judgement came from Lord Frazer of Tullybelton, who noted[33] that over this century the word 'ethnic' had been developing a wider meaning than merely that of pertaining to race. On the other hand it did not include any group which simply shared some common racial or cultural or religious or linguistic characteristics. He stressed that the 1976 Act will not apply to religious groups as such but felt the true approach was that while 'ethnic still retained a racial flavour it is used nowadays in an extended sense to include other characteristics which may be commonly thought of as being associated with common racial origin'.[34] He provided two 'essential factors' which a group must show if it is to be considered 'ethnic':

(1) a long shared history, of which the group is conscious as distinguishing it from other groups, and the memory of which it keeps alive;
(2) a cultural tradition of its own, including family and social customs and manners, often but not necessarily associated with religious observance.

In addition he thought that there were additional factors which, although not crucial, were relevant:

(1) either a common geographical origin, or descent from a small number of common ancestors;
(2) a common language, not necessarily peculiar to the group;
(3) a common literature peculiar to the group;
(4) a common religion different from that of neighbouring groups or from the general community surrounding it;
(5) being a minority or being an oppressed or a dominant group.[35]

It is possible to become a member of such a group as well as being a member of it by virtue of one's birth. He then considered the history of the Sikhs and held that they were a racial group, because of their ethnic origin, and thus came under the protection of the race relations legislation.

What other religions will be covered? The answer is not clear, although Lord Fraser did stress that a religious group as such were outside the Act. Perhaps it is easier to say what lies outside rather than in. World religions as such would seem to lie outside because of their universality, although where a particular group, although belonging to a universal religion, have enjoyed a destinctive history of their own they may come within the bounds of the definition — thus Roman Catholics and Muslims as such are outside the definition whilst for historical reasons certain groups of Catholics and Muslims may fall within. Strange results indeed may result. The religious customs of a Muslim from Saudi Arabia may be protected not because he is a Muslim (universal religion) but because of his ethnic origins of which Muslim customs are a manifestation. However, the Muslim observances of a English convert to that religion would not seem to be covered, as Muslim customs are not equated with Englishmen because of their ethnic origins — Islam, being universal, is not identified with one particular area or people (as is the case with Sikhism) so as to be an 'ethnic' group under *Mandla* v. *Lee*. Another class of religions which are clearly outside the definition are the 'new religions' (e.g. the 'Moonies') for the obvious reason that they have not been in existence long enough in order to show that they have 'a long shared history'. Perhaps this is as far as one can be certain — the Sikhs are covered by the law and the clear implication of the case is that the Jews are as well.[36] Future court decisions will have to be awaited for other religions although some of the other ramifications of the case may mean a fairly cautious approach will need to be adopted.

Given that Sikhs were covered by the law had there been unlawful discrimination here? Was the 'no turban' rule a rule which a considerably smaller proportion of Sikhs could comply with[37] than members of other groups. In the Court of Appeal Keir L.J. took the line that with the exception of nationality all of the elements which constituted racial groups for the purpose of the law were based on factors which the individual had no control over (i.e. birth rather than choice) and thus 'can comply' was to be understood in the sense of 'is factually able to comply'.[38] If this was correct none of the cases where beards or turbans were worn for religious reasons came under the ambit of the law as there is always clearly some choice involved in the wearing of such things. However the House of Lords, in keeping with the wider meaning that they had given to 'ethnic', felt that the test was: ' "can in practice" or "can consistently with the customs and cultural conditions of the racial group" '[39] comply.

Under the Race Relations Act even if you have applied such a condition you will not be guilty of unlawful racial discrimination if you can show that the use of the condition was justified 'irrespective of the colour, race, nationality or ethnic or national origins of the person to whom it applied'. Can a religious objection satisfy this? Lord Fraser considered that this was a serious matter:

[the defendant] objected to the turban on the grounds that it was an outward manifestation of a non-Christian faith. Indeed he regarded it as amounting to a challenge to that faith. I have much sympathy with the respondent on this part of the case and I would have been glad to find that the rule was justifiable within the meaning of the statute, if I could have done so. But in my opinion that is impossible. The onus ... is on the respondent to show that the condition which he seeks to apply is not indeed a necessary condition, but that it is in other circumstances justifiable "irrespective of the colour, race, nationality or ethnic or national origins of the person to whom it is applied", that is to say that it is justifiable without regard to the ethnic origins of that person. But in this case the principal justification on which the respondent relies is that the turban is objectionable just because it is a manifestation of the second appellants' ethnic origins. That is not, in my view, a justification which is admissable ...[40]

This finding is the most difficult part of the decision. The result is that the present law clearly favours the religious customs of one (the Sikh father) to those of another (the Christian headmaster). The freedom to run independent schools following the religious views of one particular religious group is clearly undermined if the law prevents such schools from imposing the customs of their religion. One may only hope that this part of the decision is reconsidered either by the House of Lords or by Parliament in the light of the traditional tolerance given to freedom of religious association. Although the law has never been understood to allow racial discrimination because of religious beliefs that is no reason to forbid what is in effect religious preference for certain religious rules. The Court of Appeal were advancing a very important point with their 'freedom of choice' approach to the question, while the House of Lords have chosen to make some freedoms of choice greater than others.

Incitement to religious hatred (Northern Ireland)

There is no general United Kingdom law against incitement to religious hatred — thus an attempt to extend what was to become the prohibition in the 1936 Public Order Act of the use of insulting words or behaviour in certain circumstances to the incitement of racial or *religious* prejudice failed,[41] and the crime of incitement of racial hatred, created by the 1965 Race Relations Act, does not apply to the incitement of religious hatred. However, to deal with the very real problem of religious hatred and public disorder in Northern Ireland[42] a special statute[43] was enacted, going much further than the common law. In passing it may be noted that this is within the legislative tradition of Northern Ireland.[44] Under the Act it is an offence if a person, with intent to stir up hatred against, or arouse fear of, any section of the public in Northern Ireland:

(*a*) publishes or distributes written or other matter which is threatening, abusive or insulting, or
(*b*) uses words of a similar nature in any public place or in any public meeting,

if the words are likely to have that effect on any section of the public in Northern Ireland on grounds of religious belief, colour, race or ethnic or national origins.[45] By dealing with incitement to fear it goes further than similar United Kingdom legislation prohibiting incitement to racial hatred.[46] It is enough if the motive behind the incitement is based upon religious grounds; there is no need for the defendant to rant against a defined religious group — an attack on bank managers, by a religion objecting to usury, could in theory constitute the crime.[47] A further offence is the spreading, with the intention of causing a breach of the peace, of a statement or report which the defendant knows to be false, or does not believe to be true, if it is likely to stir up hatred against, or arouse fear of, any section of the public in Northern Ireland on grounds of religious belief, colour, race or ethnic or national origins.[48] Here the defendant need only intend a breach of the peace, he does not have to stir up hatred. The moral may be that one should think carefully before expressing views about religions, especially those other than one's own, in Northern Ireland.[49]

Seditious libels and utterances

Sedition, as now constituted, consists of the intentional oral or written publication of words of a seditious nature with an intention to cause violence through that publication.[50] Most forms of sedition were seen as attempts to disturb the Government in some way, but there emerge two kinds from the classic definition of Stephen J.,[51] which are of importance in considering the legal protection of religious belief:

> A seditious intention is an intention to bring in hatred or contempt, or to excite disaffection against ... any matter in Church ... by law established ... or to promote feelings of ill-will and hostility between different classes of such subjects ... [provided that] to excite Her Majesty's subjects to attempt by lawful means the alteration of any matter in Church or State by law established, or to point out, in order to secure their removal, matters which are producing, or have a tendency to produce, feelings of hatred and ill-will between classes of Her Majesty's subjects, is not a seditious intention.

The protection of the established Church is not surprising in such an historic offence[52] and may be briefly alluded to — in the seventeenth century an attack on James II's religious policies in the Army resulted in a prosecution for denying the authority of the King.[53] One hundred and fifty years later, in 1822, the comments of one Williams on the hostility shown by the Durham clergy towards the late, and unfortunate, Queen Caroline, resulted in his prosecution,[54] with Wood B. finding that an attack on either the clergy of one county or the clergy of the entire country, 'for the purpose of bringing into hatred and contempt any of the establishments of the country ... is a libel, and ought to be punished'.[55]

Non-established religions would be protected where the assault upon them led, or was likely to lead, to civil disturbance. Thus in the old case of *R v Dammaree and Purchase*[56] the defendants were convicted of levying war against the Crown (High Treason) having attacked, pulled down and burnt the meeting houses of some Protestant dissenters. The words of Parker C.J. in that case are still worth quoting today:[57]

> there being a law that allows them the liberty of serving God in their own way; since that liberty is allowed them, why should anybody be concerned that they enjoy it? ... to demolish meeting-houses, and to raise seditions and riots, which are not to be borne in a civilised country; for nobody knows where popular tumults will end.

In 1732 Parliament was considering a change in the law with regard to the Jews when a bigot named Osborn falsely charged a group of Portuguese Jews with having burnt a bastard child, the offspring of a Christian and a Jew. Lord Raymond C.J. allowed the prosecution to be brought because the whole community of Jews had been struck at by the words.[58] Similar charges were levied against Jews over two hundred years later in *R v Leese*[59] where the Jewish ritual slaughter of cattle was linked with a number of unsolved deaths of young children. Arnold Leese, a British Fascist who expressed 'great admiration' for Julius Streicher,[60] was acquitted of seditious libel but convicted of effecting a public mischief.[61] The last prosecution of this type also ended in acquittal. In *R v Caunt*[62] the editor of the *Morecambe and Heysham Visitor* had attacked Zionists after two British Army sergeants had been murdered in Palestine. The offending editorial had rejoiced in the fact that so few Jews lived in the borough and concluded, 'If British Jewry is suffering today from the righteous wrath of British citizens, then they have only themselves to blame for their passive inactivity. Violence may be the only way to bring them to the sense of their responsibility to the country in which they live.' In his summing-up to the jury Birkett J.[63] stressed the importance of the liberty of the press and said that the jury should only convict if they thought that Caunt had published the libel with the intention of promoting violence by stirring up hostility and ill-will between different classes. In stating that the defendant must intend violence to take place he was not following the stricter objective test that had been laid down by a judge at first instance earlier in the century.[64] Caunt was acquitted, possibly because there were so few Jews living in the area in which the newspaper circulated — thus making actual violence there unlikely.

Under the law of sedition a prosecution will only be contemplated in the most extreme of circumstances. Some instances of inflammatory remarks about religion may fall foul of more modern statutory offences such as incitement to racial hatred[65] or the use of threatening, abusive or insulting words or behaviour in public.[66] These modern offences do leave gaps, for example a private meeting where hatred is stirred up against Roman Catholics. However if the recently expressed view of the Law Commission proves to be correct the law of sedition is not now available, even in legal theory, to plug such gaps. The Commission seriously doubts whether the modern law of sedition extends beyond the protection of the state and its organs.[67] This view is based on the 1951 Canadian case of *Boucher v R*[68] where a Jehovah's Witness pamphlet blackened the police, public officials and the Roman Catholic clergy for using their authority against that sect. The Court held that the law of sedition now only punished the incitement of violence for the purpose of disturbing constituted authority. Despite this it must be admitted that there is English authority illustrating the possibility of a charge of sedition where there has been incitement of religious hatred, although general consideration for freedom of speech coupled with dislike for the archaic connotations that 'sedition' evokes require that it be a most extreme case.

Defamatory libel

A defamatory remark about a religion as such has not been considered actionable[69] in the past and indeed Parliamentary attempts in 1952 to extend what was to become the Defamation Act 1952 to groups 'distinguished by race, *creed* or colour' met with failure.[70] Despite this there have been recent attempts by some of the more controversial modern religious cults to invoke the law on the ground that the relevant attack is also an attack on particular individuals because of their close associations with the group. Thus when a series of *Daily Mail* newspaper articles accused the 'Moonies' of brainwashing their young adherents, the leader of that cult in Britain was able to invoke the law because he must have known of the cult's activities, so the general attack on the Moonies must also have been an attack on him — thus he was possibly defamed by warrant of his position.[71] This trend perhaps started with the Scientologists, who pursued a large number of actions against those who had criticised their activities,[72] including one against the Member of Parliament in whose constituency their headquarters was situated.[73]

This stretching, albeit without a great deal of ultimate success at present, of a law designed to protect the reputations of *individuals* in an area where free speech and the right to criticise must be of the utmost importance raises the following fundamental questions.

First, should rich and powerful institutions be able to invoke the law in what is nominally an action brought by a private individual.[74]

Secondly, if it is thought right to protect religious belief from offensive remarks should not Parliament expressly deal with the matter? If thought desirable this could be done by the use of a group libel law[75] which would have the advantage of striking at the very thing complained of — the attack on the group as such. Damages could then be awarded in order to take into account such things as loss of potential membership through, say, resultant hostile Governmental action.[76] It might also make it easier for the group to clear its name.

Thirdly, another danger at present is the possibility that the ground that has been won already could be basis of an invocation of the law of criminal libel,[77] a charge which lies where there is some sufficient threat to the public domain or where the public peace is endangered.[78]

Finally, the use of the civil law in this area must always be seen as a potential two-edged sword. In the Moonie case the *Daily Mail*'s accusations received authentication and endorsement from the jury's verdict,[79] which not only led to a vast amount of adverse publicity for the sect[80] but also resulted in Parliamentary moves against them.[81]

International standards

The protection of religious freedom in general is a common feature in many national Bills of Rights.[82] Britain does not have such a guarantee of protection for human rights but it does adhere to a number of international covenants, the most significant for present purposes being the European Convention on Human Rights, in particular Article 9, which states:

(1) Everyone has the right to freedom of thought, conscience and religion; this right includes freedom to change his religion or belief and freedom, either alone or in community with others and in public or private, to manifest his religion or belief, in worship, teaching, practice and observance.
(2) Freedom to manifest one's religion or beliefs shall be subject only to such limitations as are prescribed by law and are necessary in a democratic society in the interests of public order, health or morals, or for the protection of the rights and freedoms of others.

Article 14 provides that all of the rights under the Convention, e.g. the right to a fair trial,[83] privacy,[84] freedom of expression,[85] freedom of speech and of peaceful assembly,[86] and to raise a family,[87] shall be guaranteed to all equally without religious discrimination.

Should an applicant consider that the United Kingdom is in breach of these obligations he can take the Government before the European Commission on Human Rights which may, if no other solution proves to be forthcoming, bring the United Kingdom before the European Court of Human Rights.[88] If the Court holds the relevant British law to be in breach of the Convention the country will be under an international obligation to change its law. This is a long-drawn-out process, so what is the position where an applicant attempts merely to rely on the Convention in an English Court? As will be seen shortly the Convention, in itself, is not seen directly as a source of law but is nevertheless influential in a number of ways:[89] it is presumed that Parliament does not breach its intentional obligations and thus statutes passed after Britain's adherence to the Convention will be read with this presumption in mind; the Convention in any case is evidence of what Britain thought to be basic human rights after the end of the Second World War and may thus be of use in interpreting the common law and pre-Convention statutes; the Convention may have a special effect on Common Market law directly applicable under the European Communities Act 1972, as the European Court recognises the Convention as part of E.E.C. law; and, finally, now that Parliament has come to change law as the result of decisions in the European Human Rights Court (e.g. contempt of court) statutes passed for this reason will, through the 'mischief rule', be read in the light of the Convention.

That the Convention is not a direct source of law is illustrated by *Ahmad* v *Inner London Education Authority*,[90] where Lord Denning,[91] with Orr L.J. agreeing, stated that although the Convention is not part of English law the courts may 'pay regard' to it where relevant. A stronger approach was made in the dissenting judgment of Scarman L.J.,[92] who felt that the Convention could always be employed as an aid to the interpretation of statutes.[93] In *Ostreicher* v *Secretary of State for the Environment*[94] any objector to a compulsory purchase order had the right to attend a public inquiry before such an order was confirmed. Three weeks before the day that had been chosen for the inquiry the applicant, a Chassidic Jewess, wrote saying that she had strong religious objections to attending on that particular day. This was considered to be a serious objection but it had to be balanced against the inconvenience that would be caused by changing the date for the hearing at that late stage. Things may have been different had she made her objections known earlier. Without special knowledge the Minister could not be under a duty to anticipate that some religious sect might object to the day that he had in mind. The judge[95] did not feel that Article 9 applied in such a case and criticised its indistinct nature. Lord Denning made a similar point in *Ahmad*: 'But it is drawn in such vague terms that it can be used for all sorts of unreasonable claims and provoke all sorts of litigation.' The Court of the European Communities has reached a similar conclusion about Article 9, in *Vivien Prais* v *Council of the European Communities*,[96] when considering a refusal to change the date of a civil service examination where the chosen day was objected to on religious grounds. These cases not only confirm that, as yet, the Convention is not directly applicable in our law but also show that the width and generality of Article 9 is considered a drawback in dealing with particular problems in the 'workaday' world.

The findings of the European organs on Article 9 show that the liberty provided by 9(1) is a right to be allowed to enjoy one's religion rather than a right requiring positive state action in order to advance the religious interests of individuals. So the state is under no duty to provide religious books for those in prison[97] and the state may, under 9(2), interfere with religious observances when that is in the public interest. Such justifiable interference has included: not allowing a prisoner his 'religious aids' when it is in the interests of prison discipline to keep them from him;[98] dairy farmers being required to become members of a Health Service, in spite of their religious objections, in the interests of the public health of the nation;[99] and the compulsion of a religious objector to contribute, against his will, to an insurance scheme which benefited motor accident cases.[100] It has also been stated that where a person is being lawfully held, awaiting trial, his religious rights are necessarily restricted.[101] Finally, a Jehovah's Witness conscientious objector in West Germany in the 1960s met with little success;[102] he had claimed (1) a right of conscientious objection under the Convention and (2) that he was being discriminated against as ministers of certain religions were exempted from substituted service; both claims were rejected, the first because of an exception to Article 4 and the second because his part-time activities were not the same as those of a full-time minister of religion[103] and thus he was not being discriminated against as he was not comparing like with like. Perhaps after reviewing such results it is not so surprising that Professor Jacobs[104] should write that '... taken together these decisions give the impression that the Commission is somewhat unsympathetic to complaints of interference with religious freedom'.

This section is not complete without mentioning the United Nations' Universal Declaration of Human Rights (1948) which for our purposes must be thought of as more of a moral than a legal exhortation:

Everyone has the right to freedom of thought, conscience and religion; this right includes freedom to change his religion or belief; and freedom, either alone or in community with others and in public or private, to manifest his religion or belief in teaching, practice, worship and observance. [Article 18]

In 1969 the United Nations prepared a draft convention for the elimination of all forms of religious intolerance (it covers atheism as well) which would prohibit any interference with religious adherence, religious worship, teaching, religious dietary practices, pilgrimages and so on. Parents would have the right to bring their children up in the religion of their choice provided that they were not reared in an intolerant manner.[105] The state should ensure that its benefits are enjoyed without religious discrimination. Religious discrimination performed by individuals would be outlawed, as would acts of incitement to religious hatred. All of these rights could be limited, '... as [is] necessary to protect public safety, order, health or morals or the individual rights and freedoms of others, or the general welfare in a democratic society'. This Convention has not been adopted and a new one may now be produced. Article 18 of the Universal Declaration of Human Rights covers generally what is now being spelt out.

In 1976 the Covenant on Civil and Political Rights came into force. As well as a general guarantee of religious freedom, subject to the proviso also found in Article 9 of the European Convention, it provides that:

No one shall be subject to coercion which would impair his freedom to have or to adopt a religion or belief of his choice. [Art. 18(2)]
The States Parties to the present Covenant undertake to have respect for the liberty of parents and, when applicable, legal guardians to ensure the religious and moral education of their children in conformity with their own convictions. [Art. 18(4)]

Article 20(2)[106] prohibits incitement of religious hatred.

Enforcement of the Covenant is by means of a reporting system in respect of the position of each country which is an adherent to the Covenant,[107] and such state reports are scrutinised by a Human Rights Committee. It is also possible for states in certain cases to bring complaints before the Committee about other states.[108] The Committee may also consider individual applications,[109] although unlike the European counterpart there is no direct award of damages. Indeed the whole procedure lacks coercive power against the state as such, though there is always the question of publicity, both generally and with regard to the United Nations.

Although of limited importance at the moment, such international covenants may be expected to develop in the future, and religious freedom may confidently be expected to remain a vital constituent of them.[110]

The protection of churches and ministers

Religious meetings, like any other activity, are governed by the ordinary law of public order. Thus breaches of the peace, fights, or even riots and affrays taking place at them will be dealt with under the law of the land and the religious element will neither add to nor subtract from the criminality of the acts. In the past several of the best-known cases in this area of law have involved outbursts of religious intolerance.[111] In addition there is special protection provided by the criminal law for religious services, places of worship and ministers of religion and it is to those that we now turn.

Under Section 2 of the Ecclesiastical Courts Jurisdiction Act 1860,

> Any person who shall be guilty of riotous, violent or indecent behaviour ... in any Cathedral Church, Parish or District Church or Chapel of the Church of England ... or ... in any Chapel of any Religious Denomination or ... in any (registered)[112] Place of Religious Worship ... whether during the celebration of Divine Service or at any other Time, or in any Churchyard or Burial Ground

is guilty of a criminal offence. The original aim of the Act was to give exclusive jurisdiction to the ordinary courts of the land in cases where lay persons had caused a disturbance in Church.[113] Before its passage ecclesiastical courts had a jurisdiction over criminal offences committed by the laity in Anglican Churches.[114] A somewhat controversial part of the offence is that conduct can be punishable simply because it takes place in a church, whereas similar conduct in some other place would go unpunished. Thus in *Abrahams* v *Cavey*[115] a service was held in a Methodist Chapel as part of the Labour Party Conference. Lessons were read by the Foreign Secretary and the Prime Minister. During these lessons the defendants, who were opposed to the then Government's support of American policy in Vietnam, shouted out, 'Oh, you hypocrites; how can you use the word of God to justify your policies?' Evidence was given to show that members of the Labour Party Conference were not regular attenders at that Chapel and Lord Soper testified that disputation in Church was a legitimate exercise of Methodist principles in the circumstances. Despite this the Divisional Court upheld the conviction on the grounds that 'riotous, violent or indecent' should be read in the context of creating a disturbance in a sacred place.[116] The Court turned to the old case of *Worth* v *Terrington*[117] to show that the circumstance of a religious service is the crucial factor in deciding whether the behaviour is indecent or not, '...

for it is clear that an act done in a church during divine service might be highly indecent and improper, which would not be so at another time',[118] or, more colourfully, 'A song by an Italian singer in a church, during the oratorio, may not be improper, but would be highly so if sung in the midst of the Litany.'[119]

Any serious interruption of a service can constitute the offence. In 1902 a loud shout of 'Idolatry' was considered sufficient, provided that the congregation could hear it.[120] A year before[121] a clergyman who had protested his dissent of a High Church Anglican Service by crying out, 'This is idolatry! Protestants leave the house of Baal!' and had then marched out of the church with his followers, was convicted.[122] 'Violent behaviour' has also been given a broad meaning. Thus in one case[123] a defendant pushed passed a churchwarden with the intention of sitting other than where the churchwarden wished him to go. Although there was no fight and no force used other than that required to push himself towards the seat, his action was held to be illegal under the section.

The section also extends to behaviour in churchyards. In 1973[124] a defendant held a black magic service[125] at midnight in an Anglican churchyard. He painted symbols on the ground and attempted to raise a dead spirit. He read out an incantation from a piece of paper upon which was also written, 'Await arrival of reporters'. No sexual acts took place at the ceremony and no witnesses were produced who had been shocked or disgusted by the activities. Nevertheless the acts were held to constitute indecency within a churchyard.[126] More recently still, if less spectacularly than the last case, the section was invoked in 1981[127] when a man dropped a plank of wood in the grounds of Wakefield Cathedral, thereby alarming three old people who were sitting on a bench at the time. He was fined £20 in a case where there was no likelihood of a breach of the peace — if that act had taken place outside the Cathedral yard no offence would have been committed.

The second half of Section 2 of the 1860 Act states:

> ... or who shall molest, let, disturb, vex or trouble, or by any unlawful means disquiet or misuse any preacher duly authorized to preach therein ... ministering or celebrating any sacrament, or any Divine Service, Rite, or Office, in any Cathedral, Church, or Chapel, or in any Churchyard or Burial Ground.

In *Matthews* v *King*[128] the defendants attempted to drown the officiating clergyman's voice by loud hymn-singing after one of them had shouted, 'Get out of the pulpit with those popish garments on.' They objected to the service as they considered it to be a departure from the laws of the Church of England. The Court, however, would not be drawn into argument about the technical correctness of the service and lay down that it was sufficient if outwardly what was going on appeared to be a service:

... it cannot have been intended that an Act providing for summary conviction for brawling should depend for its application upon the difficult questions which have often arisen upon the ceremonial law of the Church of England. The Act was designed to protect the clergyman from disturbance in the performance of his duties and to preserve order, decency and reverence in the Church during his performance of those duties; it has no reference to whether he performs them properly.[129]

The section will not apply if the minister performs a lay duty in Church, such as taking the collection.[130] The protection extends to any minister of any registered church.

The offence would seem to cover any type of obstructive or annoying behaviour and such behaviour, like any other offence against Section 2, can be punished with a £20 fine or up to two months in prison. More forceful action against a minister who is performing a religious office, including the burial of the dead, may result in up to two years' imprisonment under Section 36 of the Offences Against the Person Act 1861, although it has been recently suggested by the Law Commission[131] that this 'aggravated' assault be abolished so that clergymen would be placed on an equal footing with other citizens with regard to physical attacks on their persons.

For the sake of completeness it may be noted that part of the law dealing with the formalities of the marriage ceremony[132] makes it a crime for anyone who 'falsely pretends to be in Holy Orders' to solemnise a marriage according to the rites of the Church of England. This crime is committed where one carries out the act with the intention to deceive someone; should the defendant only intend a charade[133] or if it is an actor on a stage playing the part of a clergyman, then the offence is not committed.

The question of whether there should be special legal protection for religious services and related matters has recently been explored by the Law Commission.[134] That religious controversy can cause disturbance today is without doubt — there are still outbursts of anti-Catholic feeling, such as when in 1969[135] there was a demonstration near St Paul's Cathedral during a service for Christian Unity attended by the Roman Catholic Cardinal of Westminster. Some of the demonstrators hurled eggs and tomatoes as well as insults at the proceedings. The strong emotion felt amongst non-Christian religions can also lead to disturbances. Thus in Rotherham, in 1980,[136] there were serious differences of opinion between two groups of Muslims. Outside one mosque there was a fight between two hundred people and there were several outbreaks of violence in mosques over the period of Ramadan. In this instance a number were charged with general public order offences; but the Law Commission argue that there are cases, for example leaving a pig's head in a mosque, where great insult can be done to the devout in their place of worship without an offence being committed other than under Section 2 of the 1860 Act and therefore they propose[137] that the section should be replaced by an indictable offence, triable either way, with a maximum sentence of twelve months' imprisonment and a fine which would penalise those who, with intent to wound and outrage the feelings of those using the premises concerned, use threatening, abusive or insulting words or behaviour at any time in any place of religious worship of the Church of England, or in any other certified place of religious worship or in any churchyard or burial ground.

In general this proposal has received support. Against it and against the general idea of giving a special status to religious services and places of worship are, however, a number of arguments. First, cases such as *Abrahams* v *Cavey* show that words such as 'indecent' are given a special and extended meaning, with regard to offences relating to worship — this tradition means that there is always the risk of especially high standards being placed on conduct in church. Secondly, many of the earlier cases on the section were provoked by hostility towards the Anglican High Church movement, whereas *Abrahams* v *Cavey* concerned a political protest. All of these cases involved people who were driven to protest, out of sincere motives, at something they saw going on in church that they felt obliged to protest about. It is submitted that the criminal law is never at its happiest when dealing with such people and, until a pressing need is shown, is best left out of such cases. Thirdly, the present main offence under Section 2 and the Law Commission's proposed offence relate to conduct taking place inside a church whether or not a service is being held. This leaves us with the strange position that a politician giving a 'lunchtime lecture' in a London church falls under the special protection of the law,[138] whereas a religious activity (e.g. a revivalist meeting in the Albert Hall) held in a place that is not a registered place of worship will not enjoy such special protection.

Finally (Church of England places of worship apart) the crime depends on the place of worship being registered by the Registrar General — an issue which can lead to difficulty where 'fringe' groups are concerned whose belief that they are religious is not shared by that official.[139]

Notes

1. But see I. B. McKenna, 'A common law action for discrimination', *Legal Studies*, I, 1981, pp. 296–302.
2. P. Hartman, 'Racial and religious discrimination by innkeepers in the U.S.A.', *Modern Law Review*, XII, 1949, pp. 449–53.
3. See *Re Lysaght, Hill* v *Royal College of Surgeons* [1966] Ch 191 at p. 206. Of course 'religious discrimination' could be dressed-up racial discrimination; see *Annual Report of the Commission for Racial Equality*, 1979, at p. 20 for such an example.
4. C. H. Rolph, *Believe What You Like*, 1973, pp. 76–77.
5. Rolph, *Believe*, at p. 119.
6. [1972] A.C. 342.
7. [1972] A.C. 342 at p. 354 (Lord Donovan); p. 362 (Lord Simon of Glaisdale) and p. 368 (Lord Kilbrandon).
8. H.C. Deb. (1975–6), s.c. 'A', cols 84–118.
9. Ibid., col. 102.
10. Ibid., cols 102–3. Does this not assume that the outward marks of Sikhship are marks of race rather than of religion? Walter Clegg, M.P., recognised the distinction at col. 94.
11. Including those who were converts from Islam?
12. Including white English converts?
13. Ibid., col. 103.
14. Ibid., col. 109.
15. Ibid., cols 109–10.
16. *Singh* v *Rowntree Mackintosh* [1979] I.C.R. 554.
17. *Panesar* v *Nestlé Ltd* [1980] I.C.R. 144 [Note].
18. In that case it was interesting to note that twenty-four of the people working at the relevant factory appeared to have been Sikhs who had shaved off their beards — thus could it in any case have been said that Mr Panesar could not comply with the condition? See also discussion of *Malik* v *British Home Stores* in the *Annual Report of the Commission for Racial Equality*, 1980, at pp. 78–9.
19. For conflicting Birmingham County Court decisions on this see *Annual Report of the Commission for Racial Equality*, 1980, pp. 25–6 and 84–5.
20. [1981] I.C.R. 631.
21. *The Times*, 26 June 1981.
22. Thus see the *Commission for Racial Equality's Guidance Note on Sikh Men and Women and Employment*, 1980 (revised 1981), and their *Religious Observance by Muslim Employees — A framework for discussion*, 1980.
23. H.C. Deb. (1975–6), s.c. 'A', col. 96.
24. Ibid., col. 109.

25. Ibid., cols 95–6.
26. Ibid., cols 105–6.
27. [1983] 2 W.L.R. 620.
28. [1982] 3 W.L.R. 932, 936–7.
29. [1982] 3 W.L.R. 932, 941–2.
30. [1982] 3 W.L.R. 932, 947.
31. The Sikhs mounted a powerful campaign against the results, thus see *The Times*, July 31st, 1982.
32. *In Ealing London Borough Council* v. *Race Relations Board* [1972] A.C. 342 one of the factors which lead them to decide that nationality was outside the ambit of the Race Relations Act 1968 had been the consequences for the offence of incitement to racial hatred. Racial discrimination, although having civil consequences, is not a criminal offence as such.
33. [1983] 2 W.L.R. 620, 623–4.
34. [1983] 2 W.L.R. 620, 625.
35. His Lordship was particularly influenced by the judgement of Richardson J. in *King-Ansell* v. *Police* [1979] 2 N.Z.L.R. 531, 543 a decision on the New Zealand Race Relations Act of 1971 holding that the Jews were a group protected by that legislation by virtue of their 'ethnic origins'.
36. Thus see Lord Denning in the Court of Appeal, [1982] 2 W.L.R. 932 at 937. The House of Lords expressly relied on *King-Ansell* v. *Police* (above) an express finding in New Zealand that the ethnic origins of the Jews meant they were a racial group.
37. Race Relations Act, 1976, Section 1(1)(b).
38. [1982] 3 W.L.R. 932, 949.
39. [1983] 2 W.L.R. 620, 628.
40. [1983] 2 W.L.R. 620, 629.
41. 318 H.C. Deb. 55., (26 November 1936), cols 630–54.
42. See, for example, *Disturbances in Northern Ireland: Report of the Commission appointed by the Governor of Northern Ireland*, Cmnd. 532 of 1969 and *First Report of the Standing Advisory Commission on Human Rights: Annual Report for 1974–75*, H.C.P. No. 632, paras 20–5.
43. The Prevention of Incitement to Hatred Act (Northern Ireland) 1970. See A. Dickey, 'Anti-incitement legislation in Britain and Northern Ireland', *New Community*, 1972, pp. 133–8.
44. Section 5 of the Government of Ireland Act 1920 stated that there should be no Northern Ireland law: 'so as either directly or indirectly to establish or endow any religion, or prohibit or restrict the free exercise thereof.' This section was not considered a success (Kevin Boyle *et al.*, *Law and State — The case of Northern Ireland*, 1975, pp. 6–25, and see also J. Jaconelli, *Enacting a Bill of Rights*, 1980, pp. 222–43).

Moves to ban religious discrimination and hostility by law in Northern Ireland date from the 'Downing Street Declaration' of 19 August 1969, which recognised equality of treatment for every Northern Ireland citizen 'irrespective of political views or religion'. In addition to the Prevention of Incitement to Hatred Act and the Fair Employment (Northern Ireland) Act 1976, discussed in Chapter 11, important legislation in this area incluces: the Housing Executive Act (Northern Ireland) 1971 and Part III of the Northern Ireland Constitution Act 1973.

45. Prevention of Incitement to Hatred Act, Section 1.
46. Race Relations Act 1976, Section 70.
47. But see the Minister of Home Affairs for Northern Ireland at 76 H.C. Debs. (N.I.), col. 1846.
48. Prevention of Incitement to Hatred Act, Section 2.
49. The Act does not apply to conduct in other parts of the United Kingdom. In fact it has been seldom used in Ulster itself.
50. See *Law Commission Working Paper No. 72*, 1977, pp. 41–2; W. S. Holdsworth, 'The state and religious nonconformity: an historic retrospect', *Law Quarterly Review*, XXXVI, 1920, p. 339, especially at pp. 343 and 345; J. C. Spencer, *The Press and the Reform of Criminal Libel*, in P. R. Glazebrook (ed.), *Reshaping the Criminal Law*, 1978, p. 266.
51. *Digest of Criminal Law*, 1883, Article 93, approved by the Criminal Law Commissioners and by Cave J. in *R* v *Burns* (1886) 16 Cox C.C. 355, at pp. 359–60.
52. See J. Stephen, *A History of the Criminal Law of England*, II, 1883, at p. 424.
53. *R* v *Johnson* (1686), II State Trials 1339.
54. *R* v *Williams*, 2 Modern State Trials 231.
55. At p. 268.
56. (1709) 15 State Trials 521.
57. At p. 606.
58. *R* v *Osborn*, 2 Barn. 138 and 166.
59. *The Times*, 19 and 22 September 1936.
60. For Leese's background see R. Benwick, *The Fascist Movement in Britain*, 1972, pp. 44–7. Leese was interned in the Second World War, under Defence Regulation 18B, for publishing anti-Jewish propaganda.
61. A charge that would not lie today: *Withers* v *Director of Public Prosecutions* [1975] A.C. 842.
62. *The Times*, 17 November 1947, and see James Caunt, *An Editor on Trial*, 1947.
63. See H. Montgomery Hyde, *Norman Birkett*, 1964, pp. 532–5.
64. *R* v *Aldred* (1909) 22 Cox C.C. 1.
65. Contrary to Section 70 of the Race Relations Act 1976. *Mandla* v *Lee*, discussed above, will mean that this criminal offence will be available where Sikhs or Jews have been attacked. Its application to other groups is a matter of speculation.
66. Contrary to Section 5 of the Public Order Act 1936, as amended.
67. *Law Commission Working Paper No. 72*, pp. 43–4. However, the British Government feels that religious belief is fully protected under the existing law; see its reservation to Article 20 of the United Nations Covenant on Civil and Political Rights (which outlaws, *inter alia*, incitement to religious hatred).
68. [1951] 2 D.L.R. 369.
69. *R* v *Gathercole* (1837) 2 Lewin 237. If a religion feels it has been defamed in a newspaper it may always make a complaint to the Press Council. See *The Times*, 22 October 1982 where the Rajneesh sect cleared its name over a *Sun* article.
70. J. Dean, *Hatred, Ridicule or Contempt*, 1953, pp. 16–17.
71. *Orme* v *Associated Newspaper Group Ltd*, *The Times*, 4 February 1981.
72. Rolph, *Believe*, pp. 61–3 and 69.

73. *Church of Scientology* v *Johnson-Smith* [1972] 1 Q.B. 522, and Rolph, *Believe*, pp. 74–86.

74. In *Orme* it was accepted that the plaintiff was 'nominal'; during the trial he was required to pay £175,000 into court — *The Times*, 2 and 6 December 1980. The *Johnson-Smith* case (Rolph, *Believe*, at p. 86) cost £70,000 in 1970.

75. For an example of which see *Beauharnais* v *People of the State of Illinois* (1952) 343 U.S. 250 — publications prohibited which exposed racial *and religious groups* to contempt, derision and obloquy.

76. Such as that taken against the Scientologists in the 1960s — see Sir John Foster, *Enquiry into the Practice and Effects of Scientology*, 1971, paras 190–236.

77. On which see generally J.R. Spencer, *Criminal Law Review*, 1977, pp. 383 and 465. *Gathercole* (see note 69) was a successful prosecution for criminal libel.

78. *Goldsmith* v *Pressdram Ltd* [1977] 1 Q.B. 83. In its recent review of the law of criminal libel, the Law Commission concludes (see Law Com. No. 84, 1982, at para 8.19) that although the present law of criminal libel may be wider in certain respects than the civil law (see para 3.11), a modern law on the subject should not — owing to the difficulties of definition — extent to a 'group' that is not an incorporated or unincorporated body.

79. In finding for the defendants they added a rider calling for a review of the charity status that had been granted to some Moonie trusts, on the grounds that some of the group's activities were political — *The Times*, 1 April 1981. The total cost of the action was estimated at £500,000 — and 117 witnesses were called. The Court of Appeal subsequently refused to alter the verdict; see *Daily Mail*, 21 December 1982.

80. See *Daily Mail*, 1 April 1981.

81. Principally, in line with the jury's rider, that their charitable status should be removed. The Charity Commissioners, in a much criticised decision, refused to do this — *The Times*, 4 and 7 April 1981.

82. E.g. United States of America First Amendment (1791); Canadian Bill of Rights (1960), Article 1(c); [West] German Basic Law (1949), Article 4; Constitution of the Republic of India (1949), Articles 15, 16 and 25, etc.

83. Article 6.

84. Article 8.

85. Article 10.

86. Article 11.

87. Article 12.

88. For details see R. Beddard, *Human Rights and Europe*, 2nd edition, 1980.

89. For example see Jaconelli, *Enacting a Bill of Rights*, pp. 222–43.

90. [1978] Q.B. 36, and see Chapter 10, pp. 159–60, for details of this case.

91. At p. 41.

92. At p. 48.

93. In 1981 (*The Times*, 5 May 1981), the European Commission rejected MR Ahmad's claim that his rights had been breached under Article 14, as he had not shown that others in a like situation would have been treated differently.

94. [1978] 1 All E.R. 591, affirmed by the Court of Appeal, [1978] 3 All E.R. 82.

95. At p. 594.

96. [1976] E.C.R. 1589.
97. Dec. Adm. Com., 1735/63.
98. Ibid.
99. Dec. Adm. Com., 1068/61.
100. Dec. Adm. Com., 2988/66.
101. Dec. Adm. Com., 4517/70.
102. Dec. Adm. Com., 229/64.
103. The United Kingdom House of Lords reached a similar conclusion in the 1950's: *Walsh* v *Lord Advocate* [1956] 3 All E.R. 129.
104. F.G. Jacobs, *The European Convention on Human Rights*, 1975, pp. 143–50.
105. Article 2 of the First Protocol to the European Convention on Human Rights provides that in giving education the state 'shall respect the right of parents to ensure such education and teaching in conformity with their own religious and philosophical convictions'. The United Kingdom has made a reservation to this (Jacobs, *European Convention*, at p. 174), so that its special educational arrangements (see Chapter 10) cannot be challenged under this part of the Convention. The United Nations finally adopted a text in 1981.
106. See also Articles 2(1), 4(1), 24(1), 26 and 27.
107. On which see A. H. Robertson, *Human Rights and the World*, 1982, pp. 42–50.
108. Ibid., pp. 50–4. It is unlikely that there will be references from states who adhere to the European Convention: ibid., p. 53.
109. See ibid., pp. 54–60.
110. Thus see also Proclamation of Tehran 1968; United Nations International Covenant on Economic, Social and Cultural Rights 1976, Articles 2(2), 13(1) and 13(3); and Helsinki Final Act 1975.
111. E.g. *Beatty* v *Gillbanks* (1882) 9 Q.B.D. 308. — For a detailed discussion of this case see D.G.T. Williams, *Keeping the Peace*, 1967, pp. 49–53 and 101–5. See also *Wise* v *Dunning* [1902] 1 K.B. 167. For a recent example see *The Times*, 31 November 1982 (thirteen bound over to keep the peace, including six clergymen, after the Pope's visit to Britain). And see Williams, *Keeping The Peace*, pp. 105–10. The crime of inciting racial hatred (Public Order Act 1936, Section 5A, as amended by the Race Relations Act 1976) is not an offence designed to prevent incitement to religious hatred, although anti-semitic speeches have been prosecuted on the basis that the Jews constitute a race. At p. 173 Williams notes that fears that attacks against the Jews as members of a religion were outside the new law were expressed when the Race Relations Bill was before the House of Commons in 1965, and he remarks: 'The Government were disinclined to extend section 6 to cover religious incitement.' However it was thought that the Jews were covered by 'race' or 'ethnic' or 'national origins'.
112. Under the Places of Worship Registration Act 1855. See also the Burial Law Amendment Act 1880, Section 7.
113. See the Preamble to the Act and Section 1 and also *Vallancey* v *Fletcher* [1897] 1 Q.B. 265.
114. Since 1688 (the Toleration Act 1688, Section 15) the lay courts had a concurrent jurisdiction with the ecclesiastical courts.
115. [1968] 1 Q.B. 479.

116. At pp. 485–7.
117. (1845) 13 M. & W. 781.
118. At pp. 795–6.
119. At p. 793.
120. *Jones* v *Catterall* (1902) 18 T.L.R. 367.
121. *Girt* v *Fillingham* [1901] P. 176.
122. A clergyman who has committed an offence under the section may also be proceeded against in an ecclesiastical court under the Clergy Discipline Act 1892, if he is a Church of England cleric. The lay court's conviction will be conclusive on the issue of fact.
123. *Asher* v *Calcroft* [1887] 18 Q.B.D. 607.
124. *R* v *Farrant* [1973] Crim.L.R. 240, and see A. Micklewright, 'The occult and the law', *New Law Journal*, 1972, p. 1091.
125. Several such 'services' have taken place recently that have not resulted in prosecution; see J. Franklyn, *Death by Enchantment*, 1971, pp. 216–19.
126. In former times criminal activities in church were seen as signs of witchcraft. B. Rosen (ed.), *Witchcraft*, 1969, at p. 319.
127. *Daily Telegraph*, 30 September 1981.
128. [1934] 1 K.B. 505.
129. At p. 516.
130. *Cope* v *Barber* (1872) L.R. 7 C.P. 393, at pp. 402–3.
117. Criminal Law Revision Committee, *Fourteenth Report — Offences Against the Person*, 1980, Cmnd. 7844, paras 179 and 180.
132. Marriage Act 1949, Section 75(1)(*d*).
133. *R* v *Else*, *R* v *Kemp*, [1964] 2 Q.B. 341.
134. Law Commission Working Paper No. 79, *Offences Against Religion and Public Worship*, 1981, paras 12.1–12.23.
135. *Journal of Church and State*, XI, 1969, p. 352.
136. *The Times*, 13 August 1980, and the *Observer*, 24 August 1980.
137. Working Paper No. 79, para. 12.22.
138. While giving such a lecture in 1981 the Prime Minister was interrupted by seven young Communists who shouted, 'You are not a Christian, you are a murderer' — *The Times*, 5 March 1981.
139. See *R* v *Registrar General, Ex. p. Segerdal* [1970] 2 Q.B. 697.

2 Blasphemy

A State which refuses to enforce Christian belief has lost the right to enforce Christian morals.

[*per* Lord Devlin]

Historical background

The existence and use of an offence such as blasphemy in modern times can only be fully understood with the aid of a sketch of its background and development. Before the Restoration of King Charles II offences against morality and religion were the concern of the ecclesiastical courts and of the Court of Star Chamber.[2] By 1663, however, the Court of King's Bench, in a case where the libertine Sir Charles Sedley had appeared naked in public and had disported himself in such a manner so as to cause a crowd to throw brickbats at him, declared that,

> ... [The Court was] the custos morum of the King's subjects, and it was then high time to punish such profane actions committed against all modesty, which were as frequent as if not only Christianity but morality also had been neglected.[3]

This general dictum was first applied in a specially religious context in 1676 against one Taylor, who was somewhat mentally disturbed and who had cried out that 'Jesus Christ was a bastard, an imposter and a cheat.' Sir Matthew Hale was prepared to condemn Taylor for this reviling of Christ on the ground that as England was a Christian nation so Christianity is part of the law of England, and therefore 'to reproach the Christian religion is to speak in subversion of the law'.[4] It was argued many years later[5] that this belief was based upon a misunderstanding of words uttered by a Chief Justice of the Court of Common Pleas in 1458. Whether or not this was correct, actions such as Taylor's had been punished from early times, albeit by the courts Christian, and this was to continue now by the ordinary criminal courts. Thus whether or not Priscot C.J. had said 'ancient scripture' rather than 'Holy scripture' in medieval times did not alter in any way the willingness of the common law to strike down what it perceived as blasphemous after 1676.

After Taylor there was no great flood of prosecutions. In *Woolson*[6] a Cambridge don had published a series of works designed to show that the New Testament miracles were allegories and were not to be taken literally. The court proceeded on the assumption that Christianity was part of the law of the land and that its doctrines must be protected. A distinction was drawn between mere differences of opinion about religion, on the one hand, which the law did not interfere with and, on the other, situations where 'the very root of Christianity itself is struck at'. Woolson had so struck and was convicted. Prosecutions remained rare but the odd questioner of orthodoxy would be dealt with. Thus in 1762 the seventy-year-old Annet was sentenced to

be imprisoned in Newgate for a month; to stand twice in the pillory, with a paper on his forehead, inscribed Blasphemy; to be sent to the house of correction to hard labour for a year; to pay a fine of 6s. 8d; and to find security, himself in 100L and two sureties in 50L each for his good behaviour during life.[7]

After 1790 there came a marked change.[8] The first series of cases concerned Tom Paine's *Age of Reason*, where the authorities wished to prevent an attack upon the foundations of society[9] — hardly surprising since the year was 1797, and revolutionary France had been seen to guillotine its established Church leaders and its established governing orders without discrimination between them. Prosecutions for publishing this work continued for a generation, the last of importance being that of the Carliles in 1819 and 1821. In the case against Richard Carlile[10] Abbott C.J. claimed that it was possible to discuss religious topics provided that this was done with respect and moderation — it must not be mere scoffing at the subject. Carlile's sister continued to sell Paine's works after the imprisonment of her brother and she too was prosecuted.[11] The court made plain that attacks on religion were dangerous in that they undermined the moral code upon which society was structured.[12] If people were to discuss religion they were to do so with the respect that was due to the belief professed by the great majority in the country.[13] The law should also be enforced as the young and the intellectually weaker members of society deserved protection:

Books of this description may do no mischief in minds enlightened, as yours are [i.e. the educated all-male jury] ... But what [Christianity's] professors are afraid of is that those not capable of reasoning should have their minds weakened, their reason led astray, and the consolation of death taken from them, not by fair reasoning, but by abuse and scurrility.[14]

Paine was not the only writer whose works were suspect at this time. In the Court of Chancery Lord Eldon waged holy war against such poets as Shelley[15] and Byron[16] on account of their irreligious work, and in 1822 would not give legal protection to the copyright of a work which denied the immortality of the soul.[17]

A case of some interest because of the quality of the arguments used in it is that of *Hetherington*[18] in 1840. Hetherington was charged with publishing Halsam's *Letters to the Clergy of All Denominations*, a work that described the Old Testament as 'wretched stuff' and 'a disgrace to Orang-outangs'. 'Moses was the inventor of this grand cheat, and although it may have done some little towards frightening people into what is called morality, the purpose for which Moses invented it is now out of date.' The Attorney-General, later Lord Campbell L.C., advanced two reasons for the work's condemnation; first because it 'wounds and shocks the feeling of those who are entitled to the protection of the law' and secondly because the views which it advances tend to dissolve the foundation of the moral obligations on which society rests.[19] In reply, the defence criticised the prosecution for taking just one or two passages from a work of over five hundred pages;[20] pointed out that St Stephen, the first Christian martyr, had been executed for blasphemy;[21] claimed that whilst the works that Hetherington had sold were cheap, dearer, more exclusive books went untouched by the authorities;[22] and even attacked the legal roots of the law.[23] The trial judge, Lord Denman C.J., repeated that it was possible to discuss Christianity in a moderate manner[24] but

... if the tone and spirit is that of offence, and insult and ridicule, which leaves the judgment really not free to act, and, therefore, cannot be called an appeal to the judgment but an appeal to the wild and improper feelings of the human mind, more particularly in the younger part of the community [then the jury will convict].[25]

To set these words firmly in their context he went on to make clear that extreme socialistic philosophy was equally subversive.[26] Indeed antipathy between the socialists of the day and some of the clergy of the established Church contributed to the increase in the number of blasphemy trials at that time — this was due, in part, to the licensing function then performed by the clerics.[27] So the prosecutions continued (although they did little to discourage the growth in the free-thought movement).[28] One Southwell was awarded twelve months in prison for describing the bible as 'a history of lust, sodomies, wholesale slaughtering and horrible depravity ... To our minds the bible is one of the most contemptible and brutalising books that was ever penned.'[29] In the same year (1842) Holyoake received six months for suggesting that God should be treated as a surplus subaltern and placed on half pay,[30] an essentially political remark given the attacks on the finances of some of the established clergy of that time.[31] However with the failure of the Great Charter in 1848 the central authorities (unlike some local ones) set their faces against these types of prosecution.[32] The prosecution and treatment of Thomas Pooley in the late 1850s comes as a turning point.[33] Pooley was clearly insane and went round writing such things as 'Jesus Christ and T. Pooley' on the gates of his local clergyman. His prosecution was locally inspired and his sentence of nearly two years' imprisonment severe. Whilst in prison he went on hunger strike and showed signs of mental disturbance. His case was taken up by several leading men of the day and the Home Secretary ordered his release after he had served five months of his sentence.

One of the public men to be influenced by Pooley's case was J. S. Mill, whose classic essay *On Liberty* (1859) was a response to a law that penalised men for the expression of views and opinions. 1859 also saw the publication of Charles Darwin's *Origin of Species*, and following the famous Wilberforce–Huxley debates it was clear that influential opinion was changing and, to the utilitarian Victorian mind, a law that checked scientific progress was clearly suspect. Additionally times and society were secure — there was none of the panic that had been abroad at the time of the French wars or when the Chartists had seemed to be a threat to the established order. The free-thought movement was also on the increase and was out to do away with the laws that placed religion in a special position in society. The spearhead of the attack was *The Freethinker*, a journal supporting Bradlaugh's secular society and which proclaimed itself as:

... an anti-Christian organ, and is therefore to be chiefly aggressive. It will wage relentless warfare against superstition in general, and against the superstition of Christianity in particular. It will do its best in this direction, employing the arms of science, scholarship and philosophy against the Bible; and it will not scruple to employ for the same purpose any weapons or ridicule or sarcasm which may be derived from the armoury of common sense.[34]

The main target was the God of the Old Testament.

There were three trials concerning this journal — one before North J.[35] and two before Lord Coleridge C.J.[36] The last of these trials concerned some three hundred 'comical' French biblical sketches that had been reprinted in *The Freethinker*. Although the older cases had clearly taken the view that an attack on the fundamentals of religion could constitute blasphemy[37] a striking feature of those cases had been the distasteful *manner* in which the views of the defendant had been conveyed. To hold in the 1880s that the expression of certain views in itself was illegal would run counter to the progressive developments in freedom of thought that had taken place over the previous years. Therefore grasping at the legal fact that the laws relating to the Jews and other religious minorities had altered[38] Lord Coleridge declared that the special relationship between Christianity and the state had changed and so it was now possible that 'if the decencies of controversy are observed, even the fundamentals of the Christian religion may be attacked.' He relied on a passage in *Starkie on Libel*[39] but otherwise the strict legal authority in favour of this revision of the law was thin.[40] The greatest criminal lawyer of that age, Stephen J., rejected the modified form of blasphemy both because it was wrong in law[41] and also because by modifying it it became less likely that blasphemy as an offence would be abolished as Parliament would have been more likely to reject the old-style blasphemy as a clear interference with freedom of expression. Lord Coleridge's view was not immediately accepted by all the other judges[42] but it was later applied in criminal blasphemy trials.[43]

Blasphemy in recent times

After some difficulty Foote, the editor of *The Freethinker*, was eventually convicted, but this led in 1886 to the first Parliamentary attempt to abolish blasphemy. This was a Bill, introduced by Professor Courtney Kenny, which while abolishing blasphemy would have provided some measure of protection to all religions when they were unwarrantedly attacked.[44] By the beginning of the twentieth century the more respectable free-thought magazines found their main difficulty not so much the actual possibility of prosecution but rather that major magazine distributors refused to handle their works.[45] There were few cases, although Boulter[46] was prosecuted for giving blasphemous lectures in Highbury fields in London (he was conditionally discharged but was imprisoned in 1909 for breaking his pledge; he was also imprisoned in

1911). Just before the First World War there were flurries against a number of blasphemers but these were not encouraged by the Government, whose policy had become that a distinction should be drawn between 'the case of a man who shouts blasphemy in the streets where it must fall on unwilling ears' and 'a person who writes what is blasphemous in a publication of small circulation, mainly among people who would not be shocked at its language'.[47] Also there should not be a prosecution where the penalty was likely to be trivial and so the offender would be given 'a welcome advertisement' and 'would be held up as a victim of persecution'. After the conviction of Stewart in 1911 the then Attorney-General, Sir John Simon, suggested that it was time for the following changes to be made:

(1) the special protection given to the Church of England (see below) should be brought to an end; and
(2) *bona fide* opinions expressed on religious topics should only be prosecuted if they were expressed in an obscene or indecent manner.[48]

No change came from Parliament but in 1917 the pronouncements of the majority in the civil case of *Bowman* v *Secular Society*[49] seemed to restrict the ambit of the offence even more. In this case the House of Lords decided that an association whose objects included the denial of the Christian religion was not unlawful as far as the law of trusts was concerned. Lord Coleridge's view of the law was confirmed,[50] it being made clear that it was inappropriate expression that was forbidden by virtue of '[its] tendency to endanger the peace then and there, to deprave public morality generally, to shake the fabric of society and to be a cause of civil strife'.[51]

The speeches of the majority in *Bowman* clearly show that blasphemy was thought to be a developing offence and whereas at one time a denial of an essential Christian doctrine was thought worthy of punishment because of the danger it presented to the fabric of society, by the beginning of the twentieth century the danger was in expressing such views in a *manner* as to endanger the public well-being. Civil disorder would not now break out from a rational dissection of faith, although a violent lampoon might lead to disorder, especially as in 1917 Christianity was still clearly the predominant religion of the country.

After *Bowman* was to come what many believed was to be the final English case of blasphemy. J. W. Gott[52] was an active free-thinker of many years standing. He had got into a number of difficulties with the law, having been sentenced to four months for blasphemy in 1911;

fourteen days' hard labour for profanity in 1916; six weeks for blasphemy in 1917; and two months for the breach of a Defence of the Realm order in 1918. He persisted in distributing and selling anti-Christian leaflets which said such things as 'Jesus Christ had entered Jerusalem like a circus clown on the back of two donkeys.' As his trial before Avory J.,[53] the learned judge seemed to believe that to be blasphemous the writing must be such as to endanger the public peace; indeed he seems to have adopted a 'muscular Christian' test: '[The jury must ask] if a person of strong religious feelings had stopped to read this pamphlet whether his instinct might not have been to go up to the man who was selling it and give him a thrashing.'

The Criminal Court of Appeal, however, expressed a rather wider test: 'it must be offensive to any one in sympathy with the Christian religion, whether he be a strong Christian, or a lukewarm Christian, or merely a person sympathising with their ideals'. On that rather confused note and with Mr Gott's nine months' hard labour the law seemed to be done with blasphemy. The general mood of society which had influenced Lord Coleridge and, later, the House of Lords in *Bowman* seemed to permit far more without general outrage or a feeling of offence. Although attempts to abolish the law continued into the 1930s[54] it was clear that offensive works could always be dealt with under the laws against obscenity or indecency without appeal to a special religiously based law. Writers such as D. H. Lawrence (see his *The Man Who Died*, 1929) were able freely to publish material which would have met with difficulty in the times that had been before.[55] In 1949 Lord Denning considered the law to be a dead letter[56] and in 1959 the severest critics of the law thought it was finished — the Society for the Abolition of the Blasphemy Laws was disbanded in that year. Furthermore, in 1966 the Home Office was to declare that it doubted whether the law would ever be used again.[57] The repeal of the Blasphemy Act 1697 (a measure which was aimed at keeping blasphemers and heretics out of public office[58] and which never, in fact, seems to have been used) led at least one ex-Lord Chancellor to believe that all the laws against blasphemy were now dead and buried.[59]

Blasphemy was not dead. Newspaper editors and the censors of plays and films had to bear the offence in mind whilst at work. In the 1970s the British Broadcasting Company was still prepared to ban a play if it considered it was blasphemous or irreligious.[60] In 1972 there had been an outcry, led by Mrs Mary Whitehouse, after an episode of 'Till Death Us Do Part', where irreverent remarks had been made about the virgin birth.[61] Failing to get satisfaction from the B.B.C. authorities, Mrs Whitehouse got in touch with the Director of Public Prosecutions, who declined to act because:

> There is ... no likelihood of any recurrence. Bearing this in mind, and particularly after considering the extreme nature of the vilification, ridicule or irreverence which would at the present day have to be established, I have come to the conclusion that it is unlikely that a prosecution for blasphemy in respect of the episode broadcast in the course of the programme would succeed, offensive to many though it may have been. Accordingly, in the whole of the circumstances I do not consider that I would be warranted in instituting proceedings, and the Attorney-General agrees with this conclusion.[62]

Mrs Whitehouse and her organisation, the National Viewers and Listeners Association, continued to keep a watchful eye on television and in 1976 were advised that it was possible to bring a common law prosecution for blasphemy based on the content of a television programme, although there might be difficulty in proving the extreme anger that the programme must provoke in order for the prosecution to succeed.[63] This could prove a significant weapon for them as by statute[64] it is not possible to bring a prosecution for the broadcasting of an obscene television programme.

Films, too, were under scrutiny. In 1971, the Dowager Lady Birdwood took out a private summons against the makers of a film which was later withdrawn, where, it was alleged, there were crude caricatures of certain biblical figures.[65] In 1976 a Dane, Jens Jorgen Thorsen, proposed to come to Britain and make a film which would 'portray Christ at three different times — in his era, in the present and in A.D. 3,000. He is shown as indulging in explicit sex with John the Baptist, with Mary Magdalene and with a Palestinian girl of today.'[66] The idea that such a film was to be made in Britain provoked an outcry. The Archbishop of Canterbury said he would consider invoking the law of blasphemy. Another opponent of the film exclaimed, 'there are certainly some people in King's Lynn in a mood to do him a physical injury'. In fact the film was never made and so the point was never put to the test. When a poem published in the homosexual newspaper *Gay News* was put in the hands of Mrs Mary Whitehouse the law was, however, to be examined in modern conditions. Professor Kirkup's poem 'The Love that Dares to Speak its Name' was not, as had been the case with earlier blasphemous publications, a denial of or attack upon the Christian religion but rather a portrayal of the figure of Jesus Christ in a most controversial manner. It depicted Him as a homosexual during

His lifetime and described acts committed on His body after the crucifixion. To say that it was obscene or outrageously indecent was one thing, but its publishers were not prosecuted for those offences. They were in the dock for blasphemy and if this was so it has been argued that in effect blasphemy has taken a new turn and now penalises 'the indecent or offensive treatment of subjects sacred to Christian sympathies', and thus 'is no longer a crime of disbelief: it may be committed with the profoundest religious intentions if Christian sentiment is expressed in an eccentric or shocking manner'.[67] At first instance some of the arguments were wide-ranging. Thus the prosecution declared, 'This case is about whether anything is to remain sacred. If this isn't blasphemy, nothing is ... You're [i.e. the jury] being asked to set the standard for the last quarter of the twentieth century.' This was interesting, as one of the main driving motives behind those bringing the prosecution was to offer a test case which would produce such a standard[68] and it was also hoped that if this prosecution proved successful an American film, *The Passover Plot*, would not be shown in the United Kingdom.[69] The defence was not unequal to its task and advanced a number of propositions, all of which were rejected by the trial judge.[70] Thus the offence had not been impliedly superseded by such legislation as the Public Order Act 1936 or the Race Relations Act 1976. Nor could it be argued that it was a breach of the international covenants on religious freedom[71] to have such a law as blasphemy is currently defined. Blasphemous libel is not affected by the statutory prohibition[72] on prosecutions at common law, where the essence of the complaint is that the relevant article is obscene. As the intention of the author and publishers was deemed to be irrelevant it was not possible to call religious experts (as had been allowed in other important religious cases such as *Abrahams* v *Cavey*[73] and *R* v *Registrar-General, ex p. Segerdal*[74]), nor, as happens in obscenity trials, could literary experts be called, rather 'The poem must speak for itself.'

In determining whether the manner of expression is blasphemous the jury had to ask itself:

— Do you think God would like to be recognised in the poem?
— Were you shocked when you first read it?
— Would you be proud or ashamed to have written it?
— Could you read it aloud to an audience of fellow-Christians [sic] without blushing?
— Is it obscene?
— Does it hurt, shock, offend or appal anyone who reads it?

With this guidance the jury convicted; fines and a suspended prison sentence were imposed. There was an appeal to the Court of Appeal[75] but by now the issue had narrowed to whether the defendants were liable if they intentionally published what the jury considered to be blasphemous or only if by the publication they intended (or at least foresaw the possibility) that the words would be taken as blasphemous.[76] The Court of Appeal held unanimously that only an intention to publish the offending matter was necessary and by three votes to two the House of Lords upheld this view.[77] At this stage it is interesting to note that Kirkup himself (he was never tried) has denied an intention to blaspheme:

Of course, I knew this would dismay and shock some people ... As for blasphemy; that was never my intention. How could it be? It had never entered my head for one moment that the poem might be misconstrued in that way. My motives were pure — on that my conscience is clear — and all I wanted to create [was] a work of art. Audacity yes, blasphemy no.[78]

The issue dividing the House of Lords was whether an intention to blaspheme need to be shown. A search through the old authorities was inconclusive on this issue because:

(1) nearly all of them dated from before 1898, the date when it was first possible for a defendant fully to give evidence on his own behalf; and
(2) in most of the fully argued cases (see e.g. the quotation from *The Freethinker* above) the defendant clearly realised that his material could be taken by the opinion of the day as blasphemous.

Certainly the wording of some of the indictments in those trials indicated that an intention to blaspheme was necessary[79] and if one also considered that the common law, aided if not pushed by Parliament,[80] generally had a subjective goal in view in criminal matters then one could conclude that the offence of blasphemy required 'a "specific intention", namely, to shock and arouse resentment among those who believe in or respect the Christian faith' (*per* Lord Diplock). However, despite the agreement of Lord Edmund-Davies, this view was in the minority.

Viscount Dilhorne[81] took what might be regarded as a rather technical approach. *Hetherington*'s case[82] had illustrated that a publisher could be vicariously liable in the sense that he was guilty of blasphemy if he was responsible for the publication, even though he was not aware that what he published was blasphemous. Thus in 1841 no such specific intent was needed and he could find no authority to show that the law had changed in this respect. Lord Russell of Killowen believed that all that need be shown was the deliberate publication of what is in fact blasphemous.[83] The speech which has attracted the most comment was that of Lord Scarman, who agreed with Viscount Dilhorne but added some wide-ranging comments of his own. He felt no special intent need be shown because:

> It would be intolerable if by allowing an author or publisher to plead the excellence of his motives and the right of free speech he could evade the penalties of the law even though his works were blasphemous in the sense of constituting an outrage upon the religious feelings of his fellow citizens. This is no way forward for a successful plural society.[84]
>
> ... what does matter is the manner in which 'the feelings of the general body of the community' have been treated. If the works are an outrage on such feelings, the opinions or arguments they are used to advance or destroy are of no moment ... The true test is whether the works are calculated, i.e. objectively, to outrage and insult the Christian's religious feelings.

Lord Scarman's enthusiasm for the offence of blasphemy seems almost unlimited, for he not only found support for its existence from Article 9 of the European Convention of Human Rights but also criticised it, not for existing, but rather for not being sufficiently comprehensive — and so he declared that it should be extended to protect other religions as well.

The other issue that played some part in the case was whether it is necessary (as *Gott* was thought to indicate) to show that the words might lead to a breach of the peace. The Court of Appeal thought not, nor did Lord Edmund-Davies or Lord Scarman, who equated the phrase with the generally unsettling effect that blasphemy is said to have on society. Breach of the peace probably need not be shown now as a separate element[85] although it may be an aid in determining whether the works complained of do have an adverse effect on society in the sense described by Lord Sumner in *Bowman*.[86]

A short while after the original trial of *Gay News* a former editor of *The Freethinker* sent copies of the offending poem to several well-known persons, including Mrs Mary Whitehouse. He pleaded guilty, and was fined, for sending indecent matter through the post, contrary to Section 11 of the Post Office Act 1953.[87] This perhaps serves to underline a point which shortly must be explored somewhat more fully — anti-religious matter is likely to constitute some other offence, as well as blasphemy, in certain circumstances:

36 *Religion and the law*

(1) it may fall under the laws relating to obscenity or indecency;[88]
(2) it is an offence to offer for sale a 'profane' book, and 'profanity' can be punished in other situations as well[89] — 'profanity' would appear to be synonymous with blasphemy[90] and is an offence long known to English law;[91]
(3) or it might offend a local by-law;[92]
(4) or it may fall under some public order offence.[93]

However, those who share the views advanced by Lord Scarman have seen a gap, presently filled in part by blasphemy, and it is to that gap that we must now turn.

Aftermath of 'Gay News' — a future for a law of blasphemy?

The *Gay News* trial was a clash between two pressure groups of the late twentieth century. It will be remembered that at first instance the defence argued that blasphemy no longer existed and since then there has been a widespread debate on whether there is a place for such an offence and if so what its ambit should be. A secondary debate has centred around the technical difficulties of the current law coupled with the difficulties of finding an acceptable formula by which to draft a new law, should it be thought expedient to continue the offence in a modified or indeed (as Lord Scarman hopes) in an extended form.

Following the trial there was an unsuccessful move, on 23 February 1978, in the House of Lords (as a House of Parliament) to abolish the offence without replacement.[94] The main reasons for so doing were said to be that: such a law is totally out of place in modern society;[95] particular groups (i.e. Christians) should not be placed in a privileged position in law;[96] if material was offensive it could be met by existing laws, such as those against obscenity.[97] Despite these arguments the House rejected abolition of the law on the following grounds: the country, its institutions and the monarchy are still basically Christian and thus deserve protection by the law;[98] and the repeal of the law could lead to a tidal wave of blasphemous publications.[99] Otherwise there was support for the view (which was expressed by Lords Macaulay and Campbell in the last century) that the protection of the law should be extended to other religions.[100]

Comment on the trial from academics showed a similar division of opinion. Some have taken the view that 'it would not seem unreasonable for the law to restrain scurrilous or offensive comments or attacks on the religious beliefs of *any section* of the community'.[101] On the other hand there have been those, such as Professor J.C. Smith[102] who believe that the real harm today comes not so much from attacks on orthodox religion but rather from the beliefs and practices of some of the minority religious cults in this country and by the activities of, for example, extreme Islam in countries such as Iran, and that it could be very much in the public interest to describe what they believe and do with vilification, ridicule and contempt. In an article published in 1980 Peter Jones[103] analysed the problems at some length. He considers that:

(1) blasphemy may be justified on moral grounds; if so it is illogical to restrict it to abusive or offensive attacks on religion; or
(2) it may be justified as preventing public disorder; however, there are already Public Order offences which deal with likely breaches of the peace with regard to any religious or indeed political group; or
(3) religious believers should be protected from suffering offence to their feelings — perhaps the strongest argument in favour of a law of blasphemy.

However,[104] he does not accept that religion should be placed in a special position as compared, for example, with political beliefs. He regards the 'manner–matter' distinction that has developed in the modern law of blasphemy to be unrealistic:[105] 'anyone who has read Kirkup's poem and reports of the trial of Lemon and *Gay News* must feel that it was the character and deed attributed to Christ that gave offence and not any special features of the language used in the poem'. In practice[106] it is an impossible task to prove offence, as it is too hard for the jury to put themselves in the position of a reasonable member of the particular religion defamed (but it is fair to put out that juries in criminal cases and judges in civil actions are continually expected to place themselves in the shoes of others).

By far the most important comment on blasphemy comes from the Law Commission's Working Paper No. 79, published in 1981. After a description of the development of the law the paper outlines what are seen as the principal weaknesses of the current law. A general criticism is its uncertainty, given the vagueness[107] of deciding what does vilify the Christian religion; indeed it is fair to say that if some of the majority judgments in *Gay News* are followed it could constitute a serious impediment on free speech since in that case it was surely the idea of Christ being involved in homosexual activity that was offensive. Cases such as *Foote and Ramsey* and *Bowman* saw the judges attempting to modify the offence so that it might appear acceptable to the spirit of the age but by seeming to reject the 'breach of the peace' test[108] the law now seems wider than it was thought to have been. No admissible evidence can be given by the publisher or the author as to their respective intentions, as no specific intent is needed;[109] and because there is no 'public good' defence, as is the case with obscene literature, the artistic or scientific merits of the work are irrelevant. It is clear that the law protects only the Christian religion,[110] and (although this has never been put to the test) the particular doctrine, of the Church of England.[111] One point that the Law Commission has been taken to task for not emphasising in its criticism of the existing law is that 'publication' in the law of blasphemy is very widely defined and covers not only all situations where there is a 'public' element but also the passing, in private, of a paper to one desirous of reading it.[112] If this is so it would seem, as is the case with obscenity, that the law is attempting to prevent individuals from private corruption rather than just upholding standards of conduct in public or preventing public outrage.

However although a number of statutory offences have been created since the 'heyday' of blasphemy there may be instances (e.g. the sale of books and leaflets falling outside Section 5 (as amended) of the Public Order Act 1936) where blasphemy is the only possible charge for matter offensive to religion.[113] This being so the paper then goes on to consider the possible justifications for a law on blasphemy. It sees four possibilities:

1. *The protection of religion and religious belief.* By this the Law Commission means blasphemy in its purest and most historic sense as a crime against God, just as defamation of character is a civil wrong against a person. They do not feel that contemporary circumstances justify the imposition of penal sanctions for this reason.[114]

2. *The protection of society.* This, it may be remembered, was the justification for the existence of the offence of blasphemy for hundreds of years. If it is the true reason then Lord Coleridge's distinction between manner and content must be wrong, for a moderately expressed opinion that there is no God can be more damaging than the rantings of a half-crazed fanatic. If this view was accepted today it would be a clear fetter on freedom of speech[115] — one which would clearly run counter to the philosophy of Mill's *On Liberty*.

3. *The protection of individual feelings.* It is not unknown for criminal sanctions to be employed in order to prevent offence[116] — should this apply to offence to religious feelings? If so it should be shown that religious beliefs are something special, something that need the intervention of the criminal sanction.[117] This is a difficult point, for the strongly religious feel strongly about religion whilst the strongly atheistic

feel strongly about atheism and the strongly political feel strongly about politics and all *may* feel hurt or even outrage when their beliefs are attacked and ridiculed. Nevertheless the Law Commission feels that where there are 'overwhelming social pressures, ... the general presumption in favour of freedom of speech both as to matter and manner may require modification either for the benefit of particular members of society or for the benefit of society as a whole'.[118] The Commission feels that incitement to racial hatred is such a crime[119] but that the social danger of attacks on religion is not a real one, as racial attacks were in the 1960s, so as to justify the creation of that offence. It feels that such a crime should only be created if such a social need is shown. However, it may be noted that attacks on such groups as Sikhs and Jews can be religious or racial or a mixture of both and when this is the case the ambit of the offence of incitement to racial hatred may be in some doubt.[120] In any case incitement to religious hatred may be such a terrible thing that it should be unlawful even though we do not presently see it as a real danger, as is the case with actions aimed at genocide.[121] While the Law Commission does not feel that religions in a multi-racial society necessarily need special protection as such, it concludes this heading by saying that the special feelings which people hold about religion could swing the law towards retaining an offence of blasphemy.[122]

4. *The protection of public order.* After some of the speeches in *Bowman*'s case it seemed as if blasphemy could be becoming merely a public order offence. However, the modern statutory offences in this area, especially the wide-ranging Section 5 of the Public Order Act (as amended) 1936, make it most likely that insulting remarks about religion resulting in public disorder are, without the need of a special blasphemy law, in any case illegal.[123]

Although the Law Commission is against either the continuation of the common law offence of blasphemy or its replacement, it does go on to consider, should a new offence be thought expedient, the possibilities of new offences, which they consider to be:

(1) publishing insulting matter likely to provoke a breach of the peace by outraging the religious convictions of others;[124] or
(2) incitement to religious hatred;[125] or
(3) publicly insulting the feelings of religious believers.

However, they are very wary of an offence which could affect such things as public discussion of birth control (which clearly outrages the religious sensibilities of some) or would interfere with scientific debate. On balance they would favour the first of the alternatives but with a specific-intent requirement and also a defence so that one would be free to comment where:

> it is very much in the public interest that the beliefs and practices of particular religious sects should come under sharp criticism, and in those cases we think it would be inappropriate for the criminal law to give even a semblance of protection to the feelings of their adherents.[126]

Whilst blasphemy is confined to Christianity one problem that the law has not had to face is the question of definition. If the law is to now have a criminal offence based on 'outraging religious convictions' we will have to determine what is a religion, and whilst the Law Commission can find no fully satisfactory answer it would, by a small margin, protect those religions which are recognised as such for the registration of places of religious worship by the Registrar-General.[127]

The conclusions of the Law Commission will find general favour with established (if one may use the term) opinion, although it does underrate one or two matters of importance. The expression of opinion about some religions can still provoke public disorder. Thus in 1971[128] a Pakistani who lived in Manchester wrote to a newspaper in Pakistan complaining of a work circulating in Manchester which, she claimed, insulted the Holy Prophet, with the result that there were serious disturbances in Pakistan, including the desecration of several Christian churches, the looting of wine shops and the destruction of the British Council offices at Lahore. More recently, this time in Rotherham, there were riots inside and outside mosques during Ramadan (1980) over certain religious differences.[129] The other, more technical, subject worthy of some consideration would have been the possibility of a group libel law,[130] especially with the recent developments in the law of libel relating to religious groups.[131]

The Law Commission has not, it seems, followed the approach of the Williams Committee on Obscenity and Film Censorship.[132] In short that Committee would divide offending material into two classes — *restricted* and *prohibited* — with an attempt to try and describe in some detail what may not be sold at all and what may only be sold under restricted conditions.[133] Clearly to attempt such a task with religious objects would be well nigh impossible and many will agree with Williams that no matter should be prohibited on the ground of blasphemy alone.[134] Parliament has been reluctant either to implement or to propose some workable substitute to Williams and we may expect it to be even more reluctant to step into this area. Whatever happens, many will be unhappy — the old law may linger on but if so there will be many cases of religious vilification that it will not reach, any defendant prosecuted under it may expect considerable sympathy given the castigation the offence has generally received, and other controls, as does happen from time to time,[135] may be of more use to those who wish to suppress anti-religious material. Any suggestion that the law should go without replacement can confidently be expected to be met by an outcry that the 'floodgates have been opened' and 'religion is under attack'. Finally any modified and modernised law of blasphemy may result in people actually being prosecuted for the offence, an occurrence which, *Gay News* apart, would not seem to be so likely with the present state of affairs.

Notes

1. See, in particular, C. Kenny, 'The evolution of the law of blasphemy', *Cambridge Law Journal*, I, 1922, p. 127; G. D. Nokes, *A History of the Crime of Blasphemy*, 1928; Hypathia Bradlaugh Bonner, *Penalties Upon Opinion; or Some Records of the Laws of Heresy and Blasphemy*, 3rd edn, 1934; P. O'Higgins, 'Blasphemy in Irish law, *Modern Law Review*, XXIII, 1960, p. 151; L. Blom-Cooper and C. Drewry, *Law and Morality*, 1976, pp. 249–60; and Law Commission, *Working paper No. 79 — Offences against Religion and Public Worship*, 1981, Chapters II and III.

2. Thus see *Taske's Case* (1618) Hob. 236. Parliament took an interest in these matters during the Commonwealth. For example in *Naylor's Case* (1656) 5 St. Tr. 825, Lord Commissioner Whitelocke declared, 'heresy is Crimen Judicii, an erroneous opinion; blasphemy is Crimen Malitae, a reviling of the name and honour of God'.

3. *R* v *Sedley* (1663) 17 St. Tr. 155. See also *Keach* (1665) 6 St. Tr. 701.

4. (1676) 1 Vent. 293.

5. See *R* v *Hetherington* (1841) 4 St. Tr. N.S. 563 at pp. 576–8 and Kenny, 'Evolution', at pp. 130–1.

6. (1729) Fitz. 64.

7. *R* v *Annet* (1762) 1 Black W. 369. Annet was regarded as a hero by the freethinkers of the nineteenth century and his work often reprinted — see *The Infidel Tradition* in note 8. By 1825 his works were not regarded as illegal.

8. For the history of the period with regard to blasphemy see E. Royle: *Victorian Infidels*, 1974; *The Infidel Tradition from Paine to Bradlaugh*, 1976; and Chapter XIV of his *Radicals, Secularists and Republicans: Popular Freethought in Britain 1866–1915*, 1980.

9. See *R* v *Williams* (1797) 26 St. Tr. 653.

10. *R* v *Carlile* (1819) 3 B. & Ald. 161, and see 1 St. Tr. N.S., pp. 1423–6.

42 *Religion and the law*

11. *R* v *Carlile* (1821) 1 St. Tr. N.S. 1034.
12. Ibid., pp. 1045–6.
13. Ibid., p. 1046, *per* Best J.
14. Ibid., p. 1048, *per* Best J. See also Bayley J. at p. 1050.
15. See Chapter 12 at p. 185.
16. In *Murray* v *Benbow* 4 St. Tr. N.S. 1409 he refused an injunction to prevent the publication of a pirated copy of *Cain* underlining the vital point that if a work is considered to be blasphemous by the *criminal law* this has *civil law* consequences.
17. *Lawrence* v *Smith* (1822) Jac 471.
18. 4 St. Tr. N.S. 563.
19. Ibid., pp. 567–9.
20. Ibid., p. 570.
21. Ibid., p. 574.
22. Ibid., p. 575. To prove his point he initiated a successful prosecution against an established bookseller who sold an edition of Shelley's poems containing 'Queen Mab' — *R* v *Moxon* (1841) 4 St. Tr. N.S. 694.
23. Ibid., pp. 576–8.
24. *Cf.* Law Com. No. 79, para. 2.5.
25. 4 St. Tr. N.S. 563 at p. 590.
26. Ibid., at p. 592.
27. See, for example, G. J. Holyoake, *Life of Holyoake: Sixty Years of an Agitator's Life*, I, 1906, at p. 110 and at p. 141.
28. Royle, *Victorian Infidels*, at p. 174.
29. W. Carpenter, *The Trial of Charles Southwell*, 1842.
30. *R* v *Holyoake* (1842) 4 St. Tr. N.S. 1381.
31. Witness Anthony Trollope's *The Warden*, 1855.
32. Royle, *The Infidel Tradition*, pp. 205–7.
33. *R* v *Pooley* (1857) 8 St. Tr. N.S. 1089.
34. *R* v *Bradlaugh* (1883) 15 Cox C.C. 217, at p. 222.
35. For an account see A. Calder-Marshall, *Lewd, Blasphemous and Obscene*, 1972, pp. 169–92.
36. *R* v *Bradlaugh*; and *R* v *Foote and Ramsey* (1883) 15 Cox C.C. 231.
37. E.g. *Woolson* above.
38. See the Appendix.
39. 1876, 4th ed, at p. 599.
40. Being:—

   (1) Erskine's charge to a Newcastle grand jury in 1840;
   (2) the report of the Royal Commissioners on Criminal Law in 1841, who, at p. 25, said that as a matter of *practice* only material of this type (i.e. offensively expressed) was prosecuted for blasphemous libel;
   (3) the summing up of Coleridge J. in *Pooley's Case*.

41. Sir J. Stephen, *History of the Criminal Law*, II, 1883, at p. 475. See also his article in the *Fortnightly Review* of March 1884.
42. See *Pankhurst* v *Thompson, Pankhurst* v *Souter* (1886), III T.L.R. 199.
43. Kenny, 'Evolution', at p. 138.
44. Other Bills aimed at the offence's abolition or modification were

introduced in 1890, 1894, 1914, 1922, 1924, 1930 and 1936.
45. Royle, *Radicals, Secularists and Republicans*, at p. 263.
46. (1908) 72 J.P. 188.
47. Quoted in Royle, *Radicals, Secularists and Republicans*, at p. 293.
48. Drewry, *Law and Morality*, at p. 293.
49. [1917] A.C. 406.
50. [1917] A.C. 406 at: pp. 421-3 (Lord Finlay L.C.); p. 433 (Lord Dunedin); p. 446 (Lord Parker of Waddington), p. 460 (Lord Sumner) and p. 470 (Lord Buckmaster).
51. [1917] A.C. 406, at pp. 466-7 *per* Lord Sumner.
52. See Royle, *Radicals, Secularists and Republicans*, pp. 282-3, and E. Pack, *The Trial and Imprisonment of J.W. Gott*, undated.
53. See (1922) 16 Cr. App. Rep. 87. Avery J.'s summing-up was published in *The Freethinker*, 8 January 1922, p. 28.
54. Drewry, *Law and Morality*, pp. 255-6.
55. For some other examples see N. Walter, *Blasphemy in Britain: The Practice and Punishment of Blasphemy and the Trial of Gay News*, 1977, at p. 8.
56. Sir Alfred Denning, *Freedom Under the Law*, 1949, at p. 46.
57. P. O'Higgins, *Censorship in Britain*, 1972, pp. 21-2.
58. *R* v *Carlile* (1819) 3 B. & Ald. 161, at p. 166.
59. H.L.Deb., 1978, vol. 280, col. 314 (Lord Gardiner).
60. For an example of this see G. Robertson, *Obscenity*, 1979, at p. 274.
61. M. Tracey and D. Morrison, *Whitehouse*, 1979, pp. 110-15.
62. Ibid., at p. 113.
63. Ibid., pp. 5-6.
64. Obscene Publications Act 1959, Section 1(3)(*b*).
65. *The Times*, 19 February 1971.
66. *The Sunday Times*, 5 September 1976. The Danish Government was advised that the film was not blasphemous under Danish law (*The Times*, 6 September 1976). The proposed film had been causing trouble since 1973, see *The Times*, 1 September 1973.
67. G. Robertson 'Blasphemy: The Law Commission Working Paper', *Public Law*, 1981, p. 295 at p. 298.
68. Tracey and Morrison, *Whitehouse*, at p. 7.
69. Ibid., at p. 11.
70. Walter, *Blasphemy in Britain*, pp. 11-12.
71. See Chapter I, pp. 11-14.
72. Obscene Publications Act 1959, Section 2(4).
73. [1968] 1 Q.B. 479.
74. [1970] 2 Q.B. 697.
75. [1978] 3 All E.R. 175.
76. See R. Buxton, 'The Case of Blasphemous Libel', *Criminal Law Review*, 1978, p. 673.
77. [1979] A.C. 617.
78. Walter, *Blasphemy in Britain*, at p. 10.
79. See also the words of Greene B. in *R* v *Petcherini* (1855) 7 Cox C.C. 79, at p. 84.
80. E.g. Section 8 of the Criminal Law Act 1967, overruling *D.P.P.* v *Smith* [1961] A.C. 290.

81. See [1979] A.C. 617, at pp. 642–3.
82. See above.
83. [1979] A.C. 617, at pp. 657–8.
84. [1979] A.C. 617, at p. 665.
85. *Cf.* Law Com. No. 79, paras 3.3–5.
86. The related offence of criminal libel seems to have moved in the same direction; see *Goldsmith* v *Pressdram Ltd* [1977] 1 Q.B. 83.
87. *The Times*, 4 October 1977.
88. On which see Robertson, *Obscenity*.
89. See Town Police Clauses Act 1847, Section 28, Metropolitan Police Act 1839, Section 54(1), and the City of London Police Act 1839, Section 35(12).
90. Nokes, *A History of the Crime of Blasphemy*, pp. 35, 38, 82 and 86. One Jackson was convicted of profanity in 1912 (see Royle, *Radicals, Secularists and Republicans*, at p. 280) and the magistrate equated 'profanity' with 'blasphemy' (see Bonner, *Penalties Upon Opinion*, at p. 124).
91. E.g. Profane Oaths Act 1745.
92. Thus in 1941 a secularist speaker was fined for breach of the Hyde Park Regulations — Walter, *Blasphemy in Britain*, at p. 7.
93. See Chapter I, pp. 7–10.
94. H.L. Deb, 1978, vol. 389, cols 279–350.
95. Col. 286.
96. Col. 289.
97. Cols 308 and 315.
98. E.g. col. 330.
99. Cols 305 and 318.
100. Cols 311, 315, 326 and 334.
101. Sir Norman Anderson, *Liberty, Law and Justice*, 1978, at p. 120. See also F.H. Amplett Micklewright, 'Blasphemy and the Law', *Law and Justice*, 1979, 20, at pp. 30–1.
102. *Criminal Law Review*, 1979, p. 311, at p. 313.
103. P. Jones, 'Blasphemy, Offensiveness and Law', *British Journal of Political Science*, X, 1980, pp. 129–48.
104. P. 138.
105. Pp. 142–3.
106. See p. 147.
107. Para. 6.1.
108. Para. 6.2. If it remains it means that 'the exiguous or non-existent burden laid upon the prosecution to prove some possibility of disturbance to Public order compares unfavourably with the position in other areas of the law.'
109. Para. 6.7.
110. Para. 6.9.
111. *R* v *Gathercole* (1838) 2 Lewin 237, at p. 254.
112. J.R. Spencer in *Criminal Law Review*, 1981, pp. 810–20, at pp. 814–5.
113. See para. 5.7.
114. Paras 7.5–6.
115. Para. 7.7.
116. E.g. the Indecent Displays (Control) Act 1981.
117. Para. 7.14.

118. Para. 7.15.
119. See Chapter I, p. 23.
120. Thus see *Ealing London Borough Council* v *Race Relations Board* [1972] A.C. 342, and Chapter I, pp. 1–7.
121. Genocide Act 1961, which clearly protects *inter alia religious groups* defined as such.
122. Para. 7.21.
123. Para. 7.23.
124. Paras 8.3–4.
125. Para. 8.5.
126. Para. 8.15.
127. Paras 8.17–22.
128. See P. Jeffrey, *Migrants and Refugees*, 1976, at p. 43.
129. *The Times*, 13 August 1980, and the *Observer*, 24 August 1980.
130. On which see for example *Beauharnais* v *People of the State of Illinois*, 343 U.S. 250 (1952).
131. See Chapter I, pp. 10–11.
132. Cmnd. 7772, 1979.
133. See Chapter 13 of their report.
134. At p. 125.
135. In 1979 the film *The Life of Brian (of Nazareth)*, which contained jokes about the Sermon on the Mount, ex-lepers complaining about their cures, and the Crucifixion, met with bans in some areas and protests in others. There was no serious suggestion that its makers should be dealt with under the criminal law, for films are subject to a local-authority-managed licensing system.

3 Sunday laws

Maddening churchbells of all degrees of dissonance ... throbbing, jerking, tolling, as if the plague were in the city and the deathcarts were going round. Everything was bolted and barred that could by possibility furnish relief to an overworked people ... nothing to change the brooding mind, or raise it up.

[Charles Dickens, *Little Dorrit*, 1857]

Introduction[1]

When attendance at the established Church was backed by sanction of the law it was natural that Sunday activities should be restricted so that the faithful were not diverted from their duty and, indeed, the English Protestant state seems to have been more zealous in this regard than most Western European countries.[2] At one time the Christian nature of the Sabbath was seen as the primary aim of Sunday observance laws[3] and in 1947 the Gowers Commission recognised that 'the policy underlying Sunday closing depends in part on spiritual questions'.[4] Although some still see this as a primary justification for Sunday restrictions[5] they are few and are many times outnumbered by those who support such restrictions upon other grounds, namely:

(1) The special nature of Sunday should not be profaned by unseemly activities and indeed too much noise on a Sunday may disturb those who wish quietly to attend their places of worship.[6]
(2) Sunday has evolved (from whatever the background) into a 'family day' and should be preserved as such.[7]
(3) A lack of Sunday activities ensures that workers are not unduly exploited on that day, an idea which found favour with Blackstone[8] as long ago as the eighteenth century. In 1964 trade unions took the view that it was 'undesirable as a matter of social policy to make changes that would result in or encourage a substantial increase in the number of people who had to work on Sunday'.[9] It may also be noted that because many workers do not work on Sundays, an alteration to the law means an alteration to their conditions of service, which many might regard as a change for the worse.

(4) If Sunday were 'just another day' Christian church-goers would be put at a disadvantage.

Opposition to these views is both idealistic — namely, that the sum effect of the remaining Sunday laws is to hinder many in their peaceful activities — and pragmatic — in that so much of the law is ignored that Sunday observance laws provide a target for those who wish to hold the law up to ridicule.

Sunday laws still provoke controversy and it is remarkable that amongst the many social reforms that Parliament has enacted, especially in the 1960s (including the abolition of capital punishment and the changes to the law on abortion, divorce and homosexuality), the attempts to liberalise the position on Sunday entertainments meet with failure.[10] Support for restrictions on Sundays has been strong until recently in parts of Wales where a 'local option'[11] exists and there can be opposition to an extension of Sunday activities in other areas as well — as the defeat of the West Midlands County Council Bill 1976 (which would have authorised extensive commercial and trading activities and motor-racing in the streets of central Birmingham, on Sundays) illustrates.

Despite the long history of Sabbatarian legislation in England, the currently accepted common law position[12] is that what is not expressly prohibited by statute[13] on that day is, if otherwise lawful, allowed. Until recently a code of laws prevented, in theory, manual labour, entertainment, and retail trading on Sundays. Thus under the Sunday Observance Act 1677, 'no tradesman, artificer, workman, labourer or other person whatsoever, shall do or exercise any wordly labour, business or work of their ordinary callings upon the Lord's Day, or any part thereof [works of necessity and charity excepted].' By the 1860s a restrictive approach to the statute was taken,[14] and it was generally ignored in the twentieth century. A final shudder from the statute came when a limited liability company[15] attempted to avoid a contract that it had entered into, on a Sunday, with another limited liability company. Mocatta J. did not seem to have a great deal of patience with such an archaic act and in any case, 'A limited company is incapable of public workship or repairing to a church or of exercising itself in the duties of piety and true religion, either publicly or privately, on any day of the week.'[16] The entire statute went in 1969[17] with few to mourn its passing.

Sunday entertainment

By virtue of Section 1 of the Sunday Observance Act 1780,

any house, room, or other place which shall be opened or used for publick entertainment or amusement, or for publickly debating on any subject whatsoever, upon any part of the Lord's Day called Sunday, and to which persons shall be admitted by the payment of money or by tickets sold for money, shall be deemed a disorderly house or place.

These words have meant a general prohibition on commercial Sunday entertainments (somewhat wider in scope than perhaps was the original intention)[18] which, subject to the exceptions discussed below, is still of general application.

A law so out of line with the desires of so many members of society is naturally flouted by laymen, and official bodies too have been tempted to ignore it — in 1930[19] the London County Council issued a licence to a cinema which stated that no legal action would be taken against it if it presented films on a Sunday provided that a payment was made to charity for each performance. Local authorities are in no position to ignore an Act of Parliament, however, even one imposing Sabbatarian restrictions: 'the London County Council is in no better position than James II ... laws cannot be dispensed with by the authority of the London County Council, when they cannot by royal authority'.[20] Nor did the honest motive of the Council affect the outcome: 'It is said that charity covers a multitude of sins, but I have never yet heard that cited to prove that if an act is done for charitable reasons it is lawful, when it would be otherwise unlawful.'[21]

Following this striking down of what had become a common practice, Parliament passed the Sunday Entertainments Act 1932, to authorise the opening of cinemas[22] (under specified conditions). Section 5 of that Act also permits:

(1) any musical entertainment at any place licensed to be open and used on Sundays for that purpose;
(2) the opening of any museum, picture gallery, zoological or botanical garden or aquarium;
(3) any lecture or debate.

It should be borne in mind that the Act does not sanction *any* Sunday activity and thus, for instance, local authorities have no power to license such things as public dancing on Sundays.[23]

The 1780 Act may apply to any place that is used for an event, as is shown by *Cully* v *Harrison*,[24] where a motor cycle 'scramble' was held in a park. Members of the public purchased tickets in order to enable them to stand near rope barriers so that they could watch the races. 'Place' was held to include a piece of land, and the presence of buildings on the land was held not to be relevant. In a general discussion on Sunday sporting activities Lord Goddard C.J. stated:

> If we were to decide that what was done in the present case was no breach of the Act of 1780, it would follow that every racecourse could be opened on Sunday and races could take place. It is well known that races do not take place on Sunday, and I think it is because of these Acts. If we gave a decision the other way, it would be possible for race courses to be opened and for dog racing and motor racing to take place on a Sunday, provided that the organisers closed the buildings, the grandstand and refreshment rooms.[25]

The 'musical entertainment' that is permitted must be 'a concert or similar entertainment consisting of the performance of music, with or without singing or recitation'.[26] Thus where there is an ordinary music hall 'turn' that consists of a performer giving comic imitations, dialogues, and 'representations of two women nagging at each other' whilst a piano is played in the background — the piano-playing will not constitute the governing or predominant feature of the performance.[27] Bizarre results have been produced by some interpretations of the provision with the result that 'a singer may not use a false moustache or a funny hat; he may not even wear a kilt to sing 'Annie Laurie' unless he is a Scotsman and can claim that it is his normal dress'.[28] Also penalised are those who (i) advertise; or (ii) cause to be advertised; or (iii) print; or (iv) publish, advertisements relating to illegal Sunday entertainments.[29] Thus a newspaper that announces that boxing is to take place on a Sunday advertises it even though no seat price is mentioned and the fact that the paper receives no payment will not take away its guilt.[30] Where no admission price is disclosed in the advertisement the offence is committed if it is clear to the average reader from the overall circumstances that payment for admission is expected.[31]

Sports events will be illegal if they come under the terms of the 1780 Sunday Observance Act but, following the repeal of a statute, archaic even by Sabbatarian standards — the 1625 Sunday Observance Act, in 1969,[32] it is no longer illegal to assemble outside one's own parish to play sport! The 1780 Act has always been thought not to apply to participant sport and since *Culley* v *Harrison* spectator sport has continued with such devices as payment for car-parking rather than payment for entry. The law has never been taken to apply to *bona fide* clubs.[33]

Finally, it is now possible for a licensed theatre to put plays on, on a Sunday after the hour of 2 p.m.[34]

Unlike the law on Sunday trading, to be discussed presently, the law restricting Sunday entertainments receives little comment today. Possibly the exceptions now go so far that there is thought to be little merit in enforcing it — in any case since 1951[35] the police have been instructed to leave enforcement of this law to private prosecutors. Whilst remaining on the statute book the odd bite is still possible from the worn-out gums — as happened in 1978 when some New Year's Eve celebrations, falling on a Sunday, were declared to be illegal.[36]

Sunday trading

Perhaps the kindest comment to be made about the Sunday trading laws is that they reflect an idea about the working week that has long since vanished — beyond that, the comments made by Humphreys J. in 1946 on the items that may be legally bought still hold good:

I have found it quite impossible to arrive at any conclusion as to what was in the mind of those who put in this list of those things that may be sold on Sundays, unless it amounts to this (I am not saying I think it does, but it possibly may) that whenever you can think of anything which people are likely to want on Sunday, then a shop may be kept open for that purpose. So you can find excepted things which are not in the least necessary, which can never be necessary, but which are the sort of things which the ordinary person may desire to purchase on a Sunday, although he could purchase them all perfectly easily on another day. They are such things as[37] ... sweets, chocolate, ice-cream. Why should people be particularly allowed to buy sweets and ice-cream on Sundays if all shops are to be closed on Sunday? I do not know. What is the necessity for a flower shop to be open on a Sunday? It is very pleasant for some people to be able to buy flowers on Sundays, but nobody can say it is necessary. Fruit and vegetables are things which you can eat[38] and one can understand it in that case. Then you get aircraft, motor or cycle supplies or accessories. I can only imagine that that is to help the broken-down motorist or even possibly the person who is travelling by air, but it is a little unlikely that a person who is travelling by air, and who found it necessary to make a forced landing, would go to the sort of shop which would be open on a Sunday in order to get what was necessary to make his aircraft airworthy. Then, tobacco and smokers' requisites. No doubt it is a convenience for a great many people to buy tobacco on Sunday. Then, newspapers, books and stationery and so forth; guide books, postcards, photographs, reproductions, photographic film and plates and souvenirs.[39]

Some items may always lawfully be sold on a Sunday whilst others[40] may be sold if the local authority has passed a 'partial exemption order', and yet others[41] may be sold for up to eighteen Sundays in any one year, with the permission of the local authority, in a district 'which is frequented as a holiday resort during certain seasons of the year'.[42]

If an item is sold or dealt with on a Sunday and it is not in one of the lists of permitted transactions, and

(1) it is sold or dealt with in a shop or place, and
(2) by an act constituting 'a serving of customers',

an offence is committed.[43]

The transaction must be in a place which has a recognisable degree of permanence. Thus a market stall which is moved twice a year to make way for a fair, and which has mail delivered to it, is sufficiently permanent even though it can be moved in an hour and the stock is taken away every night.[44] A stall regularly erected for one day a week[45] or a sixteen-day exhibition on a single site is also sufficiently permanent.[46] On the other hand box-tricycles used for selling ice-cream[47] and motor vans used as mobile shops[48] lack sufficient permanence to be deemed shops. *Jarmain* v *Wetherall*,[49] in 1977, marks perhaps the outer ambit of what will not constitute a shop or place — there it was successfully argued that a stamp and coin fair held for only a day lacked the necessary degree of permanence.

As well as being permanent a 'retail trade or business' must be carried on[50] at the shop or place if the law is to apply. This has been held to cover the selling or buying of goods on a small scale together with the sale of services, such as the repairing of shoes or the cleaning of clothes, in circumstances similar to ordinary retail trade.[51]

There must also be a serving of customers by human, rather than mechanical,[52] agents. There need be no sale at all provided that there is some act aimed towards a possible sale, it making no difference that the conclusion of such a sale is deferred until another day. Giving information about a product on display can constitute 'a serving' and this will be especially likely if the salesmen were placed there for that purpose, or if it was clear to the proprietors that members of the public would frequently ask for information about prohibited items.[53]

When the Sunday Fairs Act 1448 was repealed[54] there was a widespread belief that the Sunday trading provisions did not apply to markets. This belief was firmly quashed in 1972[55] and the courts acted again in 1977,[56] when a company held a large Sunday market, renting 'pitches' to stall-holders. Given the large profits that were to be made a fine seemed to be a small penalty to pay and so an injunction against the market was issued, with Lord Denning M.R. declaring,[57] 'It seems to me that it should be known throughout the country that this Sunday market trading is contrary to the Shops Act 1950. It cannot therefore be carried on. It does not matter whether people think that it is beneficial or not. It is contrary to the Act.'

Special consession is made to those who observe Saturday as their Sabbath rather than Sunday.[58] 'A person of the Jewish religion' or 'members of any religious body regularly observing the Jewish sabbath' (such as Seventh Day Adventists) may open their shops for any retail trade up to 2 p.m. on Sundays provided that they close all day on Saturdays, display the requisite notices, and register with the local authority.[59] Should an occupier of a shop become so registered he may not be concerned with the running of other shops on Saturdays and the registration cannot be revoked within the first twelve months.

Until 1979 the procedure was that registration was automatic if the requisite declaration was handed in. Where disputes developed about the 'Jewishness' of the applicant a tribunal,[60] set up in consultation with the London Committee of Deputies of the British Jews or, if the person is not a Jew, with the appropriate body, will consider the issue. Registration would have been revoked if it was found that the person did not hold the religious views which he claimed.[61] There was a duty, it seemed, placed upon the local authority to register a person who handed in the requisite statutory declaration — refusal to register being countered with a High Court prerogative order.[62]

It was felt by the Home Office and by official Jewish representatives that this automatic registration process had become open to abuse.[63] Jewish nominees were being used for large-scale markets that were not in reality Jewish businesses and there were cases of Sunday markets that had been closed by the courts reopening under 'Jewish management'. The Home Office disliked the abuse of the law whereas the Jewish organisations felt that the situation was giving Jews a poor image. An example of these difficulties came in *Thanet District Council* v *Ninedrive Ltd*[64] where a company, controlled by persons of the Jewish religion, applied to have a piece of land registered for Sunday trading. It was going to allow some forty other (non-Jewish) persons onto the site and they wanted their exemption to cover all of them — they were not Jews but would be plying various trades and would pay the company for the franchise. Walton J. pointed out that each trader must seek registration in his own right and said of the exemption:

> The idea behind these provisions is the obvious one, that as a devout Jew will be prevented by the tenets of his faith from opening his shop on Saturday, it is hard on him that he should in fact be forced to close his shop for two days a week whilst his Christian neighbour is only forced to close it for one. From this simple idea of holding the scales of statutory provision equally between Christian and Jew ... there has sprung up the attempt by certain persons of the Jewish faith to exploit these provisions.[65]

These problems have now lead to a change.[66] Every applicant for registration for the Jewish exemption must now supply a certificate signed by a panel appointed by the Board of Deputies, stating that his conscientious objection to trading on Saturdays is genuine. The new system does not, like the old, appear to follow the principles of natural justice and has certainly made registration harder — thus between 1 December 1979 and 28 April 1981, of 279 applicants interviewed by a panel one-third have not been granted certificates, with no reasons being publicly given for the refusal.[67]

Sunday employment

Although the main restriction on Sunday employment went in 1969 certain prohibitions remain:

(1) there is a general restriction on shopworkers being employed for more than two Sundays a month in a shop lawfully open on Sundays and such workers must receive special time off when they do work on Sundays;[68]
(2) there are restrictions on Sunday work in factories that do not apply to Jewish persons.[69]

Such restrictions are now generally supported on the ground of protection of the work-force rather than for their role in protecting the Sabbath.

The future of Sunday legislation

The most detailed proposals for reform are to be found in the Crathorne Report (1964).[70] The Report's approach can be described as 'moderate', in that while wishing to retain Sunday as a special 'family day' it called for more opportunity for leisure,[71] with cinemas, theatres, public dancing, circuses and similar entertainments being generally available (an objective now achieved, with regard to the first two, by legislation), and sports meetings where payment is required for entry being legalised.[72] Sunday trading would remain generally prohibited,[73] although the system would be rationalised with updated lists of what may lawfully be sold on Sundays.[74] Employees would be protected by guaranteed time off in lieu of Sundays[75] — guaranteed time off which would also apply to those working in the entertainment industry.[76]

Parliamentary discussion on Sunday restrictions today tends to be concentrated on Sunday trading[77] and a strong combination of union and employer pressure matched with a marked degree of Government inertia has prevented even modified, more rational, Sunday trading legislation, whilst total abolition is something that seems far distant. Generally the provisions are defended because of the protection they are said to give to employees but this view is often based on a misunderstanding of what it is that the Sunday trading provisions actually do prohibit and may in any case be seen as rather outdated paternalism. The attempts by so many to get round some of the technicalities of the law illustrate how little it is liked by them whilst the actual possibility of enforcement of the existing legislation can provoke horror and disbelief.[78] Other parts of this work show that the need for time off work on religious grounds is a real one[79] to those who are supposed to be protected by the existing law (e.g. Christians) and to those who receive no protection (e.g. Muslims). Legislation going further than this end is an attempt to impose standards on the unwilling and should no longer have a place on the statute book.

Notes

1. See: C. L. Lewis, *A Critical History of Sunday Legislation*, 1888; W. B. Whittaker, *Sunday in Tudor and Stuart Times*, 1932, and *The Eighteenth-century English Sunday*, 1940; J. Wigley, *The Rise and Fall of the Victorian Sunday*, 1980; P. F. Skottowe, *The Law Relating to Sunday*, 1936; W. Hodgkins, *Sunday — Christian and Social Significance*, 1960; *Departmental Committee Report on Sunday Observance*, Cmnd. 2528, 1964; and St J. A. Robilliard, 'No crime on Sunday?', *Criminal Law Review*, 1980, pp. 496–502. See also *McGowan* v *Maryland* 366 U.S. 420 (1961) for an important United States Supreme Court discussion of the development of English Sunday legislation.

2. When Prince Albert arrived in England he came to the conclusion that Englishmen 'cared for nothing but foxhunting and Sunday observance' — Lytton Strachey, *Queen Victoria*, 1921.

3. For example: Bayley J. in *Fennell et al.* v *Ridler* (1826) 5 B. & C. 406, at p. 407.

4. Cmnd. 7105, 1947, para. 101.
5. In 1964 the view of the Lord's Day Observance Society was that 'the law should be based on Christian principles even if the liberty of some individuals had to be curtailed for the benefit of the community'. Cmnd. 2528, para. 43.
6. Hodgkins, *Sunday*, pp. 204–5.
7. Although as a 'day of leisure' Sunday does present problems:

> The freedom to choose how one spends Sunday poses a conflict of interest between those who wish to enjoy recreation and those who must work to provide those recreations and necessary supporting services and to lose their own Sunday and their opportunity for worship, recreation and family pursuits.

Cmnd. 2528, para. 49.

8. IV Bl., Comm. 63.
9. Cmnd. 2528, para. 46.
10. P.G. Richards, *Parliament and Conscience*, 1970, pp. 159–78, and G. Drewry, 'Sunday laws', *New Law Journal*, 1972, pp. 501–2.
11. Licensing Act 1964, Section 66.
12. The reverse is true of judicial acts — *Re N (Infants)* [1967]1 All E.R. 161. See also Skottowe, *Law Relating to Sunday*.
13. For a list see Wigley, *Rise and Fall*, pp. 204–6.
14. E.g. *R* v *Cleworth* (1864) 4 B. & S. 927; *Palmer* v *Snow* [1900] 1 Q.B. 725, and *Gregory* v *Fearn* [1953] 2 All E.R. 559.
15. *Rolloswin Investments Ltd* v *Chromolit Porgugal Cutelarias e Produtos Metalicos SARL* [1970] 2 All E.R. 673.
16. At p. 675.
17. Statute Law (Repeals) Act 1969.
18. Cmnd. 2528, 1964, at p. 16.
19. *R* v *London County Council, ex p. The Entertainment Protection Association Ltd* [1931] 2 K.B. 215.
20. *Per* Scrutton L.J. at p. 229.
21. *Per* Greer L.J. at p. 235.
22. See also the Sunday Cinema Act 1972.
23. *R* v *Hereford Licensing J.J., Ex p. Newton* [1940] 4 All E.R. 479. Sunday Entertainments Act 1932, Section 3, and see also *Roe* v *Harrogate J.J.* (1966) 64 L.G.R. 465.
24. [1956] 2 All E.R. 254.
25. At p. 256.
26. Sunday Entertainment Act 1932, Section 5.
27. *Barnes* v *Jarvis* [1953] 1 All E.R. 1061.
28. Cmnd. 2528, 1964, at p. 22.
29. Sunday Observance Act 1780, Section 3; *Cf. Green* v *Kursaal (Southend-on-Sea) Estates Ltd* [1937] 1 All E.R. 732.
30. *Green* v *Berlinger* [1936] 1 All E.R. 199.
31. *Kitchener* v *Evening Standard Co. Ltd* [1936] 1 All E.R. 48. A fiction of paying for the seat rather than for admission will make no difference to the commission of the offence.
32. Statute Law (Repeals) Act 1969.

33. Cmnd. 2528, 1964, pp. 27–34.
34. Sunday Theatre Act 1972.
35. H.C. Deb. (1978), vol. 952 (Written Answers), cols 204–5.
36. Ibid.
37. Listed in Schedule 5 of the Shops Act 1950.
38. One of the most 'fruitful' areas of case law has been over just what constitutes 'a refreshment' (which may be sold on a Sunday). *Newberry* v *Cohen's Smoked Salmon Ltd* (1956) 54 L.G.R. 343 held that a raw kipper was a 'refreshment' as it could be consumed on its own. On the other hand flour and tea leaves require further preparation before eating and are thus not 'refreshments' that may be sold without restriction on Sundays. For a decision that raw eggs and lard are not 'refreshments', see Hodgkins, *Sunday*, at p. 159.
39. *Binns* v *Wardale* [1946] 1 K.B. 451, at p. 457.
40. Listed in Schedule 6 of the Shops Act 1950.
41. Listed in Schedule 7 of the Shops Act 1950. One such item is a 'souvenir' which, according to *Hudson* v *Marshall* (1976) 75 L.G.R. 13, includes a 'Bugs Bunny' teeshirt.
42. Shops Act 1950, Section 51.
43. Ibid., Section 47.
44. *Greenwood* v *Whelan* [1967] 1 Q.B. 396.
45. *Maby* v *Warwick Corporation* [1972] 2 Q.B. 242.
46. *Randall* v *D. Turner (Garages) Ltd* [1973] 1 W.L.R. 1052.
47. *Eldorado Ice Cream Co. Ltd* v *Clark, Knighton and Keating* [1938] 1 K.B. 715.
48. *Stone* v *Boreham* [1959] 1 Q.B. 1.
49. 75 L.G.R. 537.
50. Shops Act 1950, Section 74(1).
51. *Dennis* v *Hutchinson* [1922] 1 K.B. 693; *M. & F. Frawley Ltd* v *The Ve-Ri Best Co. Ltd* [1953] 1 Q.B. 318, and *Ilford Corporation* v *Bettaclean (Seven Kings) Ltd* [1965] 2 Q.B. 222.
52. *Willesden Urban District Council* v *Morgan* [1915] 1 K.B. 349, and *Ilford Corporation* v *Bettaclean (Seven Kings) Ltd*.
53. *Waterman* v *Wallasey Corporation, Hesketh* v *Same* [1954] 1 W.L.R. 771; *Betta Cars Ltd* v *Ilford Corporation* (1959) 124 J.P. 19 and *Monaco Garage Ltd* v *Watford Borough Council* [1967] 1 W.L.R. 1069. In 1982 Whitford J. held that allowing people to 'browse' round a store did not constitute a serving: *Daily Telegraph*, 6 March 1982.
54. By the Statute Law (Repeals) Act 1969.
55. *Maby* v *Warwick Corporation* [1972] 2 Q.B. 242.
56. *Stafford Borough Council* v *Elkenford* [1977] 2 All E.R. 519.
57. At p. 528.
58. But not to those who observe other holy days. The Department Committee, Cmnd. 2528, 1964, at p. 55, believed that special provision should be made for Muslims with regard to this.
59. Shops Act 1950, Section 53. S. R. & O. 1937, No. 271.
60. Shops (Regulations for Jewish Tribunals) Regulations 1937, S. R. & O. No. 1038.
61. Shops Act 1950, Section 53(7).
62. Although refusal might be justified in an extreme case; *cf. Thanet District*

Council v *Ninedrive Ltd* [1978] 1 All E.R. 730, and *Chichester District Council* v *Flockglen Ltd* (1978) 122 S.J. 61.

63. G. Alderman, 'Jews and Sunday trading: the use and abuse of delegated legislation', *Public Administration*, LX, 1982, pp. 99-104.

64. [1978] 1 All E.R. 703.

65. At p. 705.

66. Shops Regulations 1979, No. 1294. See *R* v *London Committee of Deputies of British Jews, ex p. Helmcourt Ltd, The Times*, 16 July 1981, and also *Barking and Dagenham L.B.C.* v *Essexplan Ltd, The Times*, 20 November 1982.

67. Alderman, 'Jews and Sunday trading', at p. 102.

68. Shops Act 1950, Section 22.

69. Factories Act 1960, Section 109.

70. Cmnd. 2528.

71. See paras 76, 84, 85, 87, 90 and 96.

72. Para. 117 — but not if the sportsmen are paid to take part.

73. Para. 139.

74. Paras 163 and 165. These lists have formed the basis for many of the proposals for change that have come in recent years.

75. Paras 224 and 230.

76. Para. 226.

77. E.g. Cmnd. 2528, 1964, pp. 35-50; H.L. Deb., vol. 399 (1979), cols 558-608; vol. 368 (1976), cols 685-92; vol. 315 (1971), cols 501-30; vol. 314 (1971), cols 735-96 and 1141-52; vol. 313 (1970), cols 1095-136; vol. 291 (1968), cols 741-50 and 754-63; and vol. 290 (1968), cols 1144-76. See also H.C. Deb., vol. 999 (1981), cols 561-624; vol. 930 (1977), cols 1689-98; and vol. 919 (1976), cols 471-8 — for some recent attempts to change the law.

In early 1983 Raymond Whitney, M.P., failed by the wide margin of 106 votes to 205 to secure agreement in the Commons to a proposal to abolish *all* restrictions on Sunday trading; see H.C. Deb., vol. 36 (1983), cols 540-606. Although supported by the Association of District Councils he faced widespread opposition from employers' associations on the ground that Sunday trading would increase costs, and from the trade unions who felt that employees would be disadvantaged by the measure. Mr Whitney felt such a change in the law would encourage freedom of choice but was opposed amongst others by a Liberal, Alan Beith, M.P., who argued that 'one has to recognise the role of the state in controlling freedom when it affects the freedom of others ... there is no doubt that a change towards extensive Sunday trading would clearly affect the freedom of many people to worship and enjoy peace and quiet on Sundays' (col. 560). Mr Mellor, for the Government, laid down three tests for the use of the criminal law in such an area (cols 564-5):

> (1) is the unlawful activity so clearly defined that the citizen can be reasonably certain whether he risks engaging in a criminal activity when he embarks on a certain course of action?
> (2) does the law reasonably clearly distinguish the prohibited activity from other forms of like activity which are not criminal offences?
> (3) is the law credible and does it command the respect of the public as a whole, not just of a particular section of the community?

He felt the current law failed all three tests. Despite this encouragement from the Government the measure was clearly defeated by a combination of all sections of the House.

78. When a large number of shopkeepers in Tameside were threatened with prosecution in early 1980 there was an outcry: *Manchester Evening News*, 23 January 1980. The Court of Appeal, *The Times*, 27 April 1983, have now held that a local council may obtain an injunction to enforce the law. Lawton L.J. said that in reaching this decision it was irrelevant that: (1) Section 47 was widely disregarded, (2) many people wanted it repealed, (3) many people found it convenient to shop for non-exempt goods on Sundays, and (4) the law was enforced selectively and spasmodically.

79. See Chapters 1 at p. 12, 10 at pp. 159–60 and 11 at pp. 169–70.

4 Charitable status, taxation advantages and related matters

One other matter of substance has arisen in the course of this Enquiry which, in my view, merits further consideration, and that is the variety of privileges which the laws of this country confer upon associations of mortals who combine for religious purposes.

[*Per* Sir John Foster, Enquiry into the Practices and Effects of Scientology, 1971, para. 263]

This chapter presents a picture of the religious organisation and purpose as a legal charity and outlines the advantages that thus accrue. This is followed by a discussion of the related matter of taxation advantages. The chapter then concludes with a look at two slightly different matters — the courts' continued allowance of what may be called religious choice in private giving, and finally the doctrine of undue influence. The law on charities and taxation is indeed vast, a subject for many a full-length book, and the aim here is to give a sample of the highlights rather than a full exposition, such highlights being illuminated by the twin spots of religious privilege and religious liberty.

Advancement of religion — the advantages

Allowing organisations which 'advance religion' charitable status is justified on the ground that they are said to provide 'public benefit', the reason for allowing anything to be considered charitable in the modern law,[1] a factor which usually has to be established to the satisfaction of the courts.[2] When the courts come to consider whether a purpose advancing religion is for the public benefit a number of special factors come into play.

First, the court will not adjudicate on the merits of the religious doctrine being advanced. In *Thornton* v *Howe* in 1862[3] the court held that the advancement of the writings of the early nineteenth-century Anglican 'mystic', Joanna Southcote[4] was charitable even though it was clear that the judge thought little of the worth of those writings. Lord Davey's words in *Free Church of Scotland* v *Lord Overtoun*[5] provide a useful reminder of the traditional role of the courts with regard to doctrine: 'I disclaim altogether any right in this or any other Civil Court of this realm to discuss the truth or reasonableness of any of the doctrines of this or any other religious association.' This applies whether the religion is Christian or otherwise, which is not to say that non-Christian religions may not, because of their cultural differences and different conceptions of charity, suffer certain difficulties from time to time.[6]

Secondly, the courts tend to give encouragement to religious trusts, since 'any religion is better than none'.[7]

Thirdly, where it has been shown that the purpose in question is the advancement of religion there is a presumption that it is for the public benefit, a presumption which may only be rebutted where it is established that the relevant doctrines are subversive to the very foundations of all religion and are subversive of all morality[8] or are illegal.[9] Thus in *Re Watson* (1973) there was a bequest for the publication of a series of fundamentalist Christian writings. 'Expert evidence' was that their intrinsic worth was nil and they were unlikely to extend mankind's knowledge of the Christian religion. However the writings would probably confirm the religious prejudices of those who were likely to read them and they were not contrary to religion or morality. Thus the presumption was applied and the purpose held to be charitable, just as it was later to be applied in holding that the advancement of the Exclusive Brethren was a charitable purpose.[10] It has been argued that 'A religion which breaks up families might therefore be accounted contrary to public policy'.[11] Other parts of this work[12] reveal that there has been much public concern over some of the modern cults which, it is claimed, sometimes have this effect. As yet, there has been no conclusive decision on the point, but it may be said that the law already protects children (i.e. those under eighteen) from influences which break up the family bond, whereas parents do not enjoy any special control over their adult children. Religious differences have frequently split families but this has usually been a by-product of religious fervour rather than an express aim of the religion in question. The position may be different where it can be demonstrated that an express object of the cult is to undermine family life — that indeed might be considered 'subversive of all morality'. But just to say 'subversive of *all* morality' shows what a heavy task attackers of such a cult have although not all the past cases would place such a heavy burden upon their shoulders.[13] There must, nevertheless, be some evidence that the work advances the relevant religion in some material way (such as teaching or at least holding public services) — thus, as will be shown later, the prayers and contemplations of a closed order of nuns will not provide sufficient 'public benefit' even should the religion in question believe that this does provide spiritual benefit for the public.[14]

Where organisations are recognised by the law as charities in that they advance religion,

(1) they may be exempt from some of the controls exorcised under the charities legislation;[15]
(2) they will be exempt from certain technical rules (namely, the rule concerning certainty of objects is not so strictly applied and the rule against perpetuities does not apply at all);
(3) they will find that the *cy-près* doctrine may be invoked to transfer their assets to a likeminded body where otherwise, under the general law, they would have reverted (because of failure of the original object) back to the donors (although this may not always assist the 'fringe' cults holding near unique views);[16]
(4) they, as will be illustrated later, will be entitled to substantial tax advantages.

Definition of religion in the law of charities

English law is not called upon to answer questions in the abstract and thus one cannot say that the legal definition of religion is this or that. Rather it has been necessary to define 'religion' for particular purposes — the most 'legalistic' perhaps being where it must be determined whether something which is said to advance religion in the law of charities can be thought of as truly religious. In *Barralet* v *Attorney-General*,[17] in 1980, Dillon J. had to decide whether a humanist society could be considered to be 'religious' at the present day. The society in question was the South Place Ethical Society, whose objects included 'the study and dissemination of ethical principles, and the cultivation of a rational religious sentiment'. Such principles embrace belief in the excellence of truth, love and beauty and are said to date back to the time of Plato. They do not embrace a belief in the supernatural but rather hold that truth is a matter which may be reached through the intellect. To answer whether this added up to a religious belief as far as the law was concerned Dillon J. could have taken either a wide view, one which involved calling something religious if it was one's 'ultimate concept of life' even if it did not embrace a supernatural or, at least, superhuman deity; or a narrower one which holds that religion must involve belief in and worship of a deity.

The wider test has developed in the United States of America in the 1960s where cases had declared such things as Buddhism, Taoism, Ethical Culture and Secular Humanism 'religious' under that country's guarantees for religious freedom.[18] In particular *United States* v *Seeger*[19] was of prime significance. This was a conscientious-objector case where, under the relevant statute, the objection to military service had to be based upon 'religious training and belief'. The court was prepared to hold that this could reach 'the broader concept of a power or being, or a faith, to which all else is subordinate or upon which all else is ultimately dependent' and would thus cover 'any belief occupying in the life of its possessor a place parallel to that occupied by belief in God in the minds of theists in religion'.

Of course to say something is like a religion is not to say it is one and the United States courts sometimes tend to attempt to accommodate humanists so that they cannot be said to be favouring religion (in the orthodox sense) to the prejudice of convinced and committed non-believers. As the United Kingdom does not walk a similar constitutional tightrope it is perhaps not surprising that our courts concentrate more on finding the literal meaning of 'religion' rather than examine it against a wider background. Thus the English view is exemplified by *R* v *Registrar-General, ex p. Segerdal*,[20] where the Court of Appeal upheld the view of the Registrar-General that a chapel belonging to the Church of Scientology was not entitled to be registered as a place of religious worship under the Places of Religious Worship Act 1855. To succeed the Scientologists had to show that what took place in their chapel was *religious worship*, a point which was clear to all three judges,[21] although certainly the attitude of Lord Denning was that Scientology was not a religion because of the failure to show that there was some special deity which they worshipped. It is interesting to note that Winn L.J.[22] did recognise that by some definitions the philosophy underlining Scientology was not unlike what at least some past cultures have considered to be religious, but agreed in the result that the chapel could not be registered because the requirement of worship was missing.

Neither of these two schools of thought was binding on Dillon J., for the one was a doctrine evolved in United States constitutional law whereas the other, more narrow approach was supported by dicta in a Court of Appeal decision on a rather different legal point. Nevertheless in the *South Bank Ethical Society* case Dillon J. adopted the narrower approach. He felt that the definition of religion for charitable purposes had not changed since the legal landmark of *Bowman* v *Secular Society*[23] in 1917. Thus it describes man's relations with God (i.e. a supernatural being) as opposed to his relations with other men. Having determined this he continued:

'There is a further point. It seems to me that two of the essential attributes of religion are faith and worship: faith in a god and worship of that god,'[24] and in so holding imposed an additional restriction on the activities that may be considered religious for these purposes.

Dillon J.'s fairly conservative approach may well not be the last word. In reaching his definition he was prepared to quote from the *Oxford English Dictionary* and, of course, the dictionary meaning can alter over the years.[25] Attacks on it may come on the one hand from those who resent the present position that 'it is enough for any small group of people to come together and claim to believe in, and worship, a deity and this is clearly not good enough in light of the great economic value of the privileges concerned'.[26] While on the other humanist groups will continue to resent the privileged position of religion in the law (although in the *South Bank Ethical Society* case the Society were held to be charitable on another ground — it advanced education — something which such societies will not always be able to claim).[27] A final group to enter the field with a challenge may well be some of the newer 'cults' who feel aggrieved at not being granted equal treatment with more orthodox groups.[28]

Advancement of religion[29]

In order to achieve charitable status the purpose in question must be to advance religion by propagation, teaching, maintaining institutions and so on.[30] It must be for the public benefit — an objective test (it not being enough if the members of the relevant religion consider that what they do benefit the public) but nevertheless one which the courts have applied liberally, for 'In the diversity of form which religious expression may take — praise, petition or sacrifice manifested by words, ritual and music — it is hardly surprising that the judges have found difficulty in finding a definite criteria of public benefit.'[31] Examples of the advancement of religion include:

(1) A gift for the saying of masses. Until *Bourne* v *Keane*[32] 'superstitious uses' were believed to be illegal but by 1919 it was established that the liberating

statutes of the nineteenth century[33] had overtaken this idea with regard to the Catholic mass[34] which if held in public would stand:

> in precisely the same position as any other service of a religious body, and as the advancement of religion by providing for public worship according to the beliefs of a religion recognised by the law has never failed to gain charitable status [would thus be charitable in law].[35]

(2) Maintaining adjuncts to religion such as burial grounds, churchyards, and certain public religious memorials.[36]
(3) A gift to a religion as such, such as the 'Church of England',[37] the 'Roman Catholic Church'[38] or a body such as the 'Salvation Army'[39] will be considered charitable as a gift to the organisation that advances the religion and supports its doctrine.
(4) The upkeep of places of worship.[40]
(5) The support of the clergy.[41]
(6) Support of missionary work, the distribution of religious books and other means of propagating faith.[42]

However, to constitute religious advancement in law the activity must satisfy the requirement of public benefit.[43] In *Gilmour* v *Coates* (1949)[44] there was a trust whose object was the benefit of an order of contemplative nuns who spent their lives offering intercessory prayers, meditating and worshipping, but they performed no tangible works for the outside world. The Catholic authorities argued that this spiritual work produced an edifying result for the public at large. This was held not to constitute public benefit in law for a number of reasons:

(i) it was for the court, not the religion in question, to determine what was in the public benefit;
(ii) the benefit must be more than the mere knowledge that there are those such as these nuns who spend their lives in this way, it must be more than just being inspired to follow them;
(iii) even if the prayers did provide a benefit for the public,
  (1) it was too indirect a one to be taken into account, and
  (2) it was incapable of proof in a court of law.

Thus there was a fatal lack of public benefit and so there was no room for the argument that as only Roman Catholic women could join the order that constituted a sufficient section of the public capable of enjoying the benefit.

Gilmour v *Coates* might be taken as unfair, especially given some of the things that have been endorsed as charities without difficulty. However a dividing line such as this is inevitable, given the ground that the law has now covered. The old Church of the Middle Ages provided charity to the population out of the properties that it had been given and the monies raised through church rates and tithes.[45] However, many centuries later, in the nineteenth century, religions (as opposed to religion) were said to be entitled to equal treatment and what started life as a real benefit to the population was converted into a legal presumption carefully applied lest the courts be denounced as bigots (witness *Thornton* v *Howe*). As the area became greyer an arbitrary line had to be drawn somewhere and it came with *Gilmour* v *Coates*; but what of *Re Watson*? What was the public benefit there? Might not many think there was no more benefit to the public in that case than there was in *Gilmour* v *Coates*; *Gilmour* v *Coates* is unfair because it means that some types of religious activity are privileged over other types but then it is equally unfair that religion in general basks under the sun of its special presumption. Despite calls for reform Governments and Parliament have not shown any willingness to rationalise this branch of the law in line with twentieth-century realities.

Religion and politics

The advancement of a political ideal is not charitable in law and this includes an organisation whose aim is to change the law with regard to some religious matter.[46] Political parties and movements are thus in a weaker position than religions in law. In a recent case[47] because a bequest to a part of the Labour Party infringed the rule against perpetuities (which does not apply to charities) it failed. The Law Commission has recently pointed out that a passion for religion in one man can be countered by a passion for politics in another,[48] yet an organisation promoting one may enjoy advantages which the other may not. It has also been recognised that 'A religious body may, and usually does, engage in a number of subsidiary activities which are not purely religious, but it does not thereby lose its religious character.'[49] On the other hand where one of the express objects in non-charitable the position is different and the entire trust may not be considered charitable in law.[50] This was the position in the *Oxford Group* case (1949), where one of the objects of the Group was the acquisition of land coupled with a scheme for its colonisation by members of the Jewish race — a political object which could have led to conflict with those who then governed Palestine.

The Charity Commissioners[51]

The issue of whether or not a particular body advances religion in law must be determined by the courts, although important issues of this nature are often settled by the statutory body which is charged with the general overseeing of charities — the Charity Commissioners. Their decisions relating to registrations do not always lack controversy, as is perhaps witnessed by the outcry which took place after the 'Moonie' libel action in 1981.[52] The liberal line which they appear to take in these matters may be ascribed to the presumption of public benefit which the law applies to religion, coupled with the wish that they appear as even-handed as possible. Nor should it be overlooked that the Commissioners are limited both physically, given the vast number of organisations with which they have to deal, and legally, because of the statutory framework under which they must operate. Recent matters of interest have included:

(1) A decision not to refuse registration of a trust in favour of a named Church of England clergyman which included support for the practice of exorcism.[53]
(2) In 1976 they noted that there was a steady stream of criticism of 'fringe religious organisations' which were said to 'brainwash' their young followers, coerce them to hand over all their property and conduct questionable fund-raising activities.[54]
These complaints led the Commissioners to make a detailed statement of policy.

(*a*) With regard to cults that 'break up families' and induce their adherents to hand over money, when dealing with *adults* (i.e. those aged eighteen and over) their concern was whether the youngster had joined the movement of his own free will.[55]
(*b*) Where fund-raising methods brings charitable fund-raising *in general* 'into disrepute' this will be pointed out to the relevant trustees.[56]
(*c*) With regard to community living the Charity Commissioners could find no evidence that an unreasonably large portion of the incomes of the fringe religious groups, which they had examined, is taken up with living expenses.[57]
(*d*) They have no evidence that such groups are used as fronts for political ends in England and Wales (the activities of their co-religionists in other countries not being relevant unless connected with the trust in question).[58]
(*e*) Their role as Charity Commissioners is a restricted one given what they see as their duty under the law and given the need to have real evidence when they are to act against a registered religious charity.

In registering an organisation as a charity we are concerned only with the question whether it is established for purposes which are exclusively charitable according to the law of England and Wales. Registration is not an indication that we approve of the charity's objects, or that we are satisfied about the integrity of the trustees, the efficiency of management, or the methods by which it pursues its objects, provided that these are lawful. If there is evidence that the trustees of a charity are acting in breach of the trusts we consider such evidence carefully. But offences against the general law relating to street-collecting and street-trading etc. are matters for the police.[59]

(3) A long-running dispute has been that with the Exclusive Brethren.

In 1970[60] there was a dispute between two factions of that sect, which necessitated the division of trust property between them. Because a doctrine of the Brethren known as Separation from Evil might, in its application by one of the factions, be contrary to public policy, a special one-man inquiry was set up by the Commissioners in 1974.[61] This was to assist in deciding whether the presumption in favour of public benefit had been rebutted. The investigator concluded that the doctrine as applied by the faction in question:

> was transformed into a harsh and harmful doctrine, calculated and in fact operating to disrupt family ties and perfectly normal and proper business, professional and social relationships, and to cause widespread distress and anguish among many deeply religious and decent people.[62]

The investigator therefore concluded,

> [The faction] cannot be regarded as charitable, because the advancement of such a religion, far from being beneficial to the community, is inimical to the true interests of the community ... [and] pending a decision of the court in the matter, the Charity Commissioners should refuse to register, or permit the registration of any meeting house or room [belonging to the faction].[63]

In response the Commissioners were uncertain whether this was sufficient to rebut the presumption of public benefit and so decided that the courts or Parliament must determine the issue, but in the meantime they would 'maintain the status quo' and neither register any new trusts belonging to the faction, nor delete any from the register.[64] They also rejected the idea that their policy infringed the right of one's being able to worship according to one's own conscience. Rather the question 'is the narrower, but still important one of whether the practices of a particular sect are *so contrary to public policy* that they ought no longer to be entitled to charitable status'.[65]

Following this their action was held up to scrutiny in the High Court in *Rule* v *Charity Commissioners for England and Wales* (1979).[66] The faction claimed that there never should have been an inquiry, or if it should have been held, the one in question had been conducted unfairly, and that the Charity Commissioners should not have refused to register the new trusts. Fox J. held that as the Commissioners knew little about the Exclusive Brethren it was perfectly sensible for them to have held an inquiry. There was nothing wrong with holding an investigation into a class of religious trusts which shared common beliefs. He agreed with what the Commissioners had said about the freedom of religious worship. Given the type of investigation that had been carried out it had been conducted fairly. As regards the question of whether the Separation from Evil doctrine was contrary to public policy (not an issue in this action),[67] it was one worthy of decision by a Court which was the arbitrator upon such matters (thus the Charity Commissioners' unwillingness to decide the issue was vindicated).

Taxation[68]

The most important benefit of charitable status is tax relief. Tax exemption for religious bodies has been a long-standing feature of tax law,[69] indeed one going back to ancient times.[70] (Constantine exempted the property of the Church from taxation.) The twentieth century has seen such a privilege become, with the general raising of levels of taxation and the introduction of novel forms of raising revenues, prominent in any discussion of the role of religious bodies in our society. Religions may benefit because they, or some of their activities, are charitable in law and they also enjoy some special treatment simply by virtue of being religions in law. Relief does not and never has applied to all forms of taxation, as is illustrated by the recent difficulties that many religions have encountered with value added tax, but the reliefs that are available are considerable and religious bodies may be considered in a better position than non-religious charities. The privilege can be defended by the argument that as religions are not commercial institutions they should be treated differently simply to be in a position to survive. With rising inflation coupled with falling membership the burden of taxation could destroy any hope that some religions have of remaining afloat.[71] On the other hand the continuation of the present position has been criticised[72] as it results in some bodies being placed, by the state, in a more favourable position than other worthy bodies which are not religions (e.g. the humanists) and which may not even be charities (e.g. political parties). It has also been argued that although, the Church of England apart, the state grants these benefits, not enough is known, in return, about the finances of many religions.[73] Some church members see dangers, on ethical grounds, in a system that allows religious bodies to build up considerable assets in land and equities, thus becoming major landlords or shareholders[74] whilst others have been worried by the feelings of ill-will that such a privileged position is capable of producing.[75]

The main exemptions will now be considered in outline.

Income tax: When entitled to claim charitable status, religions are exempt from income tax on payments made from land, investments and other charges and also where they carry on trades 'in the course of the actual carrying out of the primary purpose of the charity, or ... the work in connection with the trade is mainly carried out by the beneficiaries of the charity'.[76] In these cases the income must be applied for the charitable purpose. If a religion runs a shop selling books and postcards in order to raise funds, this will be taxable, as the running of the business is not a charitable object. However, tax in this position may be minimised by having the business run by a separate company which then covenants to hand over its profits to the religion.[77] Money that is raised by such devices as bazaars and jumble sales will not be taxed provided that: they are not run on a regular basis; they are not in competition with other traders; they are clearly run for charity in the eyes of the public; and the profits that they raise are spent on charitable purposes.[78] Ministers of religion enjoy special relief with regard to their occupation of houses in connection with their offices, such relief also covering sums of money expended on the maintenance, repair, insurance and management of their houses.[79] The benefits sketched above also apply to corporation tax.[80]

The other great benefit enjoyed by charities is that they may, as non-income-tax payers, claim back the standard rate of tax on sums paid to them under a deed of covenant (which must run for more than a set period of years, or for an indefinite period which may exceed that set period[81]) under which the donor has received, and will receive, no benefit. Only the standard rate of income tax may be reclaimed and so charities are the one group that suffers a reduction of income when the standard rate is lowered as they are able to claim back less from the Inland Revenue on their covenants.

Capital taxes: Charitable trusts and charitable companies are exempt from capital gains tax when the gain accrues to the charity and is applied for charitable purposes.[82] Gifts (or transfers at the base price, or less than the base price) of assets to charities are not chargeable to the tax.[83]

The position with capital transfer tax is that an individual may make transfers to charities which will be exempt from the tax, save that there is an upper limit on death (which includes amounts paid in the year before death).[84] Existing trusts may make tax-free donations of any amount without having to pay the tax.[85] When, however, a donor has hedged the gift with conditions so that it is in effect not outright and voluntary, the exemption will not apply.[86] Transfers made by charities themselves are exempt.[87]

Rates.[88] Where a religious charity occupies property 'wholly or mainly used for charitable purposes (whether of that charity or of that and other charities)',[89] and gives written notice of this fact to the rating authority, it will be entitled to mandatory relief from paying one-half of the rates that would otherwise have to be paid. Such relief also applies to a residence occupied by a 'clergyman or minister of any religious denomination ... from which [he performs] the duties of [his] office'.[90] When such a residence has been left unoccupied no rates are payable at all.[91] Even where only half rates are payable it is open to the local rating authority to remit some or the rest of the remainder, and discretionary relief of up to one-half may also be given where premises are occupied 'for the purposes of one or more institutions or other organisations which are not established or conducted for profit and whose main objects are charitable or otherwise religious'.[92] Religious bodies are granted *total relief* from rates for:

(*a*) places of public religious worship which belong to the Church of England or to the Church in Wales (within the meaning of the Welsh Church Act 1914), or which are for the time being certified as required by law as places of religious worship; and
(*b*) any church hall, chapel hall or similar building used in connection with such place of public religious worship, and so used for the purposes of the organisation responsible for the conduct of public religious worship in that place.[93]

This relief would seem to extend[94] to ancillary buildings of the church, such as a residence used by the caretaker where he is employed by the religion and his residence can be said to form a 'single hereditament' with the church, a factor to be determined by having regard to the location of the residence and by examining the use to which it is put.

In order to enjoy the benefit of full relief the activity taking place inside the church must be 'public religious worship'. The meetings of a closed order will not qualify, as is illustrated by the Mormon temple case of 1964.[95] This religion owned a number of chapels which were open to the general public and also a temple where only selected members of the religion could attend. The House of Lords held that the temple was not entitled to the full relief.[96] In order to gain this privilege the religion must allow any member of the public to enter provided that he approaches the service in reverence and in reasonable conformity with the general customs of the religion.[97] More recently the Exclusive Brethren have experienced some difficulty over the registration of their meeting rooms for similar reasons.[98] The main problem is that the 'Separation from Evil' doctrine does not encourage non-members to attend.[99] In addition their halls do not 'look like' places of religious worship and they have not been, it is claimed, publicly advertising the times of their services. In reply the Exclusive Brethren have argued that the fact that these places are open is sufficient. The Lands Tribunal has held that the ease with which members of the public can attent is relevant and on the evidence they do attempt to make their meetings secret.

Value added tax:[100] All charities were subject to the old purchase tax and when VAT was introduced in 1972 no special exemptions were created for them. This greatly upset the charities as the new tax was far wider than the old, but their attempts to gain special treatment in the new law did not meet with success.[101] A particular problem with the more 'main-line' religions has occurred with church repairs. When the tax was being introduced there was an attempt to get a special provision to deal with this sort of work[102] on the ground that such repairs were of great expense due to the limited supply of specialist craftsmen. In 1972 the Church of England estimated that VAT would add £200 to the annual repair bill of the average Anglican church whilst the equivalent figure for the Roman Catholics was put at £134. The Government refused to make a concession on this point as the 1972 Budget had increased other tax benefits for charities and also because they thought that if such treatment was given to churches other charitable bodies would demand the same. It was also stressed that churches could be eligible for grants as 'historic buildings'. This last matter perhaps favours the Church of England more than other religious bodies since they own most of the older churches, whilst a great many churches belonging to all denominations are not of 'historic interest'.[103] The underlying rationale of such grants turns on the historic and tourist interest of such places rather than the intrinsic religious aspects of the buildings.

VAT cases since 1972 have confirmed the fears expressed by the church authorities. When a church replaced a nineteenth-century roof in a different style (the old roof itself was not in the same style as the rest of the church and also replacement in that style would have damaged the church walls) the work was held to be an alteration by way of repair and therefore susceptible to VAT.[104] A more crucial decision came in 1978.[105] A church was seriously damaged by fire and only the shell of its buildings was left. The interior was redesigned and new vestries were built, which were larger than the previous ones. Changes were made to the position of the choir and also to the seating. New toilets were installed. The roof was changed and a new organ placed where the chancel had been. The VAT tribunal held that there was a repair where the thing was restored to its former use without a change in character — this is tested by use rather than appearance. Here there was a 'restoration of efficiency in function', thus it was a repair and therefore £8,000 in VAT had to be paid. Following this case the Customs and Excise decided to bring claims against any church restoration scheme which fell under this formula. With soaring costs in the 1970s one Liverpool church was asked for £20,000 VAT for its restoration in 1978.[106]

VAT is not payable on donations (that is gifts given without the expectation of something in return) but where a religion constitutes an association that provides facilities for its members in return for charges it will be liable,[107] although:

> when a body has objects which are in the public domain and are of a ... religious ... nature, it is not to be treated as carrying on a business only because its members subscribe to it, if a subscription obtains no facility or advantage for the subscriber other than the right to participate in its management or receive reports on its activities.[108]

Where a religion carries on a business in order to raise funds it will be liable to VAT,[109] although when a committee set up a 'self-help' project to enlarge a church hall and effectively managed the building work on a day-to-day basis, entering into building contracts and so on, it was held not to be operating a business for VAT purposes.[110] It has been postulated that the religious nature of an activity could convert a *prima facie* business into a non-business, a point advanced by the Scientologists but which, at present, has made little headway,[111] and given both the intention behind, and the wording in, the 1972 Finance Act it may prove to be a non-starter.

The imposition of VAT is not fatal. Many religious activities are exempt as they do not fall within the definition of 'business' (e.g. collections). Religious groups if divided into reasonably sized units should be able to benefit from the small turnover exemption.[112] As was predicted at the time of its introduction the greatest difficulty has been over expensive church repairs.

Other duties and taxes: When a property is transferred to a charity a lesser stamp duty is payable than would have applied had the transfer been to a non-charitable body.[113] If a parsonage is purchased from the incumbent or, if he is not available, the bishop, no stamp duty is payable at all,[114] which, in 1979, could mean that a purchaser could save £1,000 on the purchase of a £50,000 parsonage.[115] Whilst development land tax was in force it did not apply to land disposed of by charities which they owned on 12 September 1974[116] and there were reliefs for a property acquired by them after that date.[117] Similar treatment was granted under the Community Land Act provisions.[118]

Giving — certainty and public policy

A common task for the courts is the construction of an instrument, such as a will, with the object of discovering whether a gift which bears a restriction relating to the religious beliefs of the recipient is valid. In determining this issue two questions must be asked:

(1) Does the form of words that has been used sufficiently define the religion in question so as to be certain in law?
(2) Is the restriction contrary to public policy?

In *Clayton* v *Ramsden*, decided in 1943,[119] a woman was a beneficiary under a will but her interest in the benefit would cease should she ever marry someone who was not 'of Jewish parentage and of the Jewish faith'. The House of Lords held that to be valid both requirements had to be ascertainable and that as 'Jewish parentage' was too uncertain a term (did it mean 'Jewish' in the religious or racial sense? Would one 'Jewish' parent be sufficient? How 'Jewish' did he/they have to be?) the entire condition was invalid and thus unenforceable in law. Some opinions were expressed as to whether 'the Jewish faith' could be sufficiently defined for legal purposes — Lord Russell of Killowen felt that it too might fail for uncertainty,[120] whereas Lord Wright leant the other way.[121] Lord Romer made the important point that 'the question whether a man is of the Jewish faith is a question of degree' and that for the condition to be valid there had to be an indication of the degree of faith required. Had the courts chosen to build on some of the dicta in *Clayton* v *Ramsden* very strict tests might now be applied where a reference to religion came to be held up against the hallmark of legal certainty. Instead, subsequent decisions have tended to view it as a special case. Thus the Court of Appeal of Northern Ireland, just a few years later,[122] had little difficulty in holding that a forfeiture provision — 'should ... become a Roman Catholic or profess that he or she is of the Roman Catholic religion' — was not legally uncertain. 'Becoming a Roman Catholic' and 'professing the Roman Catholic religion' were regarded as questions of fact.[123] Thus:

I am impressed by the words of Gavan Duffy P. in *In re McKenna*,[124] that a Protestant farmer testator knew what he meant, and practically every citizen in every walk of life, be he Catholic or Protestant, knew the meaning conveyed, by the words 'marry a Roman Catholic'; and the learned President added that the had only to construe the plain words used by a plan man in a sense plain to all of us.[125]

Thus a common-sense or at least 'man in the street' test will be used in determining the issue. As regards 'professing the Roman Catholic religion':

anyone who openly accepts the authority of the Roman Catholic Church in religious matters may reasonably and properly be said to 'profess that he is of the Roman Catholic religion'. The possibility of a difficulty of proof arising in an individual case will not render a condition void if it is clear, distinct and certain in itself.[126]

That the test of certainty will not be pushed too far is confirmed by the recent House of Lords decision in *Blathwayt* v *Baron Cowley*.[127] Here a beneficiary under a will would forfeit his bounty should he 'be or become a Roman Catholic'. Lord Wilberforce[128] felt that *Clayton* v *Ramsden* was a particular case concerning particular words used about a particular religion and it should not be extended, whereas Lord Cross[129] indicated that he was inclined towards Lord Wright's view in *Clayton* v *Ramsden* that 'Jewish faith' was not too vague as to be uncertain in law. Thus, as the earlier Northern Irish case had indicated, it is possible to apply a common-sense view to the question of fact of whether someone is or is not a Roman Catholic, and so on. *Blathwayt*'s case indicates that the courts will not concern themselves too much with 'degrees of faith' and so *Clayton* v *Ramsden* may now merely be a legal curiosity.

In *Clayton* v *Ramsden* Lord Atkin[130] had expressed disquiet that someone's freedom to marry could be influenced by such conditions (in that case the loss of her inheritance should she not marry someone of 'Jewish parentage and of the Jewish faith') and in *Blathwayt* the issue was raised of whether such restrictions and fetters upon a gift should, given such modern developments as the guarantee of religious freedom to be found in Article 9 of the European Convention on Human Rights, now be considered to be contrary to public policy. The House of Lords did not think so. Lord Wilberforce[131] denied that such personal choice in the disposal of one's assets could be considered to be discrimination and such personal choice had not yet been affected by recent changes in law and social thought. Lord Cross went even further and recognised that to hold that public policy could be a factor here would mean, in effect, that one preferred the religion of the putative donee to the religious prejudices of the donor. The freedom to dispose of one's own property as one thinks fit is an principle still dear to the law:

it is true that it is widely thought nowadays that it is wrong for a government to treat some of its citizens less favourably than others because of differences in their religious beliefs; but it does not follow that it is against public policy for an adherent of one religion to distinguish in disposing of his property between adherents of his faith and those of another. So to hold would amount to saying that though it is in order for a man to have a mild preference for one religion as opposed to another it is disreputable for him to be convinced of the importance of holding true religious beliefs and of the fact that his religious beliefs are the true ones.[132]

Giving and taking back — *the doctrine or undue influence*

The question of whether some of the smaller and newer religious groups overbear the free will of their adherents is both crucial and one yet to be fully considered by the law.[133] Where money has been given to such a group the equitable doctrine of undue influence may be of relevance. When a donor is forced to hand over property it is not surprising that the law should demand its return, but it goes further and states that where one stands in the position of 'spiritual adviser' (or some like relationship, such as guardian and ward) to another, a gift by that other to the 'spiritual adviser' is returnable unless the adviser can overcome the burden of demonstrating that his influence did not overbear the free will of the other. In the leading case of *Allcard* v *Skinner* in 1887[134] Lindley L.J. remarked, 'the influence of one mind over another is very subtle and of all influences religious influence is the most dangerous and the most powerful, and to counteract in Courts of Equity have gone very far'.[135] In the same case Bowen L.J. summed up the rule thus:

> equity will not allow a person who exercises or enjoys a dominant religious influence over another to benefit directly or indirectly by the gifts which the donor makes under or in consequence of such influence, unless it is shown that the donor, at the time of making the gift, was allowed full and free opportunity for counsel and advice outside'.[136]

Past cases where the principle has been applied in an apparent religious context have included:

(1) a case in 1840[137] where a girl, who had entered a convent, made her money over to it when she came of age — the conveyance had been drawn up by the nuns' attorney and she had not been allowed to see a relative without a nun being present;

(2) *Lyon* v *Home* (1868)[138] where a seventy-five-year-old widow was able to claim back £24,000 she had given to a spiritualist medium[139] whom she had been consulting concerning the death of her late husband, a case of some importance as it made clear that this equitable doctrine enjoys considerable flexibility — there being no need for the relationship in question to fall under the heads that had already been recognised in previous cases;

(3) *Morley* v *Loughman* (1893)[140] where it was said that the principle applied where a member of the Exclusive Brethren came to be a companion to an epileptic and obtained £140,000 from him[141] (although this was *obiter* as it was found that the money had been obtained under the 'guise' that it was for religious purposes),

(4) a case from Northern Ireland decided in 1935[142] where undue influence was found; an architect had executed work for a religious order for much less than his usual fee in return for the saying of prayers for his family and himself, the arrangement having been made at the dictation of a canon, known to the architect for twenty years past, who had promised him the spiritual benefits to be obtained from such an agreement and who had dictated most of the letter embodying it.[143]

In *Allcard* v *Skinner* the plaintiff became a member of a sisterhood and under its rule of charity had to give her property either to her relatives, the poor, or to the sisterhood. She handed over substantial sums to the sisterhood but ultimately became disillusioned and left. It was held that she had been subject to the influence of the spiritual director of the order and also had acted under the influence of its head and that but for other reasons of law (which were not related to undue influence) she could claim the return of all of the property which she had donated that had not been spent on the purposes of the order, whilst she had remained a member. The law would interfere as a matter of 'public policy'[144] given the relations which existed between the parties rather than because of any wrongdoing on the part of the recipient. The plaintiff had given the money

> as a matter of course, and without seriously thinking of the consequences to herself. She had devoted herself and her fortune to the sisterhood and it never occurred to her that she should ever wish to leave the sisterhood or desire to have the money back.[145]

The money was not for any purpose other than those for which the donor had expected it to be used. There had been no deception and no pressure other than 'the inevitable pressure of the vows and rules'.

Undue influence is open to questioning both with regard to policy and its practical application. The Victorian authorities have a paternalistic ring to them — they often spoke of protecting people (especially those of the 'weaker sex') from the consequences of their own acts in the context of fringe religious movements and closed orders. Is such an approach justifiable today? If someone works for a religious organisation and then undergoes a change of heart they cannot, fraud apart, claim anything for their 'lost work', so why should they be able to claim the return of their property? The judges, especially before *Allcard* v *Skinner*, often spoke in fairly robust language[146] about the self-evident dangers of religious pressure. Nowadays, given the general tendency of the courts to tread with care when dealing with issues of religion, such assumptions seem, in the absence of real proof, a little out of place and perhaps could be replaced by a study of the actual mental state of the donor at the crucial time.

The other difficulty is the determination of the exact scope of the rule. On the one hand, *Allcard* v *Skinner* contains dicta which could provide any expansionist judge with ammunition; on the other, many of the cases were bound up with what appears to have been actual fraud or at least where such obvious cases that they would have been decided the same way whether or not the presumption existed. Some of the more technical difficulties have been examined in the recent case of *Roche* v *Sherrington*.[147] The plaintiff had been a member of the controversial Roman Catholic group, the Opus Dei.[148] He had worked for them for several years and had made over sums of money to them. He then left and saying that he had made the payments because of the influence of the group claimed the return of these sums. *Allcard* v *Skinner* and its family of cases had been situations where the pressure was said to come from one, or two, particular individuals in a religious context (although the judges did discuss the effect of the influence of the group in, for example, a religious order), but *Roche* v *Sherrington* asks whether the presumption could apply to a group (i.e. an unincorporated association). Slade J. felt that this was a possibility and compared the situation with that of a merchant bank advising a customer — the customer could be considered to be in a relationship with the bank as a whole rather than any particular bank employee.[149] Furthermore it was possible that, when speaking of a religious group, all the members of the group at the time of the donation might be in a fiduciary relationship with the donor. If this is right it is a major extension of the principle which has been spoken of in the past as an imposition on the conscience of the one (or ones) who had received the gift as the result of their position. Slade J. did not support the claim as put forward here as he did not believe that the obligation attached to members who joined the group after the gift. If, however, he is right, another serious problem needing resolution will be Who is a member of a group for these purposes? — especially difficult where there is a loose association of those in agreement over particular religious points.

Notes

1. *Attorney-General* v *Pemsel* [1891] A.C. 531.
2. See *Re Pinion* [1965] Ch. 85.
3. 31 Beav. 14.
4. On her life see, G. R. Balleine, *Past Finding Out: The Tragic Story of Joanna Southcott and Her Successors*, 1956.
5. [1904] A.C. 515, at pp. 644–5.
6. For examples see: *Charity Commissioners' Report for 1976*, paras 109–12, and their *Report for 1979*, paras 128–31 (difficulties with a Sikh temple at Coventry).
7. *Neville Estates* v *Madden* [1962] Ch. 832, at p. 853, *per* Cross J.
8. *Re Watson (deceased)* [1973] 3 All E.R. 678, at p. 688, *per* Plowman J.
9. *Attorney-General* v *Pearson* (1817) 3 Mer. 353, at p. 399.
10. *Holmes and Others* v *Attorney-General*, *The Times*, 17 February 1981.
11. By H. Picarda, 'New religions as charities', *New Law Journal*, 1981, 436, at p. 437; see also his 'Religions and ethical movements as charities', *New Law Journal Annual Charities Review*, 1981, 1, at p. 3.
12. Thus see Chapters 1, pp. 10–11, and 6, pp. 113–14.
13. Thus in *O'Hanlon* v *Logue* [1906] 1 I.R. 247, at p. 260, Walker L.J. stated, 'It is enough that it is not illegal, *or contrary to public policy*, or opposed to the settled principles of morality', which would seem to give wider scope to public policy than seemed to be envisaged in this area in *Re Watson*.
14. *Gilmour* v *Coates* [1949] A.C. 426. However, although not charitable in law, such orders are thought by the authorities to be sufficiently worthy to be granted concessions — e.g. by the Inland Revenue, ([1980] 2 All E.R. at p. 394).

15. For details see M. Chesterman, *Charities, Trusts and Social Welfare*, 1979, pp. 124-9.
16. For this view see F. Lyall, *Of Presbyters and Kings: Church and State in the Law of Scotland*, 1980, at p. 112.
17. [1980] 3 All E.R. 918.
18. E.g. *Torcasco* v *Watkins* 367 U.S. 488 (1961).
19. 380 U.S. 163 (1965). See also, *Welsh* v *United States* 398 U.S. 333 (1970).
20. [1970] 2 Q.B. 697.
21. Thus see Lord Denning M.R. [1970] 2 Q.B. 697, at p. 707. Buckley L.J. concentrated his thoughts on the definition of *religious worship*.
22. [1970] 2 Q.B. 697, at pp. 708-9.
23. [1917] A.C. 406, at p. 445.
24. He is supported in this by the unreported decision of *Re St Saviourgate Chapel, York* (1898); see F.H. Amphlett Micklewright, 'Places of worship', *Solicitor's Journal*, 1971, 197.
25. Thus 'ecclesiastical building' can have different meanings in different ages: *Attorney-General* v *Howard Church Trustees* [1975] 2 W.L.R. 961, at p. 968.
26. Sir John Foster, *Enquiry into the Practice and Effects of Soientology*, 1971, para. 265. See also Hanbury's *Modern Equity*, 10th ed, 1976, at p. 385.
27. The Goodman Report, *Charity Law and Voluntary Organisations*, 1976, Ch. III, para. 53, suggests that ethical and moral societies should be treated on the same basis as organisations which advance religion.
28. The Scientologists being perhaps, because of *Segerdal*, the prime current example.
29. The fullest published account of religious trusts is C.E. Crowther, *Religious Trusts*, 1954.
30. See Rowlatt J., *Keren Kayemeth Le Jisroel* v *Commissioners of Inland Revenue* (1931) 17 T.C. 27.
31. Crowther, *Religious Trusts*, at p. 21.
32. [1919] A.C. 815.
33. See Appendix, passim.
34. Crowther, *Religious Trusts*, Chapter 4.
35. Ibid., at p. 57.
36. Ibid., Chapter 5.
37. *Re Barnes* [1930] 2 Ch. 80.
38. *Re Schoales* [1930] 2 Ch. 75.
39. *Re Lea* (1887) 34 Ch. D. 528.
40. See the cases cited in Crowther, *Religious Trusts*, at p. 107ff.
41. Ibid., pp. 110-13. See his Chapter 7 for the position of where the gift is to a named ecclesiastical personage.
42. Ibid., pp. 113-17.
43. See generally P.S. Atiyah, 'Public benefit in charities', *Modern Law Review*, XXI, 1958, pp. 138-54.
44. See note 14.
45. Chesterman, *Charities*, pp. 11-13.
46. *Bowman* v *Secular Society* [1917] A.C. 406, at p. 442.
47. *Re Grant's Will Trusts*]1979] 3 All E.R. 359.
48. Law Commission Working Paper, No. 79, 1981, *Offences Against Religion and Public Worship*, para. 7.16.

49. *Oxford Group* v *Inland Revenue Commissioners* [1949] 2 All E.R. 537, at p. 539. For an application of this principle see *Commissioner of Valuation* v *Trustees of the Redemption Order* [1971] N.I.L.R. 114.
50. *Oxford Group* case.
51. *Cf.* Chesterman, *Charities*, pp. 267–8.
52. Discussed in Chapter 1 at pp. 10–11; and see *The Times*, 8 April 1981 — following criticism in the House of Commons the Charity Commission is reported as deciding to re-examine the charitable status of some 'Moonie' charities.
53. *Charity Commissioners Report* for 1976, paras 65–8.
54. Ibid., paras 103–8.
55. Para. 104.
56. Para. 105.
57. Para. 106.
58. Para. 107.
59. Para. 108.
60. *Charity Commissioners Report for 1974*, paras 78–81.
61. *Charity Commissioners Report for 1976*, paras 128–32.
62. Ibid., para. 131, quoting a press release issued on 11 May 1976.
63. Ibid.
64. Para. 130.
65. Para. 132.
66. See *Charity Commissioners Report for 1979*, paras 24–36.
67. However in *Holmes and Others* v *Attorney-General, The Times*, 17 February 1981, Walton J., in a case where in effect registration of a trust had been refused because of the Commissioner's policy, held the Exclusive Brethren to be charitable. He examined their doctrine of Separation from Evil and found that they were a religious sect. They were presumed to be charitable. They were not an exclusively closed order such as that in *Gilmour* v *Coates* (above). Nor were their practices 'contrary to the public interest'. With this finding *Rule* becomes a matter of history: *Charity Commissioners Report for 1981*, paras 22–31.
68. See generally Chesterman, *Charities*, Chapter 10, and G. N. Glover, 'The tax advantages of charitable status', *British Tax Review*, 1972, pp. 346–58.
69. L. Pfeffer, *Religious Freedom*, 1977, at p. 39.
70. Thus see Ezra 7.24.
71. For a review of the financial positions and problems of the main churches in the 1970s, see D. Perman, *Change and the Churches*, 1977, Chapter 10.
72. E.g. see Sir John Foster, *Enquiry into the Practice and Effects of Scientology*, 1971, paras 263–7.
73. Perman, *Change*, at pp. 147 and 155–60.
74. Ibid., pp. 160–8.
75. Editorial, 'Churches and tax exemption', *Journal of Church and State*, XI, 1969, p. 197, at p. 203.
76. Income and Corporation Tax Act 1970, Section 360. *Cf. Oxford Group* v *Inland Revenue Commissioners* [1949] 2 All E.R. 537, at pp. 539–40 (Tucker L.J.).
77. For details see Glover, 'Tax advantages', at pp. 351–2.
78. Inland Revenue, *Extra-Statutory Concessions in operation at 1 August 1970*.

79. Income and Corporation Tax Act 1970, Section 194.
80. Ibid., Sections 250(4) and 265(2).
81. Ibid., Section 434. See Chesterman, *Charities*, at pp. 234–5.
82. Capital Gains Tax Act 1979, Section 145.
83. Ibid., Section 146.
84. Finance Act 1975, Sch. 6, para. 10.
85. Ibid., Sch. 6, para. 12.
86. See Sch. 6, para. 15.
87. See Sch. 6, para. 10.
88. G.N. Glover, 'Rating exemptions for charitable, philanthropic and similar bodies', *British Tax Review*, 1971, pp. 86–93.
89. General Rate Act 1967, Section 40(1).
90. Ibid., Section 40(9)(*a*); see *Glasgow City Corporation* v *Johnstone and Others* [1965] A.C. 609.
91. General Rate Act 1967, Sch. 1, para. 2. The term 'unoccupied' includes the case where the residence is empty but is being held by the church for the next minister to be appointed — *Bexley Congregational Church Treasurer* v *Bexley London Borough Council* [1972] 2 Q.B. 222.
92. General Rate Act 1967, Section 40(5).
93. Ibid., Section 39(1).
94. See Glover, 'Rating exemptions', pp. 88–93.
95. *Henning* v *Church of Jesus Christ of Latter-Day Saints* [1964] A.C. 420.
96. As to the mandatory half relief under Section 40(1), *Gilmour* v *Coates* [1949] A.C. 426 indicates that there might be a difficulty because of the possible lack of public benefit in such cases. However as Section 40(5) distinguishes between bodies whose objects are 'charitable *or otherwise religious*', discretionary half relief would be a possibility.
97. [1964] A.C. 420, at p. 437 (Lord Pearce).
98. See *Attorney-General* v *British Broadcasting Corporation* [1981] A.C. 303, at pp. 307–9 and 310 (in the Court of Appeal). Although relief was granted in this case this group's status in this regard may yet be resolved by a court. See also the case in the House of Lords [1981] A.C. 303, at pp. 335, 340–1, 343.
99. See H. Picarda, 'Places of religious worship and rates', *New Law Journal*, 1981, pp. 1064–5, discussing *Broxtowe Borough Council* v *Birch (and others)* at first instance. The Court of Appeal have upheld this approach, *Broxtowe Borough Council* v *Birch (and others)* [1983] 1 All E.R. 641. They must either invite (e.g. by a notice) members of the public to attend or show that members of the public do in fact attend. It is not sufficient if they would in fact admit a member of the public should one ask to attend. At 651 Stephenson L.J. commented, 'The picture presented by the evidence is very different from the picture of a place of public religious worship, as the ordinary person would, I think, derive it from such obvious places of public worship as churches and chapels. But the courts of a country with an established church must be careful not to assume that all meeting places of other faiths are readily identifiable or even that all places of Christian worship still bear the recognised, and recognisable, style and features of earlier ecclesiastical buildings. Nor must our courts deny to other religions an element of spiritual benefit to the general public ... or restrict unfairly the extension which Parliament has granted of the privilege originally reserved to

82 Religion and the law

Anglican church buildings. On the other hand, that extension must not go beyond the limits defined by Parliament ...'

100. See Glover, 'Tax advantages', pp. 355–7.
101. (1972) H.C. Deb., vol. 840, cols 1663–1722, where an amendment to exempt charities from the tax was defeated by twelve votes.
102. (1972) H.C. Deb., vol. 840, cols 1528–42.
103. See (1972) H.C. Deb., vol. 840, cols 1690–1, 1710–11 and 1719–20.
104. *Parochial Church Council of the Church of St James* v *Customs and Excise Comrs* [1974] V.A.T.T.R. 245. See also: *Parochial Church Council of All Saints Church, Wellington* v *Customs and Excise Comrs* [1979] B.T.R. 955, and *Modbury Parochial Church Council* v *Customs and Excise Comrs* [1980] B.T.R. 828 and [1979] B.T.R. 564.
105. *Parochial Church Council of St Luke's Great Crosby* v *Customs and Excise Comrs* [1978] V.A.T.T.R. 218. But see now [1982] B.T.R. 990.
106. *Daily Telegraph*, 7 December 1978.
107. Finance Act 1972, Section 45(1).
108. Ibid., Section 45(3), substituted by Finance Act 1977, Sch. 6.
109. *Leeds Kashrut Commission and Beth Din Administrative Committee* v *Customs and Excise Comrs* (1977) B.T.R. 555 shows that the activities of a religious court that grants licences for the performance of religious acts may constitute a 'business' for VAT purposes.
110. *Trinity Methodist Church, Rayton (Building Committee)* v *Customs and Excise Comrs* [1979] B.T.R. 936.
111. *Church of Scientology of California* v *Customs and Excise Comrs* [1981] 1 All E.R. 1035.
112. See (1972) H.C. Deb., vol. 840, col. 1438.
113. Finance Act 1974, Section 49(2).
114. Parsonage Measures 1938 and 1947.
115. See *Observer*, 7 October 1979.
116. Development Land Tax Act 1976, Section 24.
117. Ibid., Section 25.
118. Community Land Act 1975, Sections 4(1)(6) and 25(5)–(7).
119. [1943] A.C. 320.
120. At pp. 328–9.
121. At p. 331.
122. *McCausland* v *Young* [1949] N.I.L.R. 49.
123. See also the comments of Coleridge J. in *Shore* v *Wilson* (1842) 9 Cl. & Fin. 354, at p. 531.
124. [1947] I.R. 277.
125. [1949] N.I.L.R. 49, at p. 57, *per* Andrews L.C.J.
126. [1949] N.I.L.R. 49, at p. 61, *per* Andrews L.C.J. At p. 99 Babington L.J. regarded it as significant that as Section 2 of the Bill of Rights 1688 excludes anyone who shall 'profess the Popish Religion' from the throne, 'to profess' a religion is a term which may be defined with sufficient certainty.
127. [1976] A.C. 397.
128. At p. 425.
129. At p. 429.
130. [1943] A.C. 320, at p. 325.

131. [1976] A.C. 397, at pp. 425–7. Lord Wilberforce recognised that 'It may well be that conditions such as this are, or at least are becoming, inconsistent with standards now widely accepted'; however, the testator's choice should be upheld in that case because the will had been made in 1936, when thinking on the subject was somewhat different, and had twice been before a court in the past. 'Discrimination is not the same thing as choice: it operates over a larger and more personal area, and neither by express provision nor by implication has private selection yet become a matter of public policy.' He went on to observe that with landed estates an identity with a particular religion might be strong, and public policy does not require testators to ignore religious considerations.

132. Pp. 429–30. The position would seem to be unaltered by the decision of the House of Lords in *Mandla* v *Lee* [1983] 2 W.L.R. 620. Although racial/religious groups such as the Sikhs are now covered by the general protections in the Race Relations Act 1976, Section 34 of the Act makes unlawful a charitable instrument which confers a benefit to a group defined *by colour*. Thus a provision in favour of Black Muslims would not be acceptable and under 34(1)(a) would take effect, being in favour of Muslims in general. Subject to the principle of justification some charitable activity may be limited by the decision; thus a Roman Catholic charity which only employs Roman Catholic would now seem to (unlawfully) discriminate against Sikhs, a protected group under the Race Relations Act 1976. On the other hand because of the drafting of the Act a group that does come under it (e.g. Sikhs) may be able so to discriminate, see Section 5(2)(d).

133. See Chapter 6, pp. 113–4.
134. (1887) 36 Ch. D. 145.
135. Ibid., at p. 183. See the hostile reaction of the Lord Chancellor to 'chanting fanatics ... whose doctrines have no other tendency than to plunge their deluded votaries into the very abyss of bigotry, despair and enthusiasm' — *Norton* v *Relly* (1767) 2 Ed. 286, at p. 288.
136. Ibid., at p. 190.
137. *White* v *Meade* (1840) 2 Ir. Eq. 420.
138. L.R. 6 Eq. 655. See also *In the Estate of Harden, The Times*, 20 June 1957.
139. The reaction of Sir G.M. Gifford V.C. to the type of spiritualism employed here (see (1868) L.R. 6 Eq. 655, pp. 681–2) may be compared to the hostile reaction of the court to extreme protestants in *Norton* v *Relly* (note 135).
140. [1893] 1 Ch. 736.
141. Ibid., at p. 756.
142. *O'Neill* v *Murphy and Others* [1936] N.I.L.R. 16.
143. Best L.J. (see [1936] N.I.L.R. 16, at p. 42) had some doubts about the application of the principle to the facts of this case but supported the decision because of the jury's finding.
144. (1887) 36 Ch. D. 145, at p. 171, *per* Cotton L.J.
145. Ibid., at p. 179, *per* Lindley L.J.
146. Thus see *Norton* v *Relly* (note 135) and *Lyon* v *Home* (note 138).
147. [1982] 2 All E.R. 426.
148. For criticism of this group see *The Times*, 12 January 1981.
149. [1982] 2 All E.R. 426, at p. 432.

5 The constitutional position of the Church of England[1]

So far as we can ascertain, the place of the Sovereign [in the Church], as a symbol of national recognition and encouragement, gives rise to very little difficulty, is seldom resented by non-Christians, would not be an obstacle to Christian unity, and is much valued by many persons.

[*Church and State*, 1970]

Phillimore J. has described the position of the established Church thus:

A Church which is established is not thereby made a department of the state. The process of establishment means that the state has accepted the Church as the religious body in its opinion truly teaching the Christian faith, and given to it a certain legal position, and to its decrees, if rendered under certain legal conditions, certain civil sanctions ... the Church of England is a continuous body from its earliest establishment in Saxon times.[2]

The Church of England is a Church which, despite moves to have it disestablished in the late nineteenth century,[3] remains 'established' perhaps because since 1885 the general opposition to the idea of establishment has run out of steam as other events have seemed more pressing and as it has seemed that full religious equality before the law is possible without formal disestablishment. Those who value establishment on moral grounds have not died out,[4] whilst most of the important enemies of establishment lie within the Church itself. The position of 'no formal change' is supported by some who feel that Christianity in general would be rebuffed in the country if the ancient links between Church and state finally come to an end.[5] Nonetheless against this view it must be countered that a large number of important changes have taken place.

An examination of the Church and its institutions is important in any general discussion on freedom of religion, for two reasons. First, the establishment means that the freedom of the Church to run its own affairs is subject to certain limitations to which no other religious group is subject. Secondly, citizens in general enjoy rights in (and in previous times obligations towards) the Church even though they are not members of it.[6]

Church, Parliament and Crown[7]

'We are Supreme Governor of the Church of England' declares the preface of the Thirty-Nine Articles of Religion of the Church of England.[8] This royal supremacy is now expressed through Parliament. A simplified version of the government of the Church is shown in Figure 1. The law-making body is the General Synod,[9] which may legislate either by Measure or by Canon. A Measure is a law, about a Church matter, that applies to the entire Church and will also, where necessary, bind others as well, because it has the force of an Act of Parliament and may even repeal or amend an Act dealing with an ecclesiastical matter.[10] Measures about doctrine, ceremonials and services, and the conduct of sacraments and rites must have been agreed by the House of Bishops before final submission to the Synod,[11] whilst certain fundamental Measures (permanent changes in the services of baptism, Holy Communion or ordination, or for a change in the relationship between the Church of England and another Christian body[12] must, as well as being approved by a two-thirds vote of each House in the Synod, be passed by a majority of the Diocesan Synods.[13] Once a Measure has been passed by each House in the General Synod it must be submitted, by its legislative Committee, to the Ecclesiastical Committee of Parliament.[14] This Committee consists of fifteen members of the House of Commons and the same number from the House of Lords and is charged[15] with the consideration of each Measure sent to it, and, if it seems useful, it will hold a conference with the Legislative Committee of the General Synod. The Ecclesiastical Committee will then prepare a report on the nature and legal effect of the Measure 'especially with relation to the constitutional rights of [Her] Majesty's subjects',[16] which, with the agreement of the Legislative Committee, may then be submitted to Parliament. The Measure must then be laid before Parliament and passed, without amendment, by a resolution of each House if it is to be submitted for the Royal Assent[17] and so become law.

Thus no change in important Church law may be made without the sanction of Parliament — a control that was painfully felt in 1928 when

FIGURE 1: *The government of the Church of England*

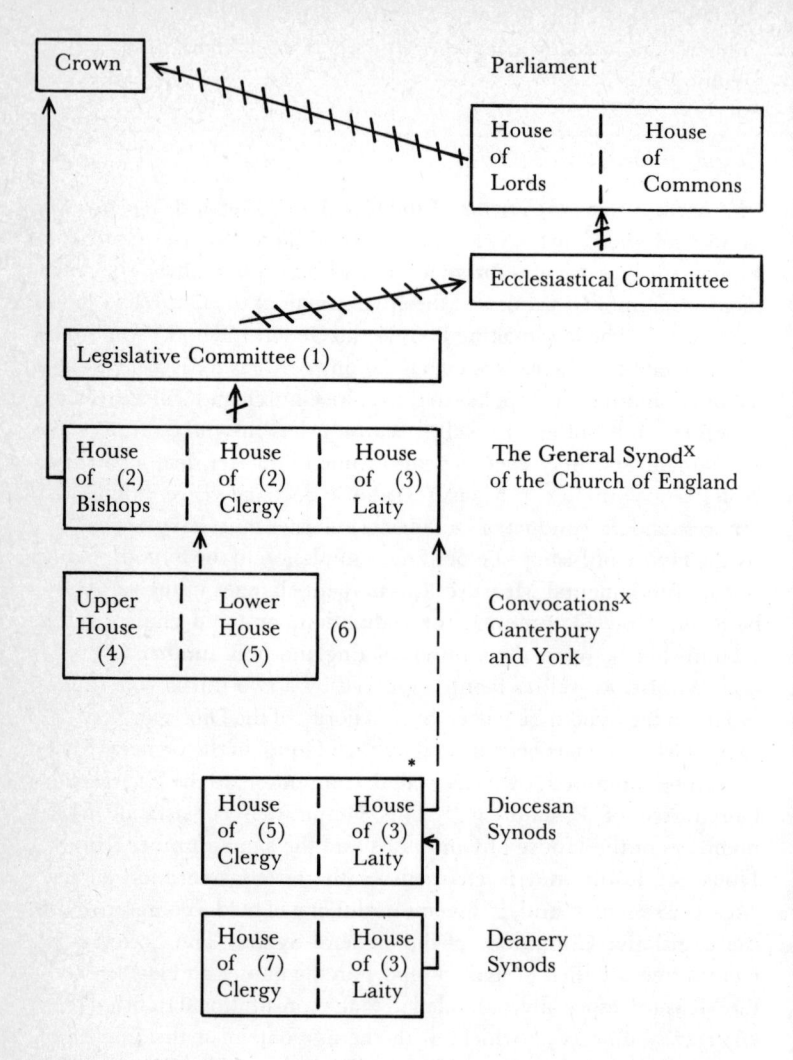

```
┌─────────┐                              Parliament
│  Crown  │◄++++++++++++┌──────────┬──────────┐
└─────────┘             │  House   │  House   │
     ▲                  │   of     │   of     │
     │                  │  Lords   │ Commons  │
     │                  └──────────┴──────────┘
     │                              ▲
     │                              ↕
     │                  ┌───────────────────────┐
     │          ◄+++++++│ Ecclesiastical Committee │
     │                  └───────────────────────┘
┌──────────────────────────────┐
│  Legislative Committee (1)   │
└──────────────────────────────┘
            ▲
            ↕
┌─────────┬─────────┬─────────┐
│ House   │ House   │ House   │    The General Synod^X
│ of (2)  │ of (2)  │ of (3)  │    of the Church of England
│ Bishops │ Clergy  │ Laity   │
└─────────┴─────────┴─────────┘
      ▲         ▲        ▲
┌─────────┬─────────┐    ¦
│ Upper   │ Lower   │    ¦          Convocations^X
│ House   │ House   │ (6)           Canterbury
│  (4)    │  (5)    │               and York
└─────────┴─────────┘    ¦
                         ¦
                     *   ¦
         ┌─────────┬─────────┐
         │ House   │ House   │    Diocesan
         │ of (5)  │ of (3)  │    Synods
         │ Clergy  │ Laity   │◄
         └─────────┴─────────┘
         ┌─────────┬─────────┐
         │ House   │ House   │    Deanery
         │ of (7)  │ of (3)  │    Synods
         │ Clergy  │ Laity   │
         └─────────┴─────────┘
```

KEY:

++++ = Measure
───── = Canon
* = Approval needed of majority for certain Measures
X = May make provision other than Measure or Canon
– – – = Power to refer

a House of Commons, suspicious of High Church influence, rejected Church proposals for changes to the Prayer Book.[18] Although time has moved on, Parliamentary approval should still not be thought of as a rubber-stamping process. The Incumbents (Vacation of Benefices) Measure was rejected by the House of Commons in 1975 because it would not have given accused incumbents a right always to state their cases, and hearings would have been in private.[19]

In 1981 Viscount Cranborne introduced the Prayer Book Protection Bill in the House of Commons under the Ten Minute Rule. The Bill provided that if twenty persons on the parochial roll signed a petition the incumbent of the parish must hold at least one 1662 Prayer Book service a month. In introducing it he argued that the 1974 Church of England (Worship and Doctrine) Measure was a concordat between Church and state, one of the conditions of which was the continuation, to some extent, of the 1662 Prayer Book. He claimed that this was being breached in those churches where no Prayer Book Service was available. He also claimed that the Prayer Book was not in use in many theological colleges at all. The Bill was opposed by the Second Church Commissioner, William Van Straubenzee, M.P., who stated that it intervened in an important area where Parliament had left the Church to be the arbitrator. Margaret Thatcher, the Prime Minister, indicated that Members of Parliament might feel bound by convention to support the General Synod and not to interfere. Despite this the Bill was given a first reading by 152 votes to 130. The following day the Bill was given a second reading in the House of Lords by 28 votes to 17. Lord Hailsham, the Lord Chancellor, stated that the Government did not support the Bill as the 1974 Measure provided adequate safeguards — the Bill was a constitutional anomaly made worse by the fact that under its provisions service could be imposed by a tiny minority on an unwilling majority. As the Bill was introduced so late in the Parliamentary session it failed to become law but it serves as a timely reminder

Notes for figure 1

1. Members drawn from each House of the General Synod.
2. The same membership as the Upper and Lower Houses of both Convocations.
3. Elected under the Church Representation Rules 1969.
4. All provincial bishops plus some elected suffragans.
5. Other clergy: some elected and some *ex officio*.
6. Each Convocation has the power to add its own House of Laity.
7. All clergy in the area.

of the control that a majority of the Members of Parliament are still prepared to consider exercising.

Such control, exercised by those who may not even be members of the Church, is naturally criticised,[21] but there have been moves, no doubt in the back of the minds of both the Prime Minister and the Lord Chancellor in the 1981 debate, which mean that the trend of convention (as opposed to strict law) is against direct intervention today because:

(1) the Church has a far more democratic structure and, since the Second World War, has moved closer towards self-government;
(2) the Church of England (Worship and Doctrine) Measure 1974 has meant that matters of worship and matters relating to the assent to, and obligations of, the doctrines of the Church may be passed as Canons, and so do not need Parliamentary consent.

There does, nevertheless, remain support for some Parliamentary involvement generally on one or both of the following grounds:[22]

(1) Parliament, as representative of the English nation as a whole, is more suited to be the ultimate arbitrator in the 'National Church' than the smaller number of (perhaps less representative) Church activists;
(2) Parliament is needed as a watchdog in order to safeguard the historic buildings and endowments which are the gifts of the past held in trust for the future, and, in addition, the complexity of some of the legislation affecting the Church over these matters means that changes to the endowments and so on can be made more easily with Parliamentary involvement than would otherwise be the case.

On the other hand the present position of Parliament with regard to the Church may prove to be a barrier to Church unity, with objections from those religions who hold that the Church and state should be fully separate.[23]

Where a change in the law is not only going to affect the Church of England but also other religions a Measure is not sufficient — the object must be achieved by an Act of Parliament passed in the usual manner — thus the Sharing of Church Buildings Act 1969 (which enables the Church of England and other religions to reach agreements over the sharing of places of worship and other buildings) was passed as an Act rather than a Measure because it was such a matter.[24]

Canons used to be made by the Convocations of Canterbury and York and are now made by the General Synod. A Canon is 'essentially a power to make rules for the clergy, and in spiritual matters, only',[25] save that they must not be 'contrary or repugnant to the royal prerogative or the customs, law or statutes of the realm'.[26] Canons are not submitted to Parliament but must receive the Royal Assent before they can become law. This assent now seems to be almost automatic unless the Crown's advisers believe that the Canon is in breach of statute or common law.[27]

As the monarch is 'Supreme Governor' of the Church; formally assents to all Church legislation; formally brings about the appointment of all archbishops and bishops; and is also the patron of many livings and other ecclesiastical appointments, she must be in communion with the Church of England and, on taking the throne, must declare that she is a Protestant and will uphold the Protestant succession to the throne.[28] The monarch, furthermore, may take no consort who is a Roman Catholic. In the summer of 1980[29] there was speculation about the possibility of the Prince of Wales marrying a Roman Catholic. This, had it happened, would have involved a change to the Act of Settlement 1700, and it would have been against constitutional convention for this to have been done without consultation with all those Commonwealth countries which still recognise the British monarch as head of state (as happened over the abdication crisis of 1936). The main domestic Parliamentary difficulty for such a change would be opposition from Unionists in Northern Ireland, as was shown when a private Member introduced a motion in the House of Commons, apparently with the Queen's permission, to change the law on the grounds that the present position was 'discriminatory, offensive and insulting to the Catholic community of the United Kingdom'. The motion was withdrawn partly because of the hostility shown by Orangemen in both Northern Ireland and Scotland. The Government thought that such a move would make the position there worse and would generate a constitutional crisis. Following its withdrawal the Government[30] stated that it saw no occasion for amending the present law.

The Lord Chancellor was historically 'keeper' of the monarch's conscience and so could not be a Roman Catholic. This was changed in 1974[31] so that a Roman Catholic may now hold the post of Lord Chancellor, save that his ecclesiastical functions (for example the appointment of certain members of the Church Courts) and his ecclesiastical patronage must be performed by the Prime Minister or some other Minister of the Crown,[32] when the Lord Chancellorship is held by a Roman Catholic. Before 1974 there had been no religious disqualifications on the holding of other political offices of state since the general removal of such disabilities in the nineteenth century,[33] although there did survive criminal offences (never in fact invoked) whereby Roman Catholics[34] or Jews[35] were prohibited from directly or indirectly giving advice to the Crown on any Church appointment.

Church in Parliament

At one time all bishops together with the heads of religious houses were members of the House of Lords, but since the time of King Edward VI this has been restricted to the two archbishops, the bishops of London, Durham and Winchester and the next twenty-one bishops according to their seniority. The fact that bishops are, or may become, members[36] of the Upper House of Parliament is probably the main justification for the continuance of the system of royal appointment.[37] In addition the two archbishops occupy positions that traditionally identify them as senior officers of state. The last major scheme for reforming the House of Lords[38] would have retained the seats of sixteen of the bishops who would, because of other changes in the composition of that House, in fact have become more influential. The Church's own reaction to this[39] was that although there is still a place for bishops in the House they would like to see more leaders of other major religions there as well.[40]

Until recent times bishops were chosen by the Prime Minister[41] after he had received advice from his appointments secretary (who forwarded the views of laity and clergy) and the archbishops[42] and:

in modern circumstances there is no question of a person [being appointed] to whose appointment he [the Prime Minister] knows the Archbishops to be entirely opposed. But this is not to say that the two or three persons from whom the final choice is made are necessarily the persons whom the Archbishop would have chosen.[43]

In 1977, following a motion passed by the General Synod in 1974, this position was changed somewhat.[44] Each diocese now sets up its own committee (such committees first came into being after 1964 so as to make a statement of needs which could be passed on to the relevant archbishop) which submits its views to the appointments committee of the General Synod. The Prime Minister's ecclesiastical appointments secretary may attend any meeting of this body. Names will be forwarded to the Prime Minister who may, exceptionally, ask for another name if he is not happy with those that he has been sent. Once the candidate has been selected in this way appointment is formal — a 'conge d'élire' will be sent to the cathedral church of the diocese and the nominee must be elected by the cathedral chapter within twelve days or else the person will be appointed by letters patent.[45]

The new system has come under strain. In 1981[46] the Prime Minister put forward Dr Leonard as the new bishop of London although the appointments commission had placed his name second and not first. It was claimed that lobbying on his behalf had been successful with both the Prime Minister and with the Leader of the Opposition. Despite the ensuing outcry both the Prime Minister and the Archbishop of Canterbury stressed that the 1976 procedures had been followed. The issue was complicated by the fact that the vacancy-in-see committee for the diocese of London had been in favour of Dr Leonard. It may also have been that his opponent was not supported by two-thirds of the appointments commission. One clear conclusion is, given the unanimous stance taken by the leading politicians involved, that there is clearly no constitutional convention that the state must accept the first choice of the Church.

There have always been those who have thought the membership of the House of Lords is a heavy price to pay for continued state supervision.[47] Additionally the theory of the royal prerogative can cause other difficulties — to resign a bishop must seek the Crown's permission and were a bishop to step down in order to do some other Church work some would take it as an insult to the Crown.[48]

Under the House of Commons (Clergy Disqualification) Act 1801,[49] 'no person having been ordained to the office of priest or deacon ... is or shall be capable of being elected to serve in Parliament as a member of the House of Commons'. Before 1662 the clergy met in their own Convocation in order to tax themselves, and therefore there was no logical reason for them to sit in the Commons. In *Re MacManaway*,[50] however, there was held to be a more general reason for justifying their continued exclusion. In that case a clergyman, who was an ordained priest of the Church of Ireland, had been elected to Parliament and it was argued that the prohibition only applies to members of the Church of England. The Judicial Committee of the Privy Council did not agree, holding that it applied to all episcopally ordained clergymen, whether or not they had been ordained by the established Church. Lord Radcliffe[51] said that this rule was based on the spiritual nature of the office of priest — priests should not get involved in mundane matters and thus should be above Parliamentary politics. Such a view of the priesthood would not seem to accord with more modern conceptions of the office, with 'worker priests' and so on. In 1801 most adults were unable to sit in the House of Commons whilst today nearly everyone has the right to stand for Parliament. The ban does not extend to ministers of the non-conformists Churches who have supplied a small number of Members of the House. In 1971 a Church Committee[52] recommended that the prohibition should be removed and later in the decade[53] moves were again afoot to change the law so as to leave the question up to the priest's conscience in future.

The financial position[54]

Although the Church is established it does not receive funds from the state and so it must 'live off its own' especially as such traditional sources of income as tithes have been abolished.[55] The main part of the Church's income now comes from:

(i) gifts and bequests from the public;
(ii) property administered by the Church Commissioners[56] (such property was originally bought from the proceeds of a tax levied on clergymen together with acquisitions down the ages);
(iii) each parish has its own endowment built up, in many cases, over many centuries;
(iv) fees, e.g. for performing marriages and burials.

Control over these assets is exercised by the Church Commissioners and the diocesan boards of finance.

Despite the general principle of no state aid there are some minor ways in which the state does, or at least can, give financial assistance:

(*a*) local authorities have the power to finance the upkeep of burial grounds;[57]
(*b*) local authorities may make grants to charities within their area of jurisdiction, a power that could be used to assist the Church with a number of aspects of its work;[58]
(*c*) the central government is empowered to make grants to the Redundant Churches Fund for the preservation of churches of historic or architectural interest.[59]

The ecclesiastical courts[60]

The Church of England is the only religious body in the land that has its own courts of law, manned by lawyers sitting as judges,[61] administering an ecclesiastical law which is 'part of the general law of England ... consisting of such Canons and constitutions ecclesiastical as have been allowed by general consent and custom within the realm'.[62] Other religious bodies may only enforce their rules through the ordinary civil law of contract.

As courts of the land the Church courts enjoy a number of advantages which the tribunals of other religious bodies do not. First, any witness, whether or not he happens to be a member of the Church, may be subpoenaed to appear before them.[63] Secondly, they may grant legal aid.[64] Thirdly, the Queen's Bench Division of the High Court will punish any contempt of a Church court as is shown by *Ex parte the Bishop of Norwich* in 1932.[65] This notorious case concerned the Rector of Stiffkey,[66] who used to spend much of his time in London reclaiming, so he said, prostitutes. The bishop, however, reached the conclusion that the Rector, a married man, was consorting with another woman and was also frequently attempting to 'pick up' prostitutes and other women whilst he was on his trips. The *Daily Herald* published an interview with the 'other woman' under the heading 'Woman's Own Story in Rector Case'. The Rector also wrote two articles that were published in the *Empire News* claiming that the allegations against him were untrue. As proceedings were pending on the issue in the consistory court at the time, these publications were held to be contempts of court on the ground that they prejudiced the fair hearing of the issue, and both newspapers were fined. The Rector of Stiffkey did not meet with greater fortune for he was deprived of his benefice and unfrocked on the ground of immorality; he started a new career as a fairground exhibit and met his end by being mauled to death by a lion. More recently, if somewhat less sensationally, a request had been made in the Salisbury consistory court for permission to sell a silver tankard.[67] The court was to sit in the local village church and at the same time a television programme was being made about the village. Permission to film the proceedings was refused because a general statutory prohibition on filming a court applied: 'when the church is being used for the purposes of the holding of a consistory court which is not a private church tribunal but one of the courts of the realm it is, in my view, a court building within the meaning of the section'.[68] Lastly, there are other advantages, such as a power to order the production of documents and the right of being able to have costs enforced by a county court.[69]

The Church courts perform two main roles today. The first is the faculty jurisdiction. A faculty is a permit to alter the fabric or the contents of a church or to effect some change in a churchyard.[70] Included are such things as: new works of decoration; changes to the pulpit, fonts, organ etc.; and the erection of monuments. Faculties may be granted for the exclusive use (e.g. by a family) of part of a graveyard and for memorials therein. An example of the latter is provided by *Re St Mary The Virgin, Ilmington*.[71] Oswald Smith, the deceased husband of the petitioner, had been a Roman Catholic whilst she was a member of the Church of England. She sought permission to have the words, 'Pray for the repose of the Soul of Oswald Smith' inscribed on his tombstone. The rector objected because he felt that these words were connected with the Roman Catholic doctrine of purgatory. Having first decided that the words were not illegal under the ecclesiastical law of the Church of England the chancellor went on to consider how he should exercise his discretion. He decided in favour of granting the faculty as there was no evidence of any feeling against it from the parish and 'if someone of another religion has a right of burial in a churchyard, it would be a hollow right if an inscription over his grave which otherwise would not offend were to be vetoed simply because it did not conform with the views of the Church of England' (although if the burial custom is thought to be 'unEnglish' — such as placing a photograph of the deceased on the headstone,[72] a different result may be reached).

The use of the faculty jurisdiction is further illustrated by *Re St Thomas's Lymington*.[73] The vicar and churchwardens of a parish church wished to erect a building in part of a churchyard. This building was to be used for meetings after services and as a Sunday School. Some parishioners, who did not usually attend the church, objected as the place was of considerable historic and architectural interest. The fact that these people were not practising members of the Church was no bar to their right to object,

The law which governs the Church of England recognises the interests of the wider community. All parishioners, regardles of whether or not they manifest or claim any allegiance to the Church, are entitled as persons having interest in proceedings such as these, and it is the duty of the court to give full and fair consideration to their representations. In particular, the law regards the Church authorities as having a special responsibility for the protection of those historic buildings and churchyards which they may be said to hold in trust as part of the national or local heritage.[74]

The chancellor then went on to hold that he could take into account the evolution of thought and practice within the Church in deciding that the building was necessary for contemporary Church circumstances. The established Church, therefore (planning permission had

had already been given in this case), may be under a greater burden than other bodies when wishing to effect changes to the use of its property.

The other main function of these courts is discipline within the clergy. From 1833 onwards the Judicial Committee of the Privy Council had been the final court of appeal in all Church matters. This was greatly resented by some members of the Church as they did not consider that a court of lay lawyers (who did not even have to be Church members) was an appropriate final arbitrator of doctrine. The decision of the board in the *Gorham* case[75] had underlined lay control over these matters, whilst, a little later on in the nineteenth century, the Public Worship Regulation Act 1874 had produced the unhappy result that laymen were sending the clergy to prison, in some cases over matters of ritual. A number of Church committees, dating from 1883,[76] recommended that this lay control by judges who were not Church members should be abolished. However the aftertaste of this unfortunate time was not removed until the passage of the Ecclesiastical Jurisdiction Measure 1963. A new system (see Figure 2) was set up with the following features:

(i) the Privy Council (none too greatly respected under the old system)[77] now only hears appeals from certain faculty cases and its decisions on matters of doctrine, ritual or ceremonial need not be followed by the new courts;
(ii) where a matter concerns doctrine, ritual or ceremonial it will be 'reserved' and heard by the Court of Ecclesiastical Causes Reserved;
(iii) in 'reserved' matters the courts will consist of Church of England theologians sitting with lawyers or judges who are in communion with the Church;
(iv) in 'reserved' matters the courts will have the benefit of guidance from a special committee of advisers;
(v) all members of all the courts (apart from the Judicial Committee of the Privy Council) must be in communion with the Church;
(vi) where the matter is about a priest's 'conduct' it will be investigated by a special committee if it is 'reserved', and by an examiner, appointed by the bishop, if otherwise, both of whom may prevent the matter form reaching the court if there is a better way of dealing with it.

The idea that a clergyman can only be deprived of his office after due process of law is a strong one, '[it] is the basis of what is known as the parson's freehold. It means that he can speak out fearlessly in the cause of righteousness, and opposition however powerful cannot deprive him of his income or drive him from the scene.'[78] In any case, despite the creation of the new system, strict judicial proceedings are not thought to be appropriate in the modern age as the first case under the new procedure,[79] where the pastoral relationship had broken down between a priest and his parish,[80] serves to point out.[81]

96 *Religion and the law*

FIGURE 2: *Courts set up under the Ecclesiastical Jurisdiction Measure 1963*

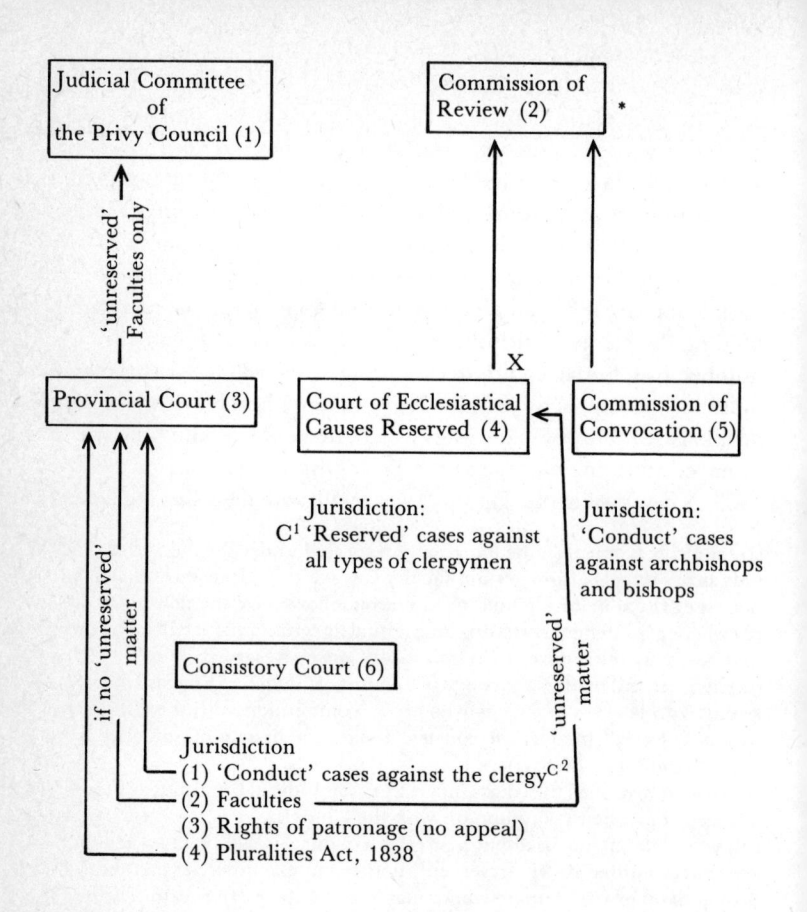

```
┌─────────────────┐              ┌─────────────────┐
│ Judicial Committee │           │ Commission of  │
│       of        │              │  Review  (2)   │   *
│ the Privy Council (1) │        │                │
└─────────────────┘              └─────────────────┘
         ↑                              ↑      ↑
    'unreserved'                        │      │
    Faculties only                      │      │
                                        │      │
                                        X
┌─────────────────┐   ┌─────────────────┐  ┌─────────────────┐
│ Provincial Court (3) │ │ Court of Ecclesiastical │←─│ Commission of │
│                 │   │ Causes Reserved  (4) │  │ Convocation (5) │
└─────────────────┘   └─────────────────┘  └─────────────────┘
    ↑  ↑  ↑
    │  │  │            Jurisdiction:              Jurisdiction:
    │  │  │            C¹ 'Reserved' cases against  'Conduct' cases
if no 'unreserved'     all types of clergymen      against archbishops
    matter                                         and bishops

                  ┌─────────────────┐
                  │ Consistory Court (6) │
                  └─────────────────┘
                    Jurisdiction
                  ─(1) 'Conduct' cases against the clergy^C²
                  ─(2) Faculties
                  ─(3) Rights of patronage (no appeal)
                  ─(4) Pluralities Act, 1838
```

KEY

──────── = Appeal

'reserved' = Matter of doctrine, ritual or ceremonial

C¹ = 'Committal' by committee of 3 members of Convocation + 2 diocesan chancellors

C² = 'Committal' by Examiner

* = In matters of doctrine joined by 5 bishops or other theologians as advisers

X = Joined by between 3 and 5 special advisers who are theologians or liturgiologists

Should a court find against a cleric the following penalties may be imposed:

(1) 'rebuke';
(2) 'monition' (an order to do or not to do something);
(3) 'suspension' (an order not to perform any rite or duty connected with the preferment for a set time);
(4) 'inhibition' (an order not to act as a clergyman at all for a set time);
(5) 'deprivation' (removal from office together with an order not to hold any clerical office in the future).[82]

Penalties (3), (4) and (5) may not be imposed on a first offender in a 'reserved' matter. None of these sentences are final because both the bishop and the archbishop have power effectively to bring them to an end. The royal prerogative of mercy may also be used to set a sentence aside.

The jurisdiction that has just been outlined is only over clergymen; the former power over lay officers of the Church was abolished in 1963.[83]

Notes for figure 2

Members of the Courts	Appointed by
1. Usually the law lords	Crown
2. Three law lords and two bishops (in House of Lords)	Crown
3. Dean of Arches and Auditor, joined in 'conduct' appeals by 2 clerks in holy orders and two judicially experienced laymen	Both archbishops with sanction of the Crown Church Church, in consultation the Lord Chancellor
4. Three spiritual (are or have been diocesan bishops) Two lay (hold or have held high judicial office)	Crown Crown
5. Dean of Arches and Auditor and four diocesan bishops	Church
6. Chancellor joined in 'conduct' cases by: two priests and two laymen	Diocesan bishop Diocesan Synod

Principal duties owed by the Church

The established position of the Church, as well as the customs produced by many centuries, means that persons resident within a parish have certain rights.

General right to attend public services

Until 1969 there was a theoretical legal obligation on all parishioners (with certain exceptions for dissenters) to attend their parish church each Sunday and so, 'by imposing a general duty to go to church, the legislature confers a general right to resort to the church on the person whom it obliges to go'.[84] The formal abolition of this obligation has probably not removed this right,[85] as in *Cole* v *Police Constable 443A*[86] Goddard J.[87] expressed the view that the right to attend was an ancient common law one, because the parish church was, by tradition, dedicated to the parishioner's use. Should the person not be a parishioner he has no such right as *Cole*'s case illustrates. At Westminster Abbey (a 'Royal Peculiar') the dean had given instructions that Cole, a self-employed guide, was to be excluded. This exclusion was upheld by the court even though it meant that he could not be present at public worship. The only parishioners of Westminster Abbey are those who live in the Close of Westminster, but even if Cole had lived there (which he did not) it seems arguable that he still could have been removed as he was present as a guide rather than as a worshipper.[88] Any person resident within a diocese would seem to have the right to attend a public service in the cathedral of the diocese.[89]

This right does not extend to sitting in a particular seat or in participating in holy communion (unless one is qualified so to do under ecclesiastical law). The right also finds expression in the legitimate expectation that divine offices will be performed at the Church.[90]

Baptism

Until recently there was a general obligation to baptise infants resident within the parish,[91] if they were presented for baptism. The present position is that a priest may object to godparents on the ground that they are not likely to fulfil their obligations towards the child and, unless the child is very ill or in danger of death, baptism may be postponed until suitable godparents are found. There is an appeal from a refusal to baptise an infant to the bishop.[92]

Marriage

Residents of a parish have a right to marry in their own parish church after the banns have been lawfully published, although there is some doubt whether this applies when both parties are unbaptised,[93] but even there the weight of opinion[94] is that the obligation exists. The only legal ground on which a priest may refuse the service is where one of the parties was married before and has been divorced.[95] Other than being obliged to conduct the service the priest could, if the parties are not regular church attenders and he wishes to bring this home to them, refuse such things as wedding bells and organ music.[96] As marriage by licence, however, is a matter of discretion, it need not be granted as of right.

Burial

A parishioner always has the right of being buried in his own churchyard[97] and a person dying in a parish has a right to be buried in that parish even though he was not resident there.[98] It does not matter what the deceased's religion was. The right does not extend to choosing a particular spot in the graveyard. Ashes from a cremation must be treated in the same way as a corpse. Under the Burial Law Amendment Act 1880,[99] the person in charge of the burial may order that the burial does not follow the Prayer Book service (which may not be used in any case where the deceased has not been baptised into any Christian Church or where he has laid violent hands upon himself) so that there is no service at all, or there may be such 'Christian [the provision does not extend to other religions] and orderly religious service', following any particular form as the person in charge of the burial thinks fit,[100] although this must not amount to an attack on any Christian religion.[101] The parish priest may say a non-Prayer Book service if it is not contrary to the doctrines of the Church of England and if it has been authorised by the bishop or the General Synod.

Notes

1. See The Archbishops' Commission on *Church and State*, 1970, 'The Church of England: Disestablishment Proposal', debated in the House of Lords, 314 H.L. Deb. (1971), cols 485–562; A. Vidler, 'The relations of Church and state with special reference to England', *Quis Custodiet?*, XXX, 1971, pp. 6–17; and R. Davies, 'Church and state', *Cambrian Law Review*, VII, 1976, pp. 11–30.

2. *Marshall* v *Graham Bell* [1907] 2 K.B. 112, at p. 126.

3. See N.J. Richards, 'Disestablishment of the Anglican Church in England in the late nineteenth century: reasons for failure', *Journal of Church and State*, XIX, 1977, pp. 193–211.
4. For example, L. S. Hunter (ed.), *The English Church: A New Look*, 1966.
5. Editorial, *Journal of Church and State*, XIX, 1977, p. 305, at p. 314.
6. In general see *Halsbury's Laws of England*, 4th edn, XIV, 1975, paras 301–1433. A useful short account is to be found in W. Dale, *Law of the Parish Church*, 5th edn, 1975.
7. See generally, Davies, 'Church and state', pp. 19–23.
8. See also Article XXXVII.
9. For the composition of this body see *Halsbury*, paras 390–8.
10. *Halsbury*, para. 399.
11. Synodical Government Measure 1969, Sch. 2, para. 7.
12. Synodical Government Measure 1969, Sch. 2, para. 8; Church of England (Miscellaneous Provisions) Measure 1978, Section 1.
13. For the composition of these bodies see *Halsbury*, para. 503.
14. Set up under Section 2 of the Church of England Assembly (Powers) Act 1919. For a useful discussion of the creation of the Church Assembly see F. A. Iremonger, *Williams Temple, Archbishop of Canterbury: His Life and Letters*, 1948, pp. 234–5 and 272–81.
15. Church of England Assembly (Powers) Act 1919, Section 3.
16. Which is taken to mean the people of England in general: *Church and State*, at p. 95.
17. Church of England Assembly (Powers) Act 1919, Section 4.
18. See Iremonger, *William Temple*, pp. 345–59; C. Garbett, *Church and State in England*, 1950, pp. 212–17; and A. Vidler, *The Church in an Age of Revolution*, 1971, pp. 163–8. The bishops were able to mitigate the problem somewhat by using their powers as 'ordinaries'. Following the difficulty a special commission was set up in 1930. Parliament's approval of the Prayer Book (Alternative and Other Services) Measure 1965 has probably removed this stain on Church/state relations although see the 1981 incident, below.
19. H.C. Deb., 1975, vol. 897, cols 1513–28. The Measure was then reconsidered. Changes were made (see the 178th Report of the Ecclesiastical Committee). A reformed Measure was passed by Parliament and given the Royal Assent in 1977. Ten years before there had been a serious (although unsuccessful) challenge to the Vestures of Ministers Measure (see H.C. Deb., 1964, vol. 699, cols 1865–1934). For difficulties encountered by Measures in the House of Lords see G. Drewry and J. Brock, 'Prelates in Parliament', *Parliamentary Affairs*, XIV, 1971, p. 222, at pp. 236–7.
20. See H.C. Deb., 1981, vol. 2, cols 959–64, and H.L. Deb., 1981, vol. 419, cols 612–67.
21. See S. Neill, *Anglicanism*, 1977, at p. 254.
22. *Church and State*, p. 16.
23. Ibid., p. 21.
24. Ibid., p. 55.
25. Dale, *Parish Church*, p. 9. The most important addition to this definition are Canons made under the Church of England (Worship and Doctrine) Measure 1974.

26. Submission of the Clergy Act 1533, Sections 1 and 3; Synodical Government Measure 1969, Section 1(3).

27. *Church and State*, p. 26. However where they wish to change the law of the land, including decisions of the ecclesiastical courts, they must proceed by way of a Measure — Davies, 'Church and state', p. 16.

28. Bill of Rights 1688, Section 1; Act of Settlement 1700, Sections 2 and 3; Accession Declaration Act 1910, Section 1.

29. See the articles and letters in *The Times*, 28, 29 and 30 July 1980.

30. H.C. Deb., 1980, vol. 989, cols 606–7 (written answers). The position has since been considered by a General Synod Working Party (see G.S. Misc. 159 of 1982), which has recognised that such a change would require the consent of Parliament and of all the countries of the Commonwealth which acknowledge the Queen as their monarch. Whilst a change regarding the consort would not directly affect the establishment of the Church, it could mean that the 'natural' succession to the throne would not be followed if a monarch married a Catholic and brought his children up as Catholics, because they would have to be treated as 'naturally dead'. Should such a thing ever come to pass it would surely cause a crisis for both the institution of monarchy and the position of the established Church. Additionally, if the monarch were to have a Catholic spouse or children, they could not worship with him in the Church of which he is Supreme Governor.

31. Lord Chancellor (Tenure of Office and Discharge of Ecclesiastical Functions) Act 1974, Section 1. And see the Appendix at pp. 202–3.

32. Section 2.

33. See the Appendix.

34. Roman Catholic Relief Act 1829, Section 18.

35. Jews Relief Act 1858, Section 4.

36. On the role of bishops as general legislators in recent times see Drewry and Brock, 'Prelates'.

37. Garbett, *Church and State in England*, p. 125 and H. Wilson, *The Governance of Britain*, 1976, p. 110.

38. Cmnd. 3799, 1968, paras 63–7.

39. *Church and State*, pp. 46–7.

40. Sometimes one is made a life peer but the numbers are negligible compared with the twenty-six *ex officio* bishops.

41. See e.g. Garbett, *Church and State in England*, 192–3; Wilson, *Governance*, pp. 108–10; and *Church and State*, chapters 3 and 4.

42. See *Crown Appointments and the Church*, 1964; Davies, 'Church and state', pp. 17–19.

43. *Church and State*, pp. 31–2.

44. Vacancy in See Regulations 1977 — see 906 H.C. Deb., 1976, col. 118 (written answers). Bishops must now retire at the age of seventy — Ecclesiastical Offices (Age Limit) Measure 1975.

45. Appointment of Bishops Act 1533. Failure to appoint (there have been minority votes against in cathedral chapters from time to time) could have resulted in praemunire, a penalty abolished by the Criminal Law Act 1967. See also the Suffragan Bishops Act 1534 and the Ecclesiastical Commissioners Act 1840.

46. See *The Times*, 31 March, 1, 2, 3, 4, 6, 7, 9 and 10 April 1981.
47. E.g. Neil, *Anglicanism*, p. 40.
48. Hunter, *English Church*, p. 80.
49. Although under the Clerical Disabilities Act 1870, a priest or deacon of the Church of England may rid himself of the disability by relinquishing his clerical office. Section 9 of the Roman Catholic Relief Act 1829 expressly excludes Roman Catholic priests from the House.
50. [1951] A.C. 161.
51. At pp. 170–1.
52. The Chadwick Commission. The matter was previously considered by Select Committees of the House of Commons in 1941 (1940–1(120)iii) and 1953 (1952–3(200)vi). These committees recommended no change.
53. *Sunday Times*, 2 September 1979, and *The Times*, 29 January 1982.
54. See E. Garth Moore, *Introduction to English Canon Law*, 1967, pp. 102–3.
55. Tithe Acts 1936 and 1951 etc. The common law right of chancel repair remains however: see *The Times*, 5 February 1982.
56. See *Church and State*, pp. 50–2.
57. Local Government Act 1972, Section 214.
58. Local Government Act 1972, Section 137. However the payment must not be authorised under some other statutory power.
59. Redundant Churches and other Religious Buildings Act 1969, Section 1(1). There is also a power to transfer small amounts of land to the Church Commissioners — Parsonages Act 1865, Section 4; Church Commissioners Measure 1947, Sections 2 and 18(2).
60. For defects with the former system of courts, see The Report of the Commission on Ecclesiastical Court, set up by the Archbishops of Canterbury and York, *The Ecclesiastical Courts. Principles of Reconstruction*, 1954.
61. The bishop's chancellor. On the modern relationship between the role of the bishop and the role of the chancellor, see *Re St Mary's Barnes* [1982] 1 All E.R. 456.
62. *Per* Lord Blackburn in *Mackonochie* v *Lord Penzance* (1881) 6 App.Cas. 424, at p. 446.
63. Ecclesiastical Jurisdiction Measure (No. 1) 1964, Section 81.
64. Ecclesiastical Jurisdiction Measure 1963, Section 59; Ecclesiastical Jurisdiction (Legal Aid) Rules, 1966.
65. [1932] 2 K.B. 402.
66. T. Cullen, *The Prostitutes' Padre*, 1975.
67. *Re St Andrew's, Heddington* [1978] Fam. 121.
68. At p. 125.
69. Ecclesiastical Jurisdiction Measure (No. 1) 1964, Section 81; Faculty Jurisdiction Measure (No. 3) 1964, Section 11.
70. *Halsbury*, para. 1306.
71. [1962] p. 147.
72. *Sunday Telegraph*, 27 July 1980, where permission to do this was refused by a consistory court sitting in Kent.
73. [1980] 2 All E.R. 84.
74. At p. 88.
75. *Gorham* v *Bishop of Exeter* (1850) Brod. & F. 64. The use of unauthorised

forms of worship or a departure from the doctrines of the Church are still grounds for disciplinary charges — *Church and State*, at p. 90.

76. The Archbishops' Commission, *Ecclesiastical Courts*, pp. 44–5.
77. Garbett, *Church and State in England*, p. 246.
78. The Archbishops' Commission, *Ecclesiastical Courts*, p. 77.
79. *Bland* v *Archdeacon of Cheltenham* [1972] Fam. 157.
80. *Cf. Re St Peter, Roydon* [1969] 2 All E.R. 1233.
81. [1972] Fam. 157, at p. 172. The breakdown of the pastoral relationship may now be dealt with under the Incumbents (Variation of Benefice) Measure 1977, thus avoiding the courts.
82. Ecclesiastical Jurisdiction Measure 1963, Section 49.
83. Ibid., Section 82. Any jurisdiction over ordinary members of the Church was considered to be obsolete by the third quarter of the nineteenth century.
84. *Taylor* v *Timpson* (1888) 20 Q.B.D. 671, at p. 682, *per* Stephen J.
85. *Halsbury*, para. 562; Dale, *Parish Church*, p. 46.
86. [1937] 1 K.B. 316.
87. At p. 333.
88. Lord Hewart C.J. at pp. 325 and 326. However du Parq J., at p. 329, seemed to indicate that if a person has a right to be in the church he could only be removed if he was acting with impropriety.
89. *In Re St Columb, Londonderry* (1863) 8 L.T. 861.
90. Dale, *Parish Church*, p. 45.
91. *Bland* v *Archdeacon of Cheltenham* [1972] Fam. 157, at p. 165. See also *Church and State*, pp. 61–3.
92. *Halsbury*, para. 993.
93. Garth Moore, *English Canon Law*, p. 87.
94. *Halsbury*, para. 1003; Dale, *Parish Church*, p. 52.
95. Matrimonial Causes Act 1965, Section 8.
96. For an example see *Journal of Church and State*, XIV, 1972, at p. 550.
97. *Ex parte Blackmore* (1830) 1 B. & Ad. 123. The Church of England (Miscellaneous Provisions) Measure 1976, Section 6(1), now provides a right of burial for anyone, in a parish, who was on the church electoral roll of the parish, even though he was not qualified at common law. See generally: M. R. Russell Davies, *The Law of Burial, Cremation and Exhumation*, 4th edn, 1974, pp. 4–8 and 32.
98. *Halsbury*, para. 1041.
99. Russell Davies, *Burial*, pp. 90–4.
100. Section 6.
101. Section 7.

6 Freedom of movement; freedom of association

Two vital parts of any consideration of religious freedom are the right to cross international frontiers for religious purposes and the right to form a free religious association in one's own country. The issues are sometimes linked, because the entering into a country of a religious personage can be important for the development of a religious group within that country, and can be seen as the international face of freedom of association.

(1) Freedom of movement

It has been a proud distinction for England to afford an inviolable asylum to men of every rank and condition, seeking refuge on her shores from persecution and danger in their own lands.

[Sir Thomas Erskine May (1906)]

In the nineteenth century Britain gained an international reputation as a refuge for many personages, including religious zealots, who were deemed to be undesirable in their own lands.[1] The first serious attempt to control the entry of aliens came with the Aliens Act of 1905 which aimed at keeping out undesirable steerage passengers. It is interesting to notice that an unrestricted right of entry was given to those escaping from political or religious persecution, even if they were going to become charges upon the state.[2] In 1914 a change occurred[3] and from then onwards[4] the Home Secretary could remove from the country, or refuse entry to, any alien whose presence in Britain was not 'conducive to the public good'. Under the current law the Home Secretary may refuse entry to alien members of religious groups on the ground that their exclusion is conducive to the public good, and there is no appeal from his decision,[5] although there is the possibility of making representations to the 'three wise men', a non-statutory group of advisers whose recommendations are not binding on the Home Secretary and who, in any case, will follow a less than 'judicial' procedure. Nor, unless perhaps one can show that he has acted from malice or at least not honestly, is there any possibility of judicial review.[6] In general 'acceptable religions' are granted favourable treatment with their ministers of religion, missionaries and members of religious orders[7] being allowed into the country without work permits[8] if they are coming to carry on their vocations and can maintain and accommodate themselves and their dependants without recourse to public funds. There is a similar exemption for members of religious orders who are coming into the country in order to teach in establishments maintained by the order. The tradition of asylum is continued and it may be granted on the ground that if the applicant had to leave the United Kingdom he might have to face *inter alia* religious persecution.[9] In dealing with all the immigration controls the authorities are enjoined to exercise them 'without regard to a person's race, colour *or religion*'.[10] The controls and their exercise are of concern from two particular viewpoints — first, how does the country stand as a refuge for those persecuted because of their religion? And second, as religions are often worldwide the question of who is admitted or not can have an important effect on those within the country.[11] A number of incidents are selected to illustrate the law and practice with regard to these controls.

Moral Rearmament

Following the end of the Second World War journeys from the United States of America to Britain were very difficult for the average man and one could only travel with a special permit. On 5 July 1946, there was an adjournment debate in the House of Commons[12] on the question of whether a sizeable number of entry permits should be given to American Moral Rearmament (or 'Oxford Group') missionaries. Tom Driberg, M.P., who thought that they should not be allowed entry,[13] made the following points:

(1) Dr Buchman, the founder of the movement, had placed a false entry in 'Who's Who';[14]
(2) the movement had attempted to bring advertising pressure to bear in a newspaper in order to prevent criticism of itself from being published;[15]
(3) the movement had been sympathetic to the Nazis;[16]
(4) and they had interfered in industry.[17]

Chuter Ede, then Home Secretary, said[18] that he had to deal with a vast number of applications for entry by persons of different religious denominations. He had admitted Mormons, having ascertained that polygamy was no longer a tenet of their faith, and he continued:

> My experience has been that there is no denomination in this country, where toleration is practised, which does not do benefit to some and harm to others. ... One has to leave these mysteries to the workings of a Power that is higher than governments and works out in its own mysterious way its influences on the souls and lives of men ... I am not prepared to apply religious or political tests to people who desire to come into this country unless it can be established that they desire to come here to carry on subversive propaganda as defined by the Acts concerned with seditious practices. Let us hear all things, for I believe the common sense of the British democracy is such that in the long run they will winnow the chaff from the wheat. A democracy that has had the long experience that ours has can be safely left to deal with these movements properly when it has heard their case expounded by themselves ... I desire that the ancient record of this country as a place of free speech, where the flow of ideas from all parts of the world is welcome, may be maintained, and while I will not guarantee that some of the people I admit may not be charlatans ... even be false prophets, on occasion, I desire to impose no censorship other than that which the law entitles me to impose against subversive propaganda on any person who desires to come to this country to meet people of his own persuasion.

Scientology

This liberal declaration of toleration for all save those who posed criminal threats for democracy came to be tested in the 1960s with the case of the Scientologists. Scientology, founded in the United States of America, was established in Britain by the late 1950s but it was in the mid-1960s that it came under the national spotlight. An incident in 1966, concerning a Karen Henslow, attracted much press comment and there was a demand for a Government inquiry into the movement.[19] In 1967 came an adjournment debate, with much criticism of the movement from several Members of Parliament, but at this stage the Minister of Health, whilst agreeing in general with the criticism, declined to take action.[20] However by 25 July 1968 he had changed his mind and announced a number of administrative measures which were to be taken so as to discourage the growth and propagation of Scientology. Included amongst these were the following:[21]

> (*b*) Foreign nationals arriving at United Kingdom ports who intend to proceed to scientology establishments will no longer be eligible for admission as students ...

(d) Foreign nationals already in the United Kingdom for study at a scientology establishment will not be granted extensions of stay to continue these studies ...
(e) Work permits and employment vouchers will not be issued to foreign nationals ... for work at a scientology establishment.

This ban remained in force until 1980 and whether or not one regards Scientology as a religion[22] the principles and lessons that may be learnt from the incident are of relevance to other controversial groups which may fall foul of these provisions.[23] At the outset it should be pointed out that Scientology was placed in this position not because the authorities believed they had committed criminal offences nor, as had been relevant with Moral Rearmament, was it alleged that they were attempting to infiltrate important institutions of the establishment,[24] but rather the main ground of objection concerned the effect that it was said to have on the minds of its adherents. It is fair to point out, however, that towards the end of the ban evidence of criminal activity did come to light relating to the activities of some of the group's leaders in the United State of America. In *Re Budlong and Kember*[25] two members of the Church of Scientology were extradited to the United States in order to face charges of complicity in acts of burglary there. It was claimed that the Church had been at odds with the Internal Revenue Services Department over their tax status and had also been in legal battles with the Food and Drugs Administration over the use of their 'E-Meters'. The Divisional Court accepted that the motivation behind these 'Watergate type' break-ins could well be that they were trying to improve their position in litigation but this did not constitute a 'political' offence enabling them to resist extradition. They were not acts aimed to bring the United States Government down but were rather aimed to improve their bargaining position with that Government. It should be stressed that at no time during the existence of the ban were any Scientologists convicted of similar acts in this country.

The major testing place for the legality of the Government's action was the Court of Appeal in the *Schmidt* case. In arguing the Scientologists' case Quintin Hogg Q.C. claimed[26] that it was action being taken against a sect and that if it was upheld action against any denomination (e.g. Christians, Roman Catholic, Moral Rearmament) would be justified simply because the Government considered it to be harmful, even though the harm did not constitute the commission of a criminal offence. This plea did not find favour with a majority of the court. Lord Denning M.R.[27] thought that the 'public good' power was a wide one and that if the Home Secretary thought Scientology harmful to society then that was a proper purpose for the exercise of his power (which was open to attack in Parliament but not elsewhere). The other judge in the majority, Widgery L.J.,[28] whilst agreeing in the result (i.e. that the two applicants in the case could be removed from the country as a result of this administrative action, without the legal right of making representations to the decision-making body), concentrated his reasoning on the fact that the aliens lacked any recognisable legal interest in the matter. Thus it was not important to him whether the Home Secretary's reasons were good or bad as they were irrelevant. On the other hand Russell L.J. thought that it could be '... arguable that the written reasons given by the Minister indicate a purpose of discouraging the institution at East Grinstead by cutting off its students rather than a purpose of keeping students away least they do harm'.[29] He, at least, did not agree that the proposed action in the case should be struck out.

The Scientologists were subsequently to meet with equally little success[30] in other courts. Their next major challenge to the ban imposed upon them was an application to the European Commission of Human Rights on the ground that the British Government's action constituted an infringement of their religious freedoms under the European Convention of Human Rights.[31] However, the Commission held that their application was inadmissible because:[32]

(i) the rights under the convention were only applicable to natural persons and not to legal ones, such as religious denominations;
(ii) the rights under the convention did not extend to persons who were foreign nationals outside the United Kingdom.

The next court they turned to was the Court of the European Economic Community, with a challenge under Common Market law claiming that the ban offended against the principle of freedom of movement of labour within the Community. In *Van Duyn* v *The Home Office*[33] that court held that a Member State could prohibit community workers from entering its territory where 'the individual was associated with an organisation which the Member State considered to be socially harmful' and that 'it was immaterial that the organisation was not subject to any restrictions under the law of the Member State'. Interestingly enough none other than Lord Denning, himself no great friend of the Scientologists,[34] has expressed the view[35] that Miss Van Duyn had a better case than the case suggests, because properly to exclude her it should have been shown that the decision was based on the particular conduct of the individual concerned rather than based on the body or organisation that she is going to associate with, regardless of her personal qualities.

Yet another avenue of attack was the immigration appeals procedure. The Scientologists were not entitled to the religious privileges in the immigration rules outlined above, and in 1974, applying *R* v *Registrar-General, ex p. Segerdal*[36] the Immigration Appeal Tribunal held[37] that Scientologists cannot be considered ministers of religion for these purposes. The Scientologists were somewhat more fortunate in 1980 when a German Scientologist won her case before an independent adjudicator.[38] She had merely wished to attend one Scientology service during a short visit to the country and it was held that this could not be objected to as it did not fall under the 1968 prohibitions.

The general effect of these legal defeats were twofold. First the cases show that only Parliament can interfere with the exercise of the Home Secretary's discretion in this area, and secondly some of the cases were somewhat unsatisfactory in that because of the nature of the cases before the courts the real issue (i.e. was Scientology harmful?) could not be tested. In 1971 the then Government asked Sir John Foster to deal with the substantive issue.[39] Whilst acknowledging the existence of the Home Secretary's legal power to do what had been done he felt it was wrong in principle to ban aliens and Commonwealth citizens from entering into the country who wished to participate in an activity which was perfectly lawful in the United Kingdom and which United Kingdom citizens could pursue without fear of penalty. If Scientology was harmful to the extent that society felt under threat then it should be controlled by a special Act of Parliament passed after a full debate and those controls should apply to both Britons and foreigners alike within the country.

But so long as none of our laws are being infringed, the classification of foreign Scientologists as 'undesirable aliens' so that they are forbidden entry through our ports, while the accident of birth permits those Scientologists who happen to be citizens of the United Kingdom to process and be processed with impunity [a Scientology practice], seems to me to constitute a use of this discretionary power which is quite contrary to the traditional policy followed by successive Home Secretaries over many years.[40]

The report contained other important recommendations such as that psychotherapy should be subject to stricter control[41] and that the privileged fiscal position of religious bodies should be re-examined,[42] but these have yet to be acted upon.

In 1980, following much canvassing from the Scientologists the ban was removed. Mr Whitelaw, the Home Secretary, declared[43] that the Government was not satisfied that 'there is clear and sufficient current evidence for continuing the existing policy with regard to Scientologists on medical grounds alone'. However, this general removal of the ban did not effect:

(1) the continued exclusion of some individual Scientologist, such as the group's founder;
(2) nor did it mean that Scientologists would be given the special treatment that is awarded to 'ministers of religion' and 'missionaries' under the Immigration Rules.

In addition to the official reason other influences may have been at work. A ban on entry is not always easy to effect — what does a Scientologist look like? His passport carries no special mark. In any case the power savours of an autocratic flavour and in the case of the Scientologists gave them a legitimate grievance and the chance to gain support from others whose concern was with the civil libertarian issues involved.

The Unification Church

The principle stated in the Moral Rearmament debate seems to be generally followed when controversial minority sects are in view. In 1976 the Government refused to ban the entry of the Children of God cult.[44] A year later there was an adjournment debate on the Unification Church (the 'Moonies').[45] Paul Rose, M.P., requested that administrative action be taken against this sect because of:

(1) its activities in the United State of America;[46]
(2) its effects on family life;[47]
(3) its alleged brainwashing tendencies;[48]
(4) the large sums donated to it by its supporters;[49] and
(5) its alleged unlawful collections of sums of money in the streets.[50]

He thought it wrong that although the Home Secretary had just removed the journalist Hosenball from the country,[51] he had done nothing against the leader of this sect.[52] Speaking for the Government Dr Shirley Summerskill said that it was a very serious matter to suggest that the Government should take action where no serious breach of the criminal law had been proved, and furthermore:

If the Government as a government took action against organisations which they regarded as wrong-headed or even worse, we should be living in a rather different kind of society. The cost of such freedom is that some people will spend their money foolishly, be led astray by charlatans and even misunderstood the motives and feelings of their families and true friends. But when we decided that people should be treated as adults from the age of eighteen, this meant that they had the right to make their own choice on the way they wished to lead their lives and to make their own mistakes.[53]

Since this debate there has been renewed pressure on the Government to act. The revelations in the 'Moonie Libel Trial'[54] plus other allegations in print[55] have contributed to this. 'Moonies' are not granted the special status attaching to ministers of religion and missionaries.

(2) Freedom of association

In the eyes of the law, Churches [other than the established Church] are merely voluntary associations, deriving their powers and authority from the consent of their members.

[*per* Professor F. Lyall] 'Religion and Law'. *Juridical Review*, 1976, 58 at p. 63.

A group of individuals sharing a common belief may come together and form what they consider to be a religion. In law they will have created an unincorporated association,[56] a simple creature of contract which is enforceable in law on that basis. Provided that the religion has not been set up in order to advance an unlawful activity[57] the task of any court that may have to deal with the legal existence of the religion is to ascertain the true meaning of the contract that has been formed. The courts have stressed that they are not concerned with the truth of any doctrine although they may, at times, have to consider whether any particular doctrine is an essential element of a sect whilst they perform such functions as the construction of trust deeds, the disposition of property rights, interference with private rights and so forth.[58] Where adherence to the original doctrine of the sect no longer seems to be dictated by the evolution of belief within the body a difficulty may occur should the original agreement not provide for amendment. When this happens the property of the religion may not belong to the reformed group which, looked at through the eyes of the original adherents, has lost its essential validity.[59] Such a result does not directly prevent the reformers from associating and advancing their new found revelation although they may be deterred at the thought of the loss of property that the change involves. The problem is not without solution — an Act of Parliament can be procured to remedy the gaps. An example of such an Act, taken at random, is the United Reform Church Act 1981. In 1980 the United Church that had already been formed between the Congregational and Presbyterian English Churches wished to join with the Reformed Association of Churches of Christ and so a special Act had to be passed in order to 'legitimise' it with regard to the existing property, rights and obligations of the Churches then in being. To perfect this the unincorporated bodies making up these religions had to be dissolved[60] and their property passed to the new ones now making up the Church.[61] At the same time rights and duties owned by the then Churches were preserved.[62] Provision was also made so that individual churches would be able to secede from the union[63] without the necessity of having to obtain yet another Act of Parliament. Courts may, at times, have to construe such Acts (just as they may be called upon to construe the 'contract' which makes up the unincorporated association). Whilst interpreting the Methodist Church Union Act 1929, Megarry J.[64] has made the important point that the chief organ of the relevant religion (in this case the Methodist Conference) is a far more suitable body for the interpretation of the relevant doctrines than is a civil court.

A religious association may of course wish to go further than mere legal existence. It may wish to claim the special legal position which is held by religious trusts.[65] and as has been shown the law will impose conditions and tests on those who seek its privileges but this should not be thought of as any issue of freedom of association as such — to deny tax status does not directly interfere with the freedom of individuals to associate, although it may indirectly discourage the growth of the relevant group.

Should the group wish to use a place for worship they will, should a large number wish to gather, need planning permission. In 1981[66] a religious sect, which believed that Jesus Christ came to Earth in a flying saucer, had been using a garage in the garden of a semi-detached bungalow. There had been complaints from neighbours due to the noise caused by visitors' cars and planning permission to use it as a place of worship was refused. An inquiry, whilst holding that the garage could not be turned into a place of religious worship, did however sanction the continuation of services there as relatively few took part. The religion may of course seek to register the place that they use for their worship under the Place of Religious Worship Act 1855, in order to obtain the privileges that registration brings.

Freedom of movement and of association 113

An issue receiving much attention in recent years has been the freedom that individuals have to join and to leave religions, particularly controversial minority sects such as the 'Moonies'. As far as adults are concerned our law is clear — given legal mental capacity an adult is free to join any group and to consent to its activities provided that they do not seriously (physically) harm him or lead to the commission of some criminal offence. This rather simple approach has now to be tested by issues posed by the activities of some of the minority groups — allegations about these cults,[67] especially from the United States of America,[68] have been disturbing. It has been stated that they use various forms of pressure, such as the use of lies, singing, chanting, a constant barrage of rhetoric and so on, so that converts loose their ordinary 'frames of reference'. In the end members are said to be deprived of control over their minds. Other pressures, it is claimed, include changes of diet, guilt pressure and promises of salvation from a world shortly coming to an end. Some of the pressures may be physical and 'privacy of body or of mind may not be allowed for days or for weeks'. Converts then become so brainwashed that for them 'reality becomes the present and includes in it elements of supernatural, magical terrifying thought'. The convert may come to reject home and parents in return for the new 'parents' that the cult leaders have become in his mind. Converts are taught to use special chants should their beliefs come under attack. This process has been described, in short, as 'depersonalisation'.[69] Those holding that some cults can work in this way believe that because of these pressures adherents are no longer acting out of their own free will and so need a form of rescue which has come to be known as 'de-programming'. 'De-programming' can include a forcible abduction followed by a period of captivity, during which the 'de-programmer' attempts to undo the 'harm' implanted by the cult.[70]

The legal problems posed by all of this have yet to be tested in this country although it seems clear that there have been some 'de-programmings' performed here. Elements of fraud, false imprisonment, assault,[71] and kidnapping may have to be balanced against such defences as consent and, perhaps, necessity. The nearest that an English Court has yet come to considering some of these questions was in an application for *habeas corpus*, heard in 1982.[72] Unification Church applicants indicated that a twenty-eight-year-old woman may have been abducted in order to get her away from the sect. The Court, on the basis of the evidence that had been produced, refused to order that the parents should reveal the woman's whereabouts and May L.J. stated that although parents were not entitled to detain an adult daughter against her wishes, they were entitled to advise and persuade their children, to refrain from action they saw as harmful, 'if they think necessary, with emphasis'.

Notes

1. C. H. R. Thornberry, 'Dr Soblen and the alien law of the United Kingdom', *International and Comparative Law Quarterly*, XII, 1963, 414, at p. 415.
2. Aliens Act 1905, Section 1(3).
3. Aliens Restriction Act 1914.
4. Although such powers might, in theory, have been available before 1914 by virtue of the Royal Prerogative — *Attorney-General for Canada* v *Cain* [1906] A.C. 542.
5. Immigration Act 1971, Section 13(5). If the alien is already in the country there is a possible appeal unless the Secretary of State is of the view that exclusion is conducive to the public good in the interests of national security, diplomatic relations or reasons of a political nature — Immigration Act 1971, Sections 14(3), 15(3) and 18(2).
6. *R* v *Leaman Street Police Inspector, ex p. Venicoff* [1920] 3 K.B. 72, and *Schmidt* v *Secretary of State for Home Affairs* [1969] 2 Ch. 149. The possibilities for a challenge to the 'public good' power were explored by the Court of Appeal in *R* v *Governor of Brixton Prison, ex p. Soblen* [1963] 2 Q.B. 243. At p. 302 Lord Denning M.R. stated that the exercise of power could be attacked if it could be shown that the exclusion had not been for the public good of this country but for some other purpose (e.g. to please a foreign government). At pp. 307–8 Donovan L.J. said that such an order could be overturned if it was a 'sham' — that is, where the Secretary of State makes the order without a genuinely formed opinion that exclusion is conducive to the public good, merely using the power in order to achieve some other object. The result of *Soblen* illustrates how hard it is to make out such an allegation. Proof will always be difficult in such a case (see Donovan L.J. at p. 308) and in any event the decision stands, it seems, if the Secretary of State honestly believes that exclusion is for the public good, even if many others do not (although the 'uniqueness' of his view and the quality of his evidence would bear on the question of whether he had genuinely formed the view).
7. *Statement of Change in Immigration Rules*, H.C. Papers, No. 394, 1979–80, para. 31.
8. For initially twelve months but under para. 108 there may be extensions, an extension being for up to three years.
9. Para. 120.
10. Para. 108.
11. Thus the removal of a Sikh priest caused consternation to the Sikh community in Bradford in 1981 — *The Times*, 13 October 1981.
12. H.C. Deb., 1946, vol. 424, cols 2562–82.
13. He later wrote a critical analysis of the group — T. Driberg, *The Mystery of Moral Rearmament: A Study of Frank Buchman and His Movement*, 1964.

14. H.C. Deb., 1946, vol. 424, col. 2566.
15. Col. 2568.
16. Col. 2572.
17. Ibid.
18. Cols 2578-81.
19. H.C. Deb., 1966, vol. 724, cols 11-12; vol. 737, col. 183 (written answers).
20. H.C. Deb., 1967, vol. 742, cols 1216-28.
21. H.C. Deb., 1968, vol. 769, cols 189-91 (written answers).
22. *R v Registrar-General, ex p. Segerdal* [1970] 2 Q.B. 697.
23. *Schmidt v Secretary of State for Home Affairs* [1969] 2 Ch. 149.
24. But see *Gaiman v National Association for Mental Health* [1971] Ch. 317.
25. [1980] 2 C.M.L.R. 125.
26. [1969] 2 Ch. 149, at p. 163.
27. At p. 169.
28. At p. 172.
29. At pp. 171-2.
30. See Sir John Foster, *Enquiry into the Practice and Effects of Scientology*, 1971, pp. 162-3.
31. See Chapter 1, at pp. 11-13.
32. Dec. Ad. Com., 3498/68.
33. [1975] 3 All E.R. 190.
34. Thus in *Ex parte Church of Scientology of California, The Times*, 20 February 1978, Lord Denning agreed not to preside over a Scientology application because of the number of times they had come before him in the past and because of the doubts that he had expressed over whether they were a 'religion' or not.
35. In *The Due Process of Law*, 1980, at p. 166.
36. [1970] 2 Q.B. 697.
37. Appeal No. TH/1326/74 — 12 September 1974.
38. *Daily Telegraph*, 17 May 1980.
39. See note 30.
40. Para. 210.
41. Paras 238-62.
42. Paras 263-7.
43. H.C. Deb., 1980, vol. 988, col. 578 (written answers).
44. H.C. Deb., 1976, vol. 905, cols 579-88.
45. H.C. Deb., 1977, vol. 926, cols 1587-98.
46. Col. 1587.
47. Col. 1588.
48. Col. 1589.
49. Col. 1588.
50. Col. 1591.
51. See *R v Secretary of State, ex parte Hosenball* [1977] 3 All E.R. 452.
52. H.C. Deb., vol. 926, col. 1594.
53. Cols 1597-8.
54. See Chapter 1, pp. 10-11.
55. E.g. C. Edwards, *Crazy for God*, 1979, and S. and A. Swetland, *Escape from Moonies*, 1982.

56. See T. Bennet, 'Free Churches and the state', *Law Quarterly Review*, XXXIV, 1918, pp. 35–48 and 174–85, and F. Lyall, 'Religion and law', *Juridical Review*, 1976, p. 58 at pp. 63–5.

57. Lord Halsbury L.C. in *Free Church of Scotland* v *Lord Overtoun* [1904] A.C. 515, at p. 613. *Mandla* v *Lee* [1983] 2 W.L.R. 620 may cause some difficulty here. Section 25 of the Race Relations Act 1976 make it unlawful for a corporate or unincorporate association which has twenty-five or more members to refuse on racial grounds to admit someone to membership. Suppose a Christian mothers' union refuses to admit a Sikh woman because of her religion. This would seem to be contrary to the Act, subject to Section 26, which provides that if the association 'is to enable the benefits of membership ... to be enjoyed by persons of a particular racial group defined otherwise than by reference to colour ...' it is lawful. The difficulty is whether the Christian mothers' union could be said to be racial, as *Mandla* v *Lee* makes clear that a mere religious grouping is not as such a racial one — if the Christian mothers cannot point to a particular 'ethnic origin' as defined in that case they would seem to fall outside the exemption granted by Section 26. This is perhaps another of the unforeseen consequences of the case. What where a particular religious group meet to further their religion? This would seem to depend on 25(1)(b), which requires that 'admission to membership is regulated by its constitution ...'. These words would hardly seem appropriate where a religious doctrine requires that only 'an elect' may be present (as in *Henning* v *Church of Jesus Christ of Latter-Day Saints* [1964] A.C. 420 — the 'Mormon Temple case') and so it may be that Section 25 does not apply. In any case the 'justification' defence in 1(1)(b) may also be of relevance in certain situations, although *Mandla* v *Lee* does not seem to give great support for it in this area. Section 35 may also be relevant in certain circumstances; it states that it shall not be unlawful to afford persons of a particular 'racial' group 'access to facilities or service to meet the special needs of persons of that group in regard to their education, training or welfare, or any ancillary benefits.'

58. Bennet, 'Free Churches', p. 177, Lyall, 'Religion and law', p. 65.

59. *Free Church of Scotland* v *Lord Overtoun* [1904] A.C. 515.

60. Section 5(1).

61. Sections 6 and 7.

62. See Sections 15, 27 and 28.

63. Section 21.

64. *Baker* v *O'Gorman* [1971] 1 Ch. 215, at p. 230.

65. See Chapter 4, at pp. 59–65.

66. *Daily Telegraph*, 27 November 1981.

67. E.g. Dr J.G. Clark, 'Investigating the effects of religious cults on the health and welfare of their converts', *American Atheist*, May 1977.

68. See in particular D.G. Hill, *Study of Mind Development Groups, Sects and Cults in Ontario*, 1980, Chapter 4.

69. Methods also used, at times, by more 'orthodox' religions; see Dr William Sargant, *Battle for the Mind*, 1959 (1970 Pan ed, at p. 79).

70. Hill, *Mind Development Groups*, Chapter 5.

71. An assault inducing an hysterical and nervous condition can constitute actual bodily harm — *R* v *Miller* [1954] 2 Q.B. 282.

72. *The Times*, 29 April 1982.

7   Clashing with the criminal law[1]

Those were not naturally cruel men who burnt heretics for not agreeing with them, and witches for being vaguely disquieting, they were simply men who refused to submit prejudice to reason'.

[Clive Bell, 'On British Freedom' (1923), at p. 47]

Witchcraft and spiritualism

Coke defined a witch as a person who, 'hath conference with the devil, to consult with him or to do some act',[2] and from early Anglo-Saxon times laws,[3] which from 1542 onwards became increasingly draconian struck at the practitioners of the 'old religion'.[4] The criminal law, as opposed to the ecclesiastical authorities, was concerned with witchcraft as it was frequently found to be a potent of sedition.[5] Additionally the criminal law intervened in order to prevent people from taking the law into their own hands. In theory the calling up of any evil spirit for any purpose was a capital crime, although the courts tended to require the witch to have produced some physical harm through her sorcery.[6] The entire mythology of devil's marks, familiars and bewitchings and the all too real occurrences of prickings, floatings and burnings[7] form an undistinguished part of our legal history — even so some of England's greatest judges, men such as Sir Edward Coke and Sir Matthew Hale, believed in the reality of witchcraft. A change of opinion occurred after Hale's time and the last execution of a witch in England was probably in 1684.[8] The Chief Justiceship of Sir John Holt, from 1689 until 1710, saw a real shift in judicial attitudes with witches being seen as wordly frauds rather than as traffickers in the supernatural. The final known trial (although there were later attempts to invoke the law that did not proceed to a trial; for example in Leicester in 1717)[9] under the old law was that of Jane Wenham in 1712,[10] where Powell J. summed up strongly in favour of an acquittal. Despite this she was, thanks to local prejudice, convicted, but the judge was able to secure a pardon in her favour. In 1735 a new Witchcraft Act was passed in order to confirm the change of attitude towards the subject. The crime would now consist of pretending to exercise or use any kind of witchcraft, sorcery, enchantment or conjuration, 'whereby ignorant persons are frequently deluded and defrauded'.

How in wholly changed circumstances would twentieth-century Spiritualism stand in the light of this historical background? In *Duncan*[11] a medium who had been acting as such for twenty-five years was convicted, as the Act in effect deemed her to pretend to converse with the spirits of the dead. There was no need to show that she had faked contact with evil or wicked spirits. Nor would the Court allow a demonstration in order to 'test' her powers.[12] Because of the difficulties this approach caused for Spiritualists the 1735 Act was replaced by the Fraudulent Mediums Act in 1951. Under this Act,

... any person who:
(a) with intent to deceive purports to act as a spiritualistic medium or to exercise any powers of telepathy, clairvoyance or similar powers, or
(b) in purporting to act as a spiritualistic medium or to exercise such powers as aforesaid, uses any fraudulent device, shall be guilty of an offence.[13]

To be convicted the false medium must have acted for a reward, either for himself or another, of money or of some other valuable thing.[14] The Act goes on to lay down that the offence is not committed if the performance has been put on merely as an entertainment.[15] As recently as 1975 five people were proceeded against for offences under Section 1 of the Act.

Section 4 of the Vagrancy Act 1824,[16] which prohibited fortune telling, was also a restriction for Spiritualists especially as it was held in 1921[17] that the offence was committed when one told fortunes and that it did not matter whether or not one had any intention to deceive or whether one actually believed that one's powers existed (although the prediction had to relate to an individual person).[18] The law reached the stage that it refused to allow that anyone could honestly consider that such powers existed.[19] However because of the wording of the Fraudulent Mediums Act[20] such prosecutions are probably not possible today — thus any fortune telling must now be knowingly deceptive to constitute the offence. Nowadays this offence has come to be little used and the Home Office feel that despite the occasional distress and nuisance that fortune telling can sometimes cause this provision may be safely repealed without replacement.

Of course black magic, witchcraft and the like can always constitute a breach of the general law. A striking example occurred in 1981[21] when a thirty-one-year-old practitioner of the black arts twice broke into a family mausoleum and on each occasion stole a skull. In passing the very severe sentence of three years' imprisonment for these offences the trial judge is reported to have said that it was hard to imagine anything so revolting as what the defendant had done.

False prophets and pious frauds

The Fraudulent Mediums Act requires both a deception and a gain, either for the medium or another, and so a crime against that statute would normally also constitute the offence of dishonestly obtaining property by deception.[22] This serious offence will be committed whenever a fraudulent representation is dishonestly made with an intention to make a gain. The idea of the pious fraud is not new — indeed such things were notorious in the Middle Ages.[23] Nowadays a court may be expected to approach the cause of one who has obtained property out of a religious motivation with real caution since '… other men's religions are always gross frauds'.[24] An example of how an English court might be expected to react in a modern pious fraud case is provided in the American decision of *United States* v *Ballard*.[25] The Ballard family claimed to be 'divine messengers' and stated that they had the power to heal the sick. They had received sums of money as a consequence of these representations. The majority of the Supreme Court held that the correct approach in such a situation is to examine whether the beliefs are sincerely held by the defendants, but at the same time not examining the truth of those beliefs, for, in the words of Douglas J.:

Many take their gospel from the New Testament. But it would hardly be supposed that they could be tried before a jury charged with the duty of determining whether those teachings contained false representations. The miracles of the New Testament, the Divinity of Christ, life after death, the power of prayer are deep in the religious convictions of many. If one could be sent to jail because a jury in a hostile environment found those teachings false, little indeed would be left of religious freedom.

Jackson J. did not feel that he could agree with the majority. He thought that it was inevitable that the less believable the jury found the claims in question to be, the more likely they were to find the beliefs to be held fraudulently. Belief was too fundamental a component of religion to be analysed by a jury. If there was to be a path of religious freedom one had to risk a few encounters with false prophets along the way. He concluded with this warning:

> when does less than full belief in a professed credo become actionable fraud if one is soliciting gifts or legacies? Such inquiries may discomfort orthodox as well as unconventional religious teachers, for even the most regular of them are sometimes accused of taking their orthodoxy with a grain of sand.

Two English civil law cases give an indication of the probable approach of the criminal law within this country. In *Phillips* v *De la Warr*[26] the defendants practised 'radionics' — a method of curing disease through treatment in the 'astral plane' by means of a device known colloquially as 'the black box'. The plaintiff had bought a black box and brought a civil action for fraud as it did not seem to help her. Although there was much evidence for and against the efficacy of the box Davies J. concentrated on the sincerity of the defendants' beliefs rather than on the truth of them, an approach which was essentially the same as that of the majority in *Ballard*. *Morris* v *Associated Newspapers Ltd*[27] saw a similar line being taken a generation earlier in an action for defamatory libel. Mrs Morris, a young spiritualist medium who had sprung to sudden fame, sued the *Daily Mail* for implying that she was a fraud. In one of the strangest actions ever heard she several times appeared to go into trances and in one of these trances said to the judge, in a deep male voice, 'Thou, who art a brother judge, hearken unto my voice.' This shook McCardie J., who later burst out, 'I care now for all the incarnate or discarnate spirits in the world. As long as I remain on the Bench, I shall resolutely seek to reach for truth and I advise the jury to do the same, although there may be ten thousand million discarnate spirits around us.' However despite these manifestations of, at least, emotion he made clear that the medium merely had to show sincerity in the exercise of 'her powers' — there was no need for the jury to believe that they existed. After much expert evidence on both sides they found that the paper had made fair comment on a matter of public interest but they did not consider that any fraud or dishonesty had been shown on the part of Mrs Morris. This rather strange verdict[28] was upheld by the House of Lords on the ground that in fact the newspaper stories had not constituted an allegation of fraud.

The Senior approach

In the nineteenth century a sect of particular concern to the criminal law grew up. They were the Peculiar People and to them prayer was a more efficacious method of curing illness than was the calling in of the medical man. When, because of this belief, they failed to obtain orthodox medical treatment for their children the law was sometimes brought in. In *Wagstaffe*[29] such failure had lead to the death of a child, and Willes J., in the ensuing prosecution for manslaughter at common law, stated that a duty of care could be carried out in different ways and that the religious beliefs of the parent could be a legitimate factor in ascertaining whether such a duty had been carried out reasonably.[30] Furthermore the issue of the sincerity of the defendants was to be resolved by determining 'whether the prisoners held the belief they hold honestly'. On the other hand it was also clear at this time that if the essential elements of the offence had been intentionally brought about a religious motive would not excuse — thus in one case a defendant was found guilty of moving a corpse from a burial ground,[31] acting on what he believed was his filial and religious duty (although in that particular case some unwillingness was expressed in confirming his conviction and only a nominal penalty was imposed upon the defendant out of respect for his sincere motive). Following alarm at the acquittal in *Wagstaffe* a statutory offence of wilful child neglect was created,[32] thus limiting the courses of action, in law, open to the parents of a sick child, as the cases that were to follow illustrate. In *Downes*[33] a member of the Peculiar People was convicted of the statutory offence through his failure to call in the physician to treat his child, who was suffering from inflamed lungs. Lord Coleridge[34] considered that the father's religious beliefs explained his motive but not his intention and were thus irrelevant to the fact that he had intentionally failed to provide medical aid. *Morby*,[35] was a similar case, save that the child died. The Court of Crown Cases Reserved quashed the conviction for manslaughter because insufficient evidence had been given at the trial. Finally came the leading case of *Senior*,[36] an unlawful-act manslaughter prosecution based on a similar failure by a father to provide medical aid for his sick child. *Senior* still provides the basic proposition that religious motive in itself is no defence to what would otherwise constitute a breach of the criminal law, because 'To permit [religious belief as a defence] would be to make the professed doctrines of religious belief superior to the law of the land, and in effect permit every citizen to become a law unto himself'.[37] The position is not the same where the religious belief is so overwhelming as to exclude intention, that is where the parent fails to see that society expects him to call in a doctor.[38] Thus, following the decision of the House of Lords in *Sheppard*,[39] the position[40] is that where a parent appreciates that an ordinary parent would call in the doctor but believes that it is in the child's better interests for prayer to be used instead the offence is committed.[41] But if he fails so to appreciate the need, not out of indifference to the child's state but through his belief about his duty, no offence is committed. Thus Senior is guilty because 'there was not any question of the accused parent being unaware that risk to the child's health might be involved in his failure to provide it with medical aid. He deliberately refrained from having recourse to medical aid with his eyes open to the child's physical health'.[42] Religious belief that is so overwhelming as to make the defendant fail to appreciate the consequences of his acts can, on the other hand, afford a defence.[43] These principles, worked out in the child-neglect cases, apply generally in criminal law.

Clashes between religion and law can involve laws that differ widely in importance from those that aim at being protective (e.g. designed to prevent harm to others) to those that paternalistically lay down a course of conduct (e.g. the wearing of crash helmets when riding a motor-cycle). A frequently discussed possible conflict[44] is that between a priest's obligation to keep confidences and his duty to give evidence in a court of law. At one time courts seemed to be indulgent towards priests in this situation[45] but by 1865, following a statement in the House of Lords by the Lord Chancellor, it was clear that there was no legal right to refuse although, in his discretion,[46] the trial judge could always protect the priest if in so doing justice could still be achieved. In line with this position in the early 1960s a Methodist minister[47] was fined twenty pounds at Bangor Petty Sessions, Belfast, for refusing to divulge information that the police had a legal right to know (the name and address of someone who had been driving a car). The minister had refused to disclose on the ground that he had learnt the information in the nature of a confession. Around the same time Lord Denning M.R. reminded us that 'the clergyman is [not] entitled to refuse to answer when directed by the judge',[48] whilst some little time later the Criminal Law Revision Committee[49] declared that as the problem presents no serious difficulty in practice the law best remains as it is, especially as there will be situations where the administration of criminal justice outweighs the conscience of the priest.

The administration of criminal justice can create other problems. If a juryman were to discuss the trial he is trying with his bishop[50] or adviser on religious matters, in order to get spiritual guidance on it, a clear contempt of court would be committed. In 1981 Slade J.[51]

noted that there was a problem with the orthodox Jews who are required to bring their disputes before the rabbis, not go to the civil courts, and to act on the decision which was based on Hebrew law. Should a party go instead to a civil court he was in peril of excommunication. Such threats were, he 'assumed' but without giving a final conclusion,[52] contempts of court. A juryman may not be excused from jury service if such service conflicts with his religious observances, although 'He may ... be excused at the discretion of the judge on the grounds of ... conscientious objection to jury service.' On the other hand jurors may be asked to 'stand down' should their religious beliefs make them unsuited to try the case in hand — as has happened when Roman Catholic jurors were not allowed to try a doctor charged with an illegal abortion at the Central Criminal Court in London during the early 1970s.[53]

Beyond this area what other clashes may nowadays occur? The difficulties of the Sikh turban and the wearing of motor-cycle helmets will be presently discussed. Other areas of difficulty include:

(1) the prosecution of Sikhs for carrying their Kirpans (ceremonial knives) in public under the offensive weapons legislation;[54]
(2) conflict between traditional Muslim leaders and Westerners on the question of what constitutes lawful 'moderate' chastisement of the children in their charge; and
(3) the Rastafarian view on smoking marijuana, which some commentators[55] have described as a key part in the evolution of their doctrine, is in inevitabler collision with western drug laws.[56]

Some solutions

One possible answer to such clashes is the enactment of an exemption to the requirement of the law, either in favour of a defined religious group or for all groups sharing a particular belief on religious grounds. A well-known field where such exemption has been long allowed is in the swearing of oaths in a court of law. It is possible to swear in any lawful manner, following either the Christian or the Jewish form, or the prescribed mode of any other recognisable religion.[57] In one case, in the 1930s, a defendant was permitted to swear by the God Apollo. Anyone, for example, who either believes that it is wrong to take a religious oath or, alternatively, has no religion, may take a solemn affirmation instead.[58] Previously the Court had to satisfy itself that the applicant came under the particular exemption[59] but under the current law it is sufficient for the applicant to object, there being no need for him to state to the Court that his objection is grounded on belief or non-belief in religion; thus he need not have any particular reason in view when he does object to the oath.

Today the exemption to the ordinary oath, unlike in the nineteenth century,[60] causes neither difficulty nor hostility as is true of some other religious exemptions,[61] but other exemptions do lead, at times, to a hostile reaction from certain sections of the community. Thus the allowance of Jewish and Muslim methods of ritual slaughter[62] has provoked criticism from animal lovers,[63] with particular objection coming in Northern Ireland, in 1980, when a large contract was made by Libya for the killing of animals in the ritual Muslim manner, on the ground that the exemption was merely designed to protect indigenous Muslims.[64] Regulations passed in 1973 had made it obligatory for all motorcyclists to wear crash-helmets, with the courts upholding them on the grounds that they were '[not] so unfair and [do not] bear so severely on the Sikh community and any others whose religion may require them to keep their heads covered'.[65] A powerful campaign was mounted and Parliament was persuaded to release members of the Sikh religion from this obligation,[66] a decision that still breeds some ill-will amongst non-Sikhs who also do not wish to wear crash-helmets.[67] The debate over this issue is illustrative of some of the problems that the creation of religious exemptions can cause, thus:[68]

(a) Who is and who is not entitled to the special treatment — that is, what is a Sikh?[69]
(b) Does not particular provision for one group lead to inevitable jealousy?
(c) How does one balance religious tolerance on the one hand with the positive policy of the criminal law on the other?

As far as the crash-helmets question was concerned the Government[70] was clearly of the opinion that, for once, the religious considerations outweighed those based upon safety.

It is not open to courts to ignore the law, no matter how unfair it may seem and no matter how much it may be seen to interfere with religious freedom. However, should a law be seen to have this effect a court may well wish to approach it as restrictively as possible — in *Kennedy* (1902)[71] a number of Protestant clergymen had attempted to bring a private summons under Section 34 of the Roman Catholic Relief Act 1829 (which imposed a heavy penalty on anyone who became a Jesuit in, and remained within, the United Kingdom). The magistrate had refused to issue the summons and the King's Bench Divisional Court held that this was not an improper exercise of his discretion and that in the light of the Section's history it was proper for the magistrate to allow only the Crown to bring such prosecutions.

General principles of statutory interpretation can lead one either to conclude that it is presumed that Parliament did not intend to restrict religious liberty in the area in question or to hold that the offending statutory instrument is invalid as the parent statute did not confer such a power. Factors in support of such a bold approach include the following:

(1) Assumptions of administrative law would seem to frown on rules that fall on particular groups with severity[72] whilst, at the same time, smiling at legitimate special treatment that work in their favour.[73]
(2) The United Kingdom adheres to international covenants that protect religious freedom[74] — a statute or statutory instrument should be read in the light of the presumption that Parliament does not intend to breach its international obligations.
(3) A somewhat weaker point is that such legislation as the Race Relations Act envisages a general Parliamentary wish to be as fair and as non-discriminatory as possible.[75]
(4) There has been a repeated assumption in Parliament and elsewhere[76] that religious observances and beliefs are always worthy of serious respect. Indeed, where a man attacked a Jehovah's Witness girl[77] the Court was prepared to regard her religious wishes as something demanding respect in determining the attacker's liability.

This general attitude was put to the test in *Graham John* in 1974.[78] The appellant believed that he had been divinely given certain healing powers which were contained in his blood. When charged with failing, without reasonable excuse, to supply a specimen of blood for a laboratory test, he claimed that his beliefs did constitute a reasonable excuse. On that Roskill L.J. had this to say:[79]

It is right to say, of course, that any state of affairs which involves persons committing criminal offences because of beliefs sincerely held by them, is, to put it at its lowest, highly distasteful for any court. Ever since the early or middle part of the eighteenth century, the courts of this country have prided themselves on the liberality of their approach to matters of conscience. That attitude had continued for the last 200 years at least. Accordingly, any argument such as that to which this court has listened on behalf of the appellant is entitled to and must receive respect. For a man to be punished for an offence which is committed by reason only of his adherence to his own religion or belief can only be justified if the court is satisfied that the clear intention of the statute creating the offence was in the interests of the community as a whole to override the privileges otherwise attaching to freedom of conscience and belief, which it must always be the duty of the courts to protect and defend.

Here the appellant was rightly convicted because:

(i) 'reasonable excuse' seemed to indicate something objective — something that the courts can judge for themselves (such as a physical illness);
(ii) in any case it should relate to only mental or physical capacity because of the general policy of the Road Traffic Acts.

Equating 'reasonable excuse' with 'is in fact able' seems a narrow approach which although perhaps justified in road traffic legislation does not necessarily mean that 'reasonable excuse' could not include refusal on religious grounds in other areas — a contention that *Wagstaffe* and *Graham John* support.

Extreme religious belief

In an old case[80] two defendants had assisted a religious fanatic in the killing of one of the constables who had come to arrest him. After the death, Thom, the fanatic, declared, 'I have killed his body, but I have saved his soul.' It was later necessary for Lord Denman C.J. to decide whether this fanatic was a person who was responsible for his actions in law:

It is not an opinion which I mean to lay down as a rule of law to be applicable to all cases, that fanaticism is a proof of unsoundness of mind, but there was in this particular instance, so much religious fanaticism — such great absurdity and extreme folly, that if Thom [who was dead by then] was now on his trial, it could hardly be said, from the evidence, that he could be called on to answer for his criminal acts.

Support has been put forward in recent times that 'fantastic superstitions' should be treated as 'insane delusions'[81] and to find those so suffering not guilty of the crime in question because of insanity. Thus in a 1976 case at the Lincoln Crown Court a man, who had killed his daughter believing that she was possessed by the devil, was found not guilty of her murder by reason of insanity; he was suffering from paranoid schizophrenia.[82] Less traditional thought,[83] however, suggests that normal persons can have their scale of values radically altered through a religious experience or conversion and yet be sane in law. The approach of deeming bizarre religious belief to be some form of mental illness is superficially attractive for it is easier to regard certain beliefs as 'mad' rather than to recognise that one's own understanding of truth might be less than perfect. The simple mental illness explanation is further frustrated by evidence[84] suggesting that those who are the most susceptible to the religious conversion process and even 'possession by demons' are not the mentally unbalanced. In a 1980 unlawful-act manslaughter case[85] an exorcism was performed where two men punched the victim unconscious and kicked her until she was dead in an attempt to remove the devil from her. Insanity was not suggested and in sentencing them the trial judge recognised that they had been acting wholly sincerely according to their own beliefs. Cases such as this indicate that a more sophisticated approach may be called for here, because clearly those who act under such beliefs are not as 'wicked' as are 'ordinary criminals'.

Deeply held religious beliefs may always lead the defendant to fail to appreciate relevant facts or to realise what the consequence of his acts will be. Until 1976 there waged a debate between those who thought that such mistakes had to be reasonable and that mistakes based on odd religious beliefs could never be considered reasonable, and Professor Glanville Williams,[86] who suggested that religiously induced mistakes negativing part of the criminal intent required for the crime in question could be a defence provided that the crime was not one of negligence (for example: gross-negligence manslaughter). Under this view, where a certain belief has to be reasonably held, as where the defendant justifies his action by the doctrine of self-defence,[87] minority religious beliefs (such as 'He is attempting to kill me by witchcraft')[88] could not provide a defence. The important House of Lords decision in *Morgan*[89] would seem to vindicate[90] Williams's views on this area in general by stating that where a belief negatives an essential pat of the requisite mental element there is no criminal liability, although the belief must still be held honestly — a minority religious view persisted in contrary to the general experiences of mankind, as seen from the viewpoint of the defendant, may well lack such honesty.[91]

These considerations only apply to a mistake of fact. That is to say had the facts, as believed by the defendant, been the truth then no offence would have been committed. If the mistake is one of law, such as a divine command to kill[92] whilst fully appreciating that you are carrying out the acts that do breach the law, there is no defence at all.

Notes

1. See St J.A. Robilliard, 'Religion, conscience and law', *Northern Ireland Legal Quarterly*, XXXII, 1981, pp. 358–72.
2. Edward Coke, *Institutes*, Chapter VI.

3. C. L'Estrange Ewen, *Witchhunting and Witch trials*, 1929, pp. 1-29.
4. E.g. 33 Hen. VIII, c. 8 (1542); 5 Eliz., c. 16 (1563); 23 Eliz., c. 2 (1580); and 1 Jac. I, c. 12 (1604).
5. B. Rosen (ed.), *Witchcraft*, 1969, p. 22. In particular with regard to ascertaining the likelihood of the death of the monarch.
6. Ibid., p. 23.
7. See, for example, T. S. Szasz, *The Manufacture of Madness*, 1971.
8. L'Estrange Ewen, *Witchhunting*, p. 43.
9. Ibid., pp. 314-16.
10. *An account of the trial and condemnation of Jane Wenham on an indictment of witchcraft, for bewitching of Mathew Gilston and Anne Thorne of Walcorne, in the County of Hereford, 1712.*
11. [1944] 1 K.B. 713.
12. At p. 715.
13. Section 1(1).
14. Section 1(2).
15. Section 1(5).
16. See Home Office, *Working Party on Vagrancy and Street Offences*, 1974, pp. 24-7.
17. *Stonehouse* v *Masson* (1921) 27 Cox C.C. 23.
18. *Barbanell* v *Naylor* [1936] 2 All E.R. 66.
19. See D. Aikenhead Stroud, *Law Quarterly Review*, XXXVII, 1921, p. 488, and Denman J., *Penny* v *Hanson* (1887) 18 Q.B.D. 478, at p. 480.
20. If *R* v *Martin* [1981] Crim L. Rev. 109 is correctly decided, no prosecution for fortune-telling would now seem possible under Section 4 of the Vagrancy Act 1824.
21. *Daily Telegraph*, 29 September 1981.
22. Contrary to the Theft Act 1968, Section 15; see J. C. Smith, *The Law of Theft*, 4th edn, 1979, paras 116-17.
23. See R.C. Finucane, *Miracles and Pilgrims: Popular Beliefs in Medieval England*, 1977.
24. M. R. Konvitz, *Fundamental Liberties of a Free People*, 1957, p. 101.
25. 322 U.S. 78 (1944).
26. *The Times*, July 1960, and see Christmas Humphreys, *Both Sides of the Circle*, 1978, pp. 202-6.
27. *The Times*, April 1932, and see H. Montgomery Hyde, *Norman Birkett*, 1964, pp. 340-9; J. Dean, *Hatred, Ridicule or Contempt*, 1953, pp. 56-79.
28. Interestingly Lord Justice Greer, in the Court of Appeal, thought that a court of law was a very bad body for deciding this type of question — Dean, *Hatred*, p. 79.
29. (1868) 10 Cox C.C. 530.
30. See also *R* v *Hines* 13 Cox C.C. 114n.
31. *R* v *Sharpe* (1857) 7 Cox C.C. 214.
32. Poor Law Amendment Act 1868, Section 37, and see J. Lewis, 'The outlook for a devil in the colonies: a colonial viewpoint on witchcraft, homicide and the supernatural', *Criminal Law Review*, 1958, p. 661, at pp. 668-70.
33. (1875) 1 Q.B.D. 25. Lord Coleridge stated that he had 'grave doubts' whether the same result would have been reached at common law. The case

is probably wrongly decided on its facts; *cf. R* v *Sheppard* [1981] A.C. 394, at pp. 418–19 (Lord Keith of Kinkel), and Glanville Williams, *Criminal Law: The General Part*, 2nd edn, 1961, pp. 143–4. Downes, because of his state of mind, did not appreciate that medical aid was necessary and thus did not wilfully refuse it.

34. (1875) 1 Q.B.D. 25, at p. 30.
35. (1882) 15 Cox C.C. 35.
36. [1899] 1 Q.B. 283.
37. *Reynolds* v *United States* 98 U.S. 145 (1878), and see also *R* v *Bourne* [1939] 1 K.B. 687, at p. 693.
38. Glanville Williams, *Textbook of Criminal Law*, 1978, pp. 88–91.
39. [1981] A.C. 394.
40. Under Section 1(1) of the Children and Young Persons Act 1933.
41. See Lord Diplock, [1981] A.C. 394, at pp. 405–7.
42. Ibid. On the facts, Russell, *On Crime*, 12th edn, vol. 1, 1964, at p. 76, has suggested that the defendant could have been convicted of gross negligence manslaughter at common law without recourse to the unlawful-act manslaughter doctrine.
43. Which may be the correct interpretation of the facts in *Downes*.
44. For example: J. R. Lindsay, 'Privileged communications with a priest' *Northern Ireland Legal Quarterly*, XIII, 1959, pp. 160–72; A. Phelan, 'Legal privilege for the priest?', *Quis Custodiet?*, 1966, pp. 8–10; The Archbishops' Commission, *Church and State*, 1970, pp. 58–60; Criminal Law Revision Committee, *Eleventh Report Evidence (General)*, Cmnd. 4991, 1972, paras 272–5, and Sir Rupert Cross, *On Evidence*, 5th edn, 1979, pp. 295–6.
45. *Broad* v *Pitt* (1828) 3 C. & P. 518; *R* v *Griffin* (1853) 6 Cox C.C. 219.
46. *Cf. Hunter* v *Mann* [1974] 1 Q.B. 767, at p. 775 (medical profession).
47. *Daily Telegraph*, 25 July 1963.
48. *Attorney-General* v *Mulholland*; *Attorney-General* v *Foster* [1963] 2 Q.B. 477, at p. 489. See also *McTaggart* v *McTaggart* [1949] P. 94, at p. 97, *Mole* v *Mole* [1951] P. 21, at p. 24, and *Pais* v *Pais* [1971] P. 119. The view has now been endorsed by the House of Lords, *British Steel Corporation* v *Granada Television Ltd* [1981] A.C. 1096. These judgments stress that the confidentiality will only be breached where that is necessary in the interests of justice.
49. Eleventh Report, para. 274.
50. See *Daily Telegraph*, 8 August 1978.
51. *The Times*, 21 July 1981.
52. In the absence of the relevant rabbis and the Attorney-General.
53. *Journal of Church and State*, XV, 1973, pp. 154–5.
54. Contrary to Section 1 of the Prevention of Crime Act 1953.
55. C. D. Yawney, *Herb and the Chalice: The Symbolic Life of the Children of Slaves in Jamaica*, 1972. See also Lord Scarman, *The Brixton Disorders of 10–12 April 1981*, Cmnd. 8427, 1981, p. 44.
56. A particular problem in the United States of America has been over the use of peyote and the Native American Church, see: B. F. Simmons, 'Implications of court decisions on peyote for the users of L.S.D.', *Journal of Church and State*, XI, 1969, pp. 83–91; *People* v *Woody* 394 P 2d. 813 (1964) (Supreme Court of California); and T. Szasz, *Ceremonial Chemistry: The Ritual Persecution*

of Drugs, Addicts and Pushers, 1974, pp. 126–9 and 198–9.

57. Oaths Act 1978, Section 1. See D. Schofield and O. Nath Channon, 'Oaths of Hindu, Sikh and Muslim witnesses', *New Community*, I, 1974, p. 409.

58. Section 5.

59. Oaths Act 1888, Section 1; *cf. R v Clark* [1962] 1 All E.R. 428.

60. Thus see the amount of legislation that was needed before the Oaths Act 1888, listed in the Appendix.

61. E.g. Powers of Criminal Courts Act 1973, Section 15(3) — community service orders not to conflict with the offender's religious beliefs if that is practicable.

62. Slaughterhouses Act 1974, Section 36(3).

63. See *The Times*, 11 February 1982 — petition, signed by 10,000 people, served on the Government, calling for an abolition of this exemption. Moves in the House of Lords to restrict the export of ritually slaughtered meat failed in December of 1981.

64. *The Times*, 10 and 11 July 1980.

65. *R v Aylesbury Crown Court, ex p. Chahal* [1976] R.T.R. 489, at p. 497.

66. Motor-cycle Crash Helmets (Religious Exemption) Act 1976.

67. Thus one motor-cyclist has been jailed on twenty-one occasions for failing to wear a crash helmet — *Daily Mail*, 29 August 1981.

68. See H.C. Deb., 1975–6 session, Standing Committee F, 23 June 1976. See also the exemption from the Sunday trading law for members of the Jewish religion, Chapter 3, pp. 52–3.

69. A familiar problem in prisons, see Chapter 8, pp. 135–6.

70. H.C. Deb. 1975–76 session, Standing Committee F, 23 June 1976, col. 11.

71. 20 Cox C.C. 230; see, in particular, the comments of Darling J. at p. 239.

72. See Lord Russell C.J. in *Kruse v Johnson* [1898] 2 Q.B. 91, at pp. 99–100.

73. In *Dodd v Venner* (1922) 27 Cox C.C. 297 the King's Bench Divisional Court had no difficulty in finding that a by-law which provided that the Jewish method of ritual slaughter was exempt from a requirement of stunning animals intended for slaughter was not *ultra vires*.

74. See Chapter 1, pp. 11–14.

75. This idea was advanced at first instance by the defence in *R v Lemon and 'Gay News' Ltd* (1977), unreported, but see N. Walter, *Blasphemy in Britain: The Practice and Punishment of Blasphemy and the Trial of Gay News*, 1977. It was not taken up when the case went on appeal.

76. E.g. Sir Alfred Denning, *Freedom Under the Law*, 1949, p. 46.

77. *R v Blaue* [1975] 3 All E.R. 446, at p. 450: 'It does not lie in the mouth of the assailant to say that his victim's religious beliefs which inhibited him from accepting certain kinds of treatment were unreasonable.'

78. [1974] 2 All E.R. 561.

79. Ibid., at p. 564.

80. *R v Tyler and Price* (1838) 8 Car. & P. 616.

81. Kenny, *Outlines of Criminal Law*, 19th edn, 1966, p. 60.

82. Diminished responsibility would be another possibility and was recently attempted, although unsuccessfully, by the notorious 'Yorkshire Ripper', Peter Sutcliffe: see *The Times*, 12 May 1981.

83. For example Dr William Sargant, *Battle for the Mind*, 1959, and *The Mind Possessed*, 1973, and Dr John G. Clark, 'Investigating the effects of religious cults on the health and welfare of their converts', *American Athiest*, May 1977. D.G. Hill, *Study of Mind Development Groups, Sects and Cults in Ontario*, 1980, especially Chapter 4.

84. Sargant, *Mind Possessed*, p. 31.

85. *The Times*, 9 September 1980.

86. 'Homicide and the supernatural', *Law Quarterly Review*, LXV, 1949, p. 491.

87. Glanville Williams, pp. 499–500. See also, Law Commission, *No. 102: Attempt and Impossibility in Relation to Attempt, Conspiracy and Incitement*, 1980, p. 52.

88. In 'Witch murder and mens rea: a problem of society under radical social change', *Modern Law Review*, XXVIII, 1965, p. 46, R.B. Seidman points out that a not uncommon feature of African life at the time was '[the] case ... in which the defendant was tried because he had killed a supposed witch in imagined self-defence against her diabolical craft. With monotonous relularity, courts have convicted, sentenced to death, and — in the same breath — recommended executive clemency.'

89. [1976] A.C. 182.

90. But see D. Cowley, 'The retreat from *Morgan*', *Criminal Law Review*, 1982, pp. 198–208.

91. H. Gross, *A Theory of Criminal Justice*, 1979, p. 268.

92. For a discussion of divine commands contrary to the criminal law see Glanville Williams, *Criminal Law: The General Part*, 1st edn, 1953, Section 46.

8 Prisons and the armed services

People may be placed in a situation where their ability to choose to observe their faith is limited by the demands of the institution.

[Prison Chaplain, 1979]

Prisons[1]

Historically religion of the orthodox variety has always been advanced in prison as one of the traditional means of attempting the reclamation of society's waifs. As will be seen shortly this continues to be so under the current conditions and perhaps for 'orthodox' one should now read 'respectable'. As will be shown, privileges attach to the recognition of a body as a 'religion' but an overall survey of practice within prison has discovered two particular problems. The first relates to the growing numbers of prisoners from the 'mainstream' non-Christian religions (e.g. Muslims, Sikhs, Hindus) which although recognised as religions present practical difficulties due to cultural differences between them and Western Christian culture, a problem seen, in part, as a race-relations matter.[2] The second difficulty arises when the authorities do not recognise a group as a 'religion', on the grounds either that it is not in fact based upon spiritual values of some sort or, even if it is, that its encouragement would be subversive to the prison regime.

Upon entry into prison a man is required to register his religious belief (if he has any) and, provided that the registration is accepted as *bona fide*, he is able to enjoy the privileges attaching to that particular religion. Where he writes what is clearly not a religion (e.g. 'Free Mason' or the name of some political party) this will be pointed out to him. At the end of the 1970s three groups in particular were not, despite their own claims, recognised as 'religions' for prison purposes. They were:

(1) the Black Muslims, who were objected to both because they were felt to be political rather than religious and because of their alleged involvement with acts of violence;
(2) Scientology, in line with the then Governmental policy[3] and because the courts had not considered it to be a religion;[4]
(3) the Rastafarians.

The official attitude with regard to this last group has changed somewhat and it now seems possible that a *via media* position may be granted, partially because of the racial element, to this group. Thus special concessions may be granted over some of their customs (e.g. in 1981 they were allowed to retain their own special form of hair-cut in detention centres) even though 'the faith cannot be accorded formal recognition as a religion'.[5] Of the groups not formally recognised the Rastafarians seem to encounter the greatest difficulties[6] (however, the Ethiopian Orthodox Church is a 'recognised religion'). Nonetheless in a prison context, at least, they are not without controversy, with one leading commentator on conflict in modern Britain[7] stating that they are 'intensely racist' and when organised in Borstals practise a strict colour bar against white inmates.

Under the Prison Rules[8] it is possible to change registration with the permission of the governor. This control is enforced so that one who is not considered to be sincere is not allowed to be a member of a religion simply in order to gain some benefit. Where the application is, however, considered to be made 'in good faith' the request is likely to be granted as a matter of course.

Provided that a religion has been accepted ministers of that religion may make visits to prisoners of their own faiths and thus by virtue of Rule 12 of the Prison Rules.

(1) The chaplain shall visit regularly the prisoners belonging to the Church of England.
(2) A prison minister shall visit the prisoners of his denomination as regularly as he reasonably can.
(3) Where a prisoner belongs to a denomination for which no prison minister has been appointed, the governor shall do what he reasonably can, if so requested by the prisoner, to arrange for him to be visited regularly by a minister of his denomination.

All prisons have Anglican chaplains.[9] There are also a number of Roman Catholic priests and Methodist ministers with prison appointments,[10] with the result that every prison has an Anglican, Roman Catholic and Methodist attached to it.[11] Official policy favours these appointments, because chaplain and ministers are said to 'have a special role in the field of moral education, and in a world of uncertain values, where even the basic concepts of good and evil are questioned, they can help to educate men and women in their basic acceptance of the human dignity of the individual'.[12] Whether chaplains or ministers hold a full-time appointment or not will depend upon the size of the institution, and sometimes ministers of other religions are given official appointments. In any case where no minister for a particular religion has been appointed to an institution an ordinary minister of that religion may visit members of the religion[13] where a prisoner has asked the governor to arrange such a visit.[14] Ministers may only visit prisoners who have registered as members of their own faith,[15] and these prisoners have the right to refuse to see them.[16] Any prisoner may ask to see the chaplain (i.e. Church of England), whatever faith the prisoner himself might be registered as.[17] The chaplain should in any case visit all those who are sick or who are under special confinement each day, if their own minister (who should attempt in any case to visit them) is unable to see them, but non-Anglicans must be 'willing' that a visit from the Anglican chaplain occur.[18] A survey conducted in 1979[19] showed that all prisons had 'regular visits' from the 'big three' (Anglican, Roman Catholic and Methodist) whilst over sixty per cent had visits at least once a month from the Jews and Salvation Army. Over forty per cent had visits from the Christian Scientists, Muslims and Quakers whilst between twenty and forty per cent had visits from the Jehovah's Witnesses and the Mormons. Some ten other groups, ranging from the Buddists to the Seventh Day Adventists, made visits, although in under twenty per cent of all penal establishments.

There do not seem to be particular problems over the holding of services, which, with the exception of detention centres, are not compulsory. Anglican services must be held on Sundays, Christmas Day and Good Friday[20] whilst services for other denominations are held by arrangement.[21] The growth of the number of different faiths has meant that about half of all prisons use rooms (such as class-rooms) for services as well as the chapel, some of the largest prisons having more than one chapel. In 1979[22] it was shown that whilst the Anglicans and Roman Catholics always held services in penal establishments Methodists held services regularly (i.e. at least once a month) in only just over half, whilst the only other distinctive services of note were those of the Jews and Muslims (who held them in between twenty and forty per cent of all establishments). Some nine other groups were recorded as holding services but in no more than ten per cent of the establishments. Although

Protestant Christians often receive visits from their own ministers it seems that when it comes to services they will attend the Church of England or the Methodist (possibly because of the relative smallness of their numbers) rather than hold their own. Under the Prison Rules,[23] 'Arrangements shall be made so as not to require prisoners of the Christian religion to do any unnecessary work on Sunday, Christmas Day or Good Friday or prisoners of other religions on their recognised day of religious observance.' It is a rule that has been criticised by those who have no religion on the ground that the Sabbatarian principle which this advances can make Sunday a rather flat, boring day for them.

As well as making visits and holding services, chaplains and ministers play a part in the parole system. Any chaplain or minister has the right to prepare a parole report on a member of his own faith, provided that he knows him personally. In 1974, for example, one chaplain reported that he, and his assistants, conducted over eighty interviews a month in connection with this aspect of his work.[24]

How far may a man be allowed to follow his religion, given the confines of prison life? The official answer is to be found in the 'instructions' circulated by the Home Office to each prison governor.[25] Negotiations are held with the 'Head Quarters' or the principal representatives of all recognised groups[26] about what is acceptable in matters of diet, dress and work. The keynote of what is to be agreed is — what is reasonable and practical given the prison environment? For example, it might be that a religious group lays down that meat be prepared in a certain way; this may be expensive and there may be few cooks qualified to deal with it. In such a case a vegetarian diet will be provided so that members of the relevant religion need not be forced to partake of 'unclean' food. Of course zealous members of the religion may not agree with what has been negotiated on their behalf — at least one very orthodox Jew has gone on hunger strike when offered vegetarian alternatives to the specially prepared meat he had requested.

One group which has received special attention are the Sikhs. The prison authorities allow uncut hair, a beard and the turban together with other physical symbols. Sometimes substitutes only are allowed — thus although, not surprisingly, Sikhs are not allowed a knife (one of the 'five symbols') they are allowed to mark the comb (another Sikh religious symbol) with the engraving of a knife. To wear these symbols the person claiming to be a Sikh must show that he has been baptised. Often the crucial question of whether or not a man is a member of a particular religion will be referred to an accredited 'minister' of that religion. Non-Christian religions tend to be fairly strict in acknowledging members,[27] and the Sikhs have seemed to 'disown' persons claiming to be of that faith from time to time.[28] Thus if a man claims to be a Sikh in order to grow long hair and enjoy a special diet his claim will not be accepted unless the Sikh priest is satisfied that he is *bona fide*.

'Days off' from work[29] are negotiated in the same way. Religious days that have come to be recognised in this manner now include the Greek Orthodox Easter and the main Jewish religious days. Muslims observe Ramadan and the feasts of Eid-Ul-Abha and Id-Ul-Fitr with food provided by the Islamic Culture Centre.[30]

Under official policy only those privileges that have been agreed in the manner just outlined should be provided and thus, for instance, whilst a Sikh priest may take in a small amount of holy food for use in a religious service or the Jews may bring in special food for the Passover, no group should have food brought in for consumption by the prisoners in the place of what the authorities normally provide.[31]

Finally, 'there shall, so far as reasonably practicable, be available for the personal use of every prisoner such religious books recognised by his denomination as are approved by the Secretary of State'.[32]

In general these provisions appear to be satisfactory, especially as some of the privileges that have been outlined would appear to go beyond the strict legal minimum. The authorities have interpreted the rules on food, dress, work and so on with the presumption that all *bona fide* religious observances must be taken seriously and should be treated with respect. In the light of the constitutional guarantees of religious freedom in the United States of America it has been stated:

we do not suggest, of course, that every religious sect or group within a prison — however few in number — must have identical facilities or personnel. A special chapel or place of worship need not be provided for every faith regardless of size; nor must a chaplain, priest or minister be provided without regard to the extent of the demand. But reasonable opportunities must be afforded to all prisoners to exercise the religious freedom guaranteed by the First and Fourteenth Amendments without fear of penalty.[33]

The present position here is not so different. Services create little problem. The registration process is perhaps a little formal — much weight is placed upon what is first written and a man may mistakenly put down the wrong definition (sometimes there is confusion between Christian Science ['C. Sci:'] and Church of Scotland ['C. S.']. It has been claimed that some members of the smaller religions have to wait several weeks before their religions are informed about them. To the civil libertarian the greatest worry must be the power to 'recognise' or 'not recognise' religions for the purposes of prison administration — a power which is probably not open to challenge in the courts.[34] To others however the greatest obstacle to religious freedom does not relate to the formal structure of religious observance in prison but rather, in the words of one prison chaplain, 'the main inhibitor to the practice of religious faith is the prison "inmate culture" itself. The criminality and prejudices people bring with them when they arrive often remain with them whilst in prison.' But it is fair to say that some find it easier to follow a religion in prison than they do in the normal world.

Military service

The armed forces create different issues with regard to religious liberty, depending on whether service is compulsory or not. In this country universal military service has only applied in the second half of the First World War, over the whole of the Second World War and for the period of National Service thereafter. When compulsory service was first introduced in 1916 regard was given to conscientious objectors,[35] that is those who resist military service 'on the ground of a conscientious objection to the undertaking of combatant service'.[36] The issue was determined by local tribunals which, given the general atmosphere in society with regard to the war, took a severe view, especially when dealing with those who did not belong to well-established pacifist Christian religions. The provision was re-enacted in 1939,[37] with the issue being determined by local tribunals subject to an appeal to an appellate tribunal. As there was no possibility for the findings of the tribunals to be tested in the courts of law[38] we have not been left with an authoritative exposition of 'conscientious', although during the Second World War one judge did remark, *obiter*, 'A true conscientious objector, which is what Parliament had in mind, is one who on religious grounds thinks it wrong to kill and to resist force by force — he thinks that that is the teaching of Christ.'[39] These words were spoken in an effort to contrast such a person with one who objected on political grounds. The practice at the time, however, was wider, encompassing the ethical objector as well.

The other relevant exemption enacted in the First World War was for 'men in holy orders or regular ministers of any religious denomination'.[40] To be in holy orders is to hold a particular status but to qualify as a 'regular minister' one must not only minister to a flock after a regular fashion but the appointment must be one that could be said to be 'regular'. The terms were designed as alternatives in order to provide for those religions that do not recognise an ordained priestly function — thus where the religion was one with ordained priests there was no room for other members of the religion (even if they did regularly lead a flock) to claim the exemption if they were not ordained.[41] Whether or not one was a regular minister was said to be a question of degree which depended upon such factors as: the method of selection; the number of services that such a minister could normally be expected to perform; whether or not he usually performed some other full time job, and so on.[42] The exemption was continued in the same form during the Second World War[43] but it was during the period of National Service[44] that it was to be given its fullest examination. In *Walsh* v *Lord Advocate*[45] a young Jehovah's Witness, 'pioneer publisher' and 'congregation servant', claimed to be a regular minister of religion. It was shown that all baptised members of that religion were considered to be 'ministers' and it was claimed that this particular applicant was, because of his onerous church duties, a 'regular minister'. It was made clear, by the House of Lords, that a man could not be a minister merely because his religion regarded him as such. The term 'regular minister' was thought to be purposefully wide so as to 'avoid any semblance of religious discrimination'.[46] Several of the judges felt that it was descriptive of a status rather than descriptive of what the particular applicant did — thus the overall duties that were expected of the office-holder were crucial; if they attached to that office it mattered not that this particular applicant was currently following them.

'A regular minister' connote[s] a class which forms but a part of the denomination as having a superior and distinct standing of its own in spiritual matters ... [the term] postulates the co-existence in the same denomination of at least two elements, namely, a ministering or clerical element and a lay element which it can minister.[47]

The Jehovah's Witnesses did not recognise a separate class from their general laity so no matter how much time a Jehovah's Witness occupies himself with his religion he cannot be considered to be a 'regular minister'.

The minister must minister to what may be considered a 'religious denomination'. Although this element was not fully explained some points of interest emerge from the earlier cases. There must be some shared belief: thus a 'missionary' of the Incorporated Seamen and Boatmen's Friendly Society[48] could not claim the exemption as his society was formed to do good in general by keeping sailors out of public houses, but it did not advance any distinctive spiritual truths as opposed to having a general Protestant outlook on life. Thus it was 'a denomination with no common denominator'.[49] The search for shared agreement on a religious philosophy, founded on the pronouncements in *Free Church of Scotland* v *Lord Overtoun*,[50] did lead the courts to hold that the Mormons were a religious denomination,[51] as members of that religion agreed over certain religious tenets and principles of worship, discipline, and church government. They also had 10,000 followers in this country at that time. On the other hand a body which existed in only one village and that could number only about fifty adherents[52] was found, as a question of fact, not to be large enough to constitute a distinctive denomination.

At the present time there is no compulsory military service within this country and the above discussion is but historic. However, should it be re-introduced at any time exemptions such as those just outlined may be expected with confidence. There are perhaps, however, some problems posed by the approach adopted in the past:

(1) Is conscientious objection on (non-religious) moral and ethical grounds sufficiently protected? Should a modern exemption make clear that objection is allowable on non-religious grounds?[53]
(2) What of those who make a conscientious objection to a particular war rather than to war in general?[54]
(3) Given the difficulties which have been encountered in the past with the use of such terms as 'regular minister' and 'religious denomination', are they really adequate or should some more precise formulation be used? — perhaps even a list?
(4) Should clergymen and ministers, who do not object on grounds of conscience, be exempt from service even when they are not needed by a congregation?

The modern forces are manned by volunteers. However, once undertaking to serve in them a man might undergo a religious conversion or profoundly change his ethical values and so come to object to being involved in the potential use of force. Where this has happened release from further service may be allowed by the service authorities on the grounds of conscience, 'conscience' being understood in the same way as it was in the Second World War and in the days of National Service. Most of these cases are dealt with by the military authorities but where the applicant wishes to contest a decision that has not been in his favour he may apply to an Advisory Committee,[55] which advises the Secretary of State for Defence and is, to some degree, the successor to the old appellate tribunal created under the war-time legislation. The members of this Committee are appointed by the Lord Chancellor and those applying to it appear before it in person. When the Committee do not consider conscientious objection is genuinely held it is possible for the case to be reconsidered at a later date should fresh evidence be forthcoming. Hearings of the Committee are public. The Committee was first used in 1971 and since that time has considered thirty-three cases. The Committee is also used where reservists claim conscientious objection as a reason for not being recalled.

Inside the modern forces chaplains and religious services are available as optional items. Until the late 1940s church parades used to be compulsory, a clear challenge to religious liberty,[56] especially where men had been conscripted into the forces. Compulsion was abolished at that time[57] but not without controversy, as it had its defenders, who based their case on paternalism and on the need to maintain military discipline.

Notes

1. See St J. A. Robilliard, 'Religion in prison', *New Law Journal*, 1980, 800.
2. Thus see *Report of the Work of the Prison Department for 1981*, Cmnd. 8543, 1982, para. 147.
3. See Chapter 6, pp. 106–10.
4. *R v Registrar-General, ex p. Segerdal* [1970] 2 Q.B. 697.
5. *Report of the Work of the Prison Department for 1981*, para. 148.
6. See Robilliard, 'Religion in prison'.
7. R. Clutterbuck, *Britain in Agony*, 1980, p. 254.
8. Prison Rules, S.I. 1964, No. 388, Rule 10(2).
9. Prison Act 1952, Section 7(1) and (4).
10. Home Office, *Prisons and the Prisoner*, 1977, pp. 40 and 127.
11. Strictly only Church of England priests are 'chaplains' or 'assistant chaplains'. Priests from other faiths, who are appointed under Section 10(1) and (2) of the Prison Act 1952, are 'ministers'.
12. *Prisons and the Prisoner*, p. 41.
13. Prison Act 1952, Section 10(3).
14. Rule 12(3).
15. Prison Act 1952, Section 10(5).
16. Section 10(4).
17. Ibid.
18. Rule 11(2) and (3).
19. Robilliard, 'Religion in prison'.
20. Rule 13(1).

21. Rule 13(2).
22. Robilliard, 'Religion in prison'.
23. Rule 15.
24. *Report of the Work of the Prison Department for 1974*, Cmnd. 6148, 1974; p. 45.
25. E.g. A/5947/72.
26. *See Report of the Work of the Prison Department for 1981*, para. 148, where it is stated that with the Rastafarians 'one difficulty has been that there is no central authority or point of reference for guidance on what constitutes Rastafarian custom and practice'.
27. R. Harebin, *Problems of Asians in Penal Institutions*, pp. 14–15.
28. As have the Jews and the Mormons — Robilliard, 'Religion in prison'.
29. Rule 15.
30. *Report of the Work of the Prison Department for 1981*, para. 147.
31. Note the complaint recorded by Harebin, *Problems of Asians*, pp. 14–15.
32. Rule 16.
33. *Cruz* v *Beto* 405 U.S. 319 (1972). See also Chapter 1, p. 13, for decisions on minimum religious standards in prison under the European Convention on Human Rights.
34. *Arbon* v *Anderson* [1943] K.B. 252, at p. 255; *Becker* v *Home Office* [1972] 2 Q.B. 407, at p. 418.
35. See generally J. Rea, *Conscience and Politics*, 1949.
36. Military Service Act 1916, Section 2(1)(*d*).
37. National Service (Armed Forces) Act 1939, Section 5.
38. Ibid., Section 5(12).
39. *Newell* v *Gillingham Corporation* [1941] 1 All E.R. 552, at p. 553 (*per* Atkinson J.).
40. Military Service Act 1916, Sch. I, para. 4.
41. *Simmonds* v *Elliott* (1917) 26 Cox. C.C. 54, at p. 57.
42. See *Kipps* v *Lane* (1917) 116 L.T. 95, and *Nock* v *Malins* (1917) 26 Cox C.C. 38.
43. National Service (Armed Forces) Act 1939, Section 11(1)(*e*).
44. National Service Act 1948, Sch. I, para. 2.
45. [1956] 3 All E.R. 129.
46. At p. 135 (*per* Lord Macdermott).
47. Ibid.
48. *Bratt* v *Auty* (1917) 26 Cox C.C. 67.
49. At p. 72 (*per* Darling J.).
50. [1904] A.C. 515.
51. *Hawkes* v *Moxey* (1917) 25 Cox C.C. 689.
52. *Kick* v *Donne* (1917) 33 T.L.R. 325.
53. As has been done with closed-shop legislation: see Chapter 11, pp. 174–8.
54. E.g. to the use of the British Army in Northern Irland: Cf. T. Young and M. Kettle, *Incitement to Disaffection*, 1976, pp. 81–94.
55. See H.C. Deb., 1970, vol. 807, col. 423 (written answers).
56. C. Northcott, *Religious Liberty*, 1948, pp. 23–4.
57. H.C. Deb., 1946, vol. 421, cols 705–41.

9 Religion, medicine and the law

When a woman died in childbirth because Christian Science kept the doctor from the house, the profane murmured that a mother and her baby had been murdered by the zealots of a craze.

[H. A. L. Fisher, *Our New Religion*, 1933, p. 47]

General observations

As far as his own life is concerned, the rational adult has the right to refuse medical treatment upon religious grounds. Until 1961 a person who refused medical aid knowing that it was highly probable that such a refusal would directly lead to his own death might have been guilty of the crime of suicide, or, if he survived, an attempt to commit that offence, and medical action taken against his will would have been justified as necessary action for the prevention of crime. Such reasoning was adopted by the Supreme Court of New Jersey in *John F. Kennedy Memorial Hospital* v *Heston*,[1] where a hospital had applied for permission to give a blood transfusion to an adult Jehovah's Witness. This was probably against her will (there was a conflict of evidence on this point but it was assumed, for the purposes of the decision, that she would not have consented). The court stated that a religious belief ordaining death where such death would be contrary to state law could not be upheld under the constitutional right to religious freedom and that the principle in *Reynolds* v *U.S.*[2] applied. There was also a public-interest consideration in seeing that a patient gets medical treatment in extreme situations. Such opinions would at one time also have been given by the English courts[3] but now that suicide has ceased to be a crime in English law[4] there is freedom to refuse aid even at the risk of death and one was reminded of this in 1979 when a member of the Court of Appeal said that a sane man has the right to starve himself to death for any reason that he wishes.[5] A doctor who treats a patient against his will may be liable for battery in civil law and also for assault in criminal law.[6] On the other hand if the patient is legally insane[7] the operation of the Mental Health Act may justify forcible intervention.[8]

Religious interests may sometimes be in jeopardy from medical treatment. In 1978 a Roman Catholic woman was sterilised in the course of a Caesarian section. She was thirty-five years old and the hospital had a standing policy of sterilising women such as herself. In law it was held that although she had given her consent to the operation she could still be awarded three thousand pounds in damages as the medical authorities had not given her sufficient advice on the matter before the operation.[9] Thus damage to religious sensibilities were recognised in a tortious situation.

The position is different where a person's religious beliefs lead him to object to orthodox medical treatment for one in his care. A parent is under a legal obligation to obtain treatment for his child, aged under sixteen, where the average parent would call in such assistance and, as the *Senior*[10] line of cases show, refusal to do this out of sincerely held religious grounds cannot generally furnish an excuse in law. The view of Jehovah's Witnesses on blood transfusions has caused difficulty in the past, although it now appears that they are more likely to give their consent for necessary blood transfusions when their children are at risk.[11] When an adult has undertaken the care of another and causes that other's death by a very careless refusal to call in medical aid when it is necessary he can be liable for the offence of gross-negligence manslaughter[12] if it would have been reasonable to foresee a risk of death or serious harm should medical aid not be sought. Subject to whatever importance may be placed on *Wagstaffe*[13] today, religious motive will provide no defence for the defendant. This principle will also come into play where a doctor, after having undertaken the care of a patient, has refused to act out of religious motivation:

A person who holds such an opinion [i.e. that an operation, in this case abortion, is contrary to his religious beliefs] ought not to be a doctor practising in that branch of medicine, for it a case arose where the life of a woman could be saved by performing this operation and the doctor refused to perform it because of his religious opinions and the woman died, he would be in grave peril of being brought before this court on a charge of manslaughter by [gross] negligence. He would have no better defence than would a person who, again for some religious reason, refused to call in a doctor to attend his child, where a doctor could have been called in and the life of the child saved.[14]

There are no particular difficulties with the state medical institutions. When the National Health Service was set up in 1946 some of the hospital secretaries and management committees were under the impression that only ministers of the established Church should be allowed to visit patients in an official capacity. However, the general liberalisation of attitudes in hospital administrations coupled with the growth of interdenominational co-operation has long since made such dictats a thing of the past. The only occasion today when a minister of religion will be excluded from a hospital is where it is a mental institution and the visit is thought to be 'dangerous' or 'not in the patient's interests'. The state educational system is under a duty to provide medical inspections and also to offer free medical treatment to the pupils in its care, subject to parental objection to the giving of such treatment. When a parent objects the 'pupil shall not be encouraged or assisted', by the authorities, with regard to such treatment.[15]

Minority medical beliefs — Christian Science

Subject to the general considerations outlined above, groups not sharing the orthodox medical beliefs of the country have few problems with the law. They must guard against acting where only a qualified person may act (the main example being midwifery)[16] and should bear in mind that any attempt to pass oneself off as a registered medical practitioner[17] or registered nurse[18] will be met with up to a five-hundred-pound fine.[19] Should a group set up what constitutes a nursing home (or mental nursing home), which is:

any premises used, or intended to be used, for the reception of and the providing of nursing for, persons suffering from any sickness, injury or infirmity ... [or] for the reception of, and the provision of nursing or other medical treatment ... for, one or more mentally disordered patients ... whether exclusively or in common with other persons',[20]

it must be specially licensed save that since 1927 there has been a special exemption for nursing homes that are run 'in accordance with the practice and principles of the body known as the Church of Christ Scientist'.[21] Where the exemption is granted the home must call itself a 'Christian Science home' and the exemption may be withdrawn if it appears to the Minister of Health that the home in question is no longer being carried out according to Christian Science principles.

Non-subscribers to orthodox medical beliefs may, through the doctrine of non-disclosure, encounter difficulty with insurance policies unless they make their heterodoxy clear when taking them out.

The Christian Scientists have drawn up a 'Christian Science Insurance Rider' which many companies accept for use in car insurance policies. It not only makes clear that the insured is a Christian Scientist but also states that the policy will, in lieu of the usual medical expenses, provide for the cost of a Christian Scientists practitioner's fees and, if necessary, for a stay in a Christian Science house.

Another possible area of difficulty occurs with state sickness benefits. Christian Scientists have reached an understanding with the authorities whereby a certificate signed by the applicant and endorsed by a Christian Science practitioner is acceptable as an alternative to the ordinary 'doctor's sick-note', subject to a right to test it by medical examination should the authorities consider that to be necessary. This agreement is only valid as far as the state institutions are concerned so their standing with private employers is a matter of negotiation and reasonable industrial practice.

Abortion

The debate on the change in the law on abortion[22] was a testing time for the position of religious integrity in Britain. Under the law in force before 1967 abortion was illegal unless it constituted an act of necessity[23] performed to conserve the patient's health in extreme circumstances. As the *obiter dictum* of MacNaughten J. from *Bourne*'s case, quoted above, shows it was not thought that a doctor had any right to refuse treatment because of his personal religious beliefs where he had undertaken the care of a woman who should be aborted according to the common law. Despite the major defeat that devout Roman Catholics suffered over the general principle of the Bill there was general support for a 'conscience clause' so that workers within the medical profession would not be legally forced to participate in abortions authorised under the new provisions.[24] There was, for example, particular concern for nurses, with one member of the Standing Committee, which considered the Abortion Bill, stating: 'Many girls are inspired to take up nursing by the belief that they can help in saving life. These young people may be easily discouraged, or their idealism shattered, and their conscientious objection should be respected'.[25]

An allied difficulty was the possibility of discriminatory measures being taken against those whose religious belief prevented them from taking part in such operations. Thus it was of some comfort that, in January of 1967, the then Minister of Health declared:[26]

(1) there should be no discrimination on the grounds of religious belief (or unbelief) in the appointment or promotion of nurses or of other staff;
(2) an employee's religious belief was his own affair, not his employer's;
(3) job application forms should not contain questions about the applicant's religious beliefs; and
(4) applicants should not be forced to answer questions about their religious beliefs at interviews.

As this was merely a Ministerial edict many wanted a prohibition on religious discrimination in the Health Service to be expressly enacted. This was resisted on the ground[27] that where an applicant's work was likely to bring him into the abortion area it was only reasonable for the authorities to know in advance what his opinions on abortion were so that they could prepare workable rotas of available staff. In any case it was felt that a non-discrimination provision would be difficult to enforce.

Following much discussion the following 'conscience clause' was enacted,

(1) Subject to subsection (2) of this section, no person shall be under any duty, whether by contract or by a statutory or other legal requirement, to participate in any treatment authorised by this Act to which he has a conscientious objection: Provided that in any legal proceedings the burden of proof of conscientious objection shall rest on the person claiming to rely on it.
(2) Nothing in subsection (1) of this section shall affect any duty to participate in treatment which is necessary to save the life or prevent grave permanent injury to the physical or mental health of a pregnant woman.[28]

These words have been carefully chosen so that the right bestowed is limited.

First, the right of objection applies to actual participation in treatment — it does not include the giving of advice beforehand and thus where a doctor has the general duty of caring for a patient (who qualifies for an Abortion Act abortion) he should tell her to go to a doctor who is not a conscientious objector, as the section will not prevent liability arising from a failure to give advice in such circumstances.[29]

Secondly, the burden of proof lies on the person claiming the conscientious objection (for example, to avoid a duty in tort that would otherwise arise from a duty of care) so that 'it reduces any risk of a doctor who is simply negligent escaping liability for his negligence by claiming a spurious conscientious objection'.[30]

Thirdly, subsection (2) was inserted because the rule in *Bourne* was thought not only to be correct but also worthy of preservation; in inserting the 'conscience clause' Parliament was balancing the rights of the doctors and nurses to their beliefs with the welfare of the patient. Where the woman is facing grave permanent injury[31] her interests will be paramount, even to the point that another must subordinate his deeply held religious convictions.

Fourthly, the words in the section do not create an express right not to be discriminated against because of one's religion although they are of great importance in answering such questions as whether a nurse is in breach of a disciplinary rule or not.

'Conscientious objection' is not defined in the Act and the meaning of the term in this context is yet to be considered by the courts. In the Standing Committee it was said that:

> The concept of conscience is nebulous ... it is not clear what objections the courts would regard as 'conscientious'. The doctor whose conscientious objections were not on religious grounds might be in a particular difficulty. I do not think there would be so great a difficulty with someone whose conscientious objections were on the grounds of religion. The fact that a doctor was a Roman Catholic would, presumably, be accepted as evidence in support of a claim of conscientious objection.[32]

It seems then that the religious objector should be secure — the (non-religious) ethical objector seems, if this extract represents the law, to be under greater difficulty, although some of the cases on the closed-shop legislation do indicate that, given a sincere applicant, the courts take a fairly generous attitude towards 'conscience' today.[33] Furthermore given the wording of Article 9 of the European Convention on Human Rights[34] the ethical objector should have a good chance of achieving parity with his religious neighbour.

The lot of the conscientious objector in practice was examined by the Lane Committee, which reported on the working of the Abortion Act in 1974.[35] In general such objectors seem to be well treated within the National Health Service[36] although refusal to take part in abortions can be a bar to promotion in the fields of obstetrics and gynaecology[37] — a situation that the committee feels is justified by the priority which should be placed on the needs of patients.[38]

Notes

1. 58 N.J. 576 (1971).
2. 98 U.S. 145 (1878); see Chapter 7, p. 000.
3. *Leigh* v *Gladstone* (1909) 26 T.L.R. 139.
4. Suicide Act 1961.

5. *Per* Lawton L.J. in *R* v *Relf*; see (1979) 1 Cr.App.R.(S.) III.
6. Subject to, in certain situations, the defence of necessity; on the possibilities of the defence, see *Report on Defences of General Application*, Law Com. No. 83, 1977, paras 4.1–4.33.
7. On the relationship between insanity and religious fanaticism see Chapter 7, pp. 126–7.
8. See B. Hoggett, *Mental Health*, 1976, pp. 129–31.
9. M. Brazier, 'Informed consent to surgery', *Journal of Medicine, Science and Law*, XIX, 1979, p. 49 at p. 54.
10. See Chapter 7, pp. 120–2.
11. Glanville Williams, *Textbook of Criminal Law*, 1978, p. 88.
12. *R* v *Stone* [1977] Q.B. 354.
13. See Chapter 7, p. 121.
14. *Per* MacNaghten J., *R* v *Bourne* [1939] 1 K.B. 687, at p. 693.
15. Education Act 1944, Section 48(4).
16. Nurses, Midwives and Health Visitors Act 1979, Section 17.
17. Medical Act 1956, Section 31.
18. Nurses, Midwives and Health Visitors Act 1979, Section 14.
19. Criminal Law Act 1977, Section 31 and Schedule 6.
20. Nursing Homes Act 1975, Sections 1 and 2.
21. Ibid., Section 18.
22. See P.G. Richards, *Parliament and Conscience*, 1970, pp. 85–112, and K. Hindell and M. Simms, *Abortion Law Reformed*, 1971,
23. *R* v *Bourne*; and see Hindell and Simms, *Abortion Law Reformed*, pp. 69–72.
24. For a discussion of the civil law consequences of the change, see R. A. G. O'Brien, 'The Abortion Act and legal liability', *Quis Custodiet?*, XVIII, 1968, pp. 16–27.
25. H.C. Deb., 1966–67 s.c. 'F', vol. 10, col. 551 (*per* Mr Braine, M.P.).
26. H.C. Deb., 1967, vol. 740, cols 78–9 (written answers).
27. H.C. Deb., 1966–67 s.c. 'F', vol. 10, col. 585 (*per* Alice Bacon, M.P.).
28. Abortion Act 1967, Section 4. *Cf.* Hindell and Simms, *Abortion Law Reformed*, pp. 204–5.
29. See H.C. Deb., 1966–67 s.c. 'F', vol. 10, col. 586 (*per* Norman St John-Stevas, M.P.).
30. Ibid., cols 565–6.
31. An Abortion Act abortion may be given where the continuance of the pregnancy

> involves risk to the life of the pregnant woman, or of injury to the physical or mental health of the pregnant woman or any existing children of her family, greater than if the pregnancy were terminated;
> or
> [where] there is a substantial risk that if the child were born it would suffer from such physical or mental abnormalities as to be seriously handicapped

[Abortion Act 1967, Section 1(1).] In assessing the risk to health the actual or foreseeable environment is taken account of: Section 1(2).

32. H.C. Deb., 1966-67 s.c. 'F', vol. 10, col. 566.
33. See Chapter 11, pp. 174-8.
34. See Chapter 1, p. 11.
35. Cmnd. 5579.
36. Ibid., vol. I, Appendix to Section K, pp. 260-1.
37. Ibid., vol. I, paras 31(3), 340, 351, 360 and 373.
38. Ibid., vol. I, para. 607.

10 Public education[1]

Here we have freedom of thought as well as freedom of conscience. Here we have been the pioneers of religious toleration. But side by side with all this has been the fact that religion has been the rock in the life and character of the British people upon which they have built their hopes and cast their cares. This fundamental element must never be taken from our schools.

[Winston S. Churchill in a broadcast to the nation, May 1943]

Compulsory state education was borne in 1870 with schools being allowed an option as to whether to include religious teaching or not. The vast majority did, with statutory protection for those who did not wish to participate.[2] At the same time many denominational schools continued and ran alongside the new creations of the state and in many areas education was only a possibility where the child attended a church school. This particular problem for those who did not wish their child to receive a religious education (usually of the Church of England variety) was aggravated by the financial provisions of the 1902 Education Act which gave birth to the term 'passive resisters' for those Nonconformists who refused to 'contribute through local rates to the maintenance of Anglican schools from which Nonconformist teachers were often barred by tests. The problem was most acute in rural districts, where it most invariably proved the case that Anglican control was exclusive.'[3]

Other problems existed as well in the state schools of those times — informal control was often kept over the religious views of teachers;[4] there were difficulties in effecting the withdrawal of pupils from religious services in the smaller schools;[5] and there were strong feelings about the organisation of church visits to them.[6] These problems, the views of the Churches, the teachers' unions, the Nonconformists and so on were thought to add up to a very hot political potato indeed[7] but the state of many schools forced those concerned to realise that there must be changes. Following the wartime production of the Government's *Education After The War*[8] there was a serious and prolonged debate between (i) the Church of England, which owned many schools that it could no longer afford to maintain, (ii) the Roman Catholics, who were determined to keep their own schools, (iii) the Nonconformists who were not over-enthusiastic about the state advancement of religion through education, (iv) the teachers, who were against denominational intrusion in their profession, and (v) the state.[9] Against this background the 1944 settlement was arrived at,[10] and a 'concordat' agreed between the religious bodies and the state whereby the church schools came under the state's general direction in exchange for financial grants. Given the history of the existing state schools coupled with the intermixing of the church schools, religion was seen also as a necessary part of all the schools connected with the state.

Under the 1944 arrangements there are two types of school:

(1) the 'county' (or ordinary state) school;
(2) the 'voluntary' (one of the forms of church) school.

The law that applies to both types is broadly similar but the religious background of the voluntary schools produces some differences.[11] There are three types of voluntary school:

(1) controlled schools — whose religious education must follow the agreed syllabus for the area unless the parent requests that his child be taught along the terms of the trust deed of the school, if there is one, or if there is no trust deed by the practice observed in the school before it became controlled;
(2) aided schools; and
(3) special agreement schools.

Religious instruction in these last two types follows the trust deed or former practice unless the parent elects for the child to be taught from the agreed syllabus for the area. Controlled schools are wholly financed by the state whereas the religious bodies still contribute something towards the running of the other two types and, in effect, play a very large part in their management. Voluntary schools are mainly Roman Catholic or Anglican.

The 1944 Education Act provisions on religion in schools do not apply to independent schools that are free of state aid, but it should not be overlooked that the law will act where it considers that religious doctrines are in conflict with a child's better interests — the religious upbringing of children being a parental matter, subject to judicial control.[12]

The duty of the local education authority

Two general provisions are of note when considering the local education authorities' duty to provide religion in their schools.

First, their general duty is to contribute towards the spiritual, moral and physical development of the children in their charge through the provision of efficient education.[13]

Secondly, 'local education authorities shall have regard to the general principle that, so far as is compatible with the provisions of efficient instruction and training and the avoidance of unreasonable public expenditure pupils are to be educated in accordance with the wishes of their parents'.[14]

Thus the wishes of the parents with regard to religion must be balanced against the general educational policy of the authority coupled with considerations of cost. In *Watt* v *Kesteven County Council*[15] the plaintiff, a Roman Catholic, wished to send his two sons to Roman Catholic secondary schools. The defendant council did not provide any secondary schools at all in their area but they were prepared to pay for the boys to go to another independent school. They are also prepared to pay some of the cost in sending the boys to the Roman Catholic school but would not meet the full cost should they be sent there. The Court of Appeal held that the section did not mean that the council had to meet the cost of sending the boys to any school that the father chose. The section did not create an independent right but was merely a gloss upon the other duties contained in the Act. The authority had discharged its general duty to provide education by offering to pay for the places at the school that it had chosen and the section did not justify the finding that there was a fresh duty to pay for schooling elsewhere. In *Cumings* v *Birkenhead Corporation*[16] a local education authority had decided that children who had attended Roman Catholic primary schools could only attend Roman Catholic secondary schools since the other secondary schools in the area were overcrowded. Those who had attended Roman Catholic primary schools could only go to non-Roman Catholic secondary schools if there were 'exceptional circumstances'. This policy was upheld by the Court which felt that it was a reasonable one to adopt and thus the parental wishes could be outweighed by the other circumstances there. These decisions in so far as they affect *admission* to a particular school must now be reviewed in the light of Section 6 of the Education act 1980. Under it parents are entitled to express a preference for the school which they wish their child to attend. The authority must comply with their wishes save where to do so would,

(a) prejudice the provision of efficient education or the efficient use of resources; or
(b) be in breach of an arrangement applying to an aided or special agreement school; or
(c) be incompatible with a method of selection based upon ability or aptitude.[17]

The two cases remain relevant when considering whether an authority may refuse to comply with the wishes of a parent because of the first of these grounds but it should also be borne in mind that (a) is qualifying a right created by statute, whereas Section 76 of the 1944 Act was not said to create any independent right.

The growth of the non-Christian religions has meant that the general cultural differences between the average English school and, say, a strict Muslim background has produced problems.[18] These have included clashes between traditional Muslim dress and obligatory school uniforms[19] and religious (and/or cultural) objections to the mixing of the sexes. The teaching of sex education has also presented problems for Muslims. The position with regard to this is that although a parent has the right to discover what it is that is taught in sex education lessons[20] he has no right to demand that his child be withdrawn (unlike the position with regard to religious education).[21] It may also be noted that the European Court of Human Rights has ruled[22] that Article 9 of the European Convention on Human Rights[23] is not infringed by compulsory sex education, this decision being justified on the grounds that the school curriculum is a matter of policy for each member country in accordance with the social conditions prevailing at the time and to allow withdrawal would undermine the whole basis of institutional teaching. To the strictest Muslims even the principle of comprehensive education is objectionable. The challenge is met by pressurising the state authorities to continue existing single-sex schools and also by raising funds for the foundation of independent Muslim schools.[24] Independent schools have their attractions to the minority faiths as they sometimes complain that when the compulsory state religious instruction covers their faith on a comparative basis with Christianity the non-Christian religion often appears in an unfavourable light.[25]

The agreed syllabus

In Cambridge in 1924 a group of Anglicans, Freechurchmen and teachers met and drew up an 'agreed syllabus' of the content of religious education for all state schools in the area.[26] The system was much copied up and down the country and was given statutory effect in 1944. Under the relevant provisions[27] every local authority must convene a conference of:

(a) such religious denominations as, in the opinion of the authority, ought, having regard to the circumstances of the area, to be represented;
(b) except in the case of an area in Wales or Monmouthshire, the Church of England;
(c) such associations representing teachers as, in the opinion of the authority, ought, having regard to the circumstances of the area, to be represented;
(d) the authority.

The conference may only adopt a syllabus of religious education unanimously (each of the groups is known as a 'committee' and each 'committee' may only cast one vote — there may be dissenting votes within a 'committee') and should it fail to do this or should an authority fail to adopt the syllabus proposed by the conference the Minister may appoint his own committee to prepare what can become the agreed syllabus for the area should he assent to it. This has never in fact had to be done.[28] Once the syllabus has been approved it remains in force until the local education authority decides to go through the machinery again. There is no particular lifetime for an agreed syllabus.

It seems[29] that, as well as all the major Christian religions, representatives of non-Christian religions should now join in the conference when they constitute a large enough group in a particular area. Christian religions have found the conference system helpful in that it has encouraged ecumenism.[30] However some teachers feel that they should play a far larger role in the production of the syllabuses and there has also been criticism as syllabuses drawn up locally can vary widely from one area to another. One suggestion is that the present system should be replaced with a scheme drawn up on a national basis which would only be concerned with the educational value of religious education with sectional interests no longer being allowed to 'veto' schemes that they do not approve of.[31] Another general improvement would be to give greater publicity to the system[32] — even many teachers are not aware of the syllabus in force in their areas.[33]

The agreed syllabus must be of 'religious instruction' and it must not bear the distinctive marks of any particular denomination.[34] The limits to which they may go was illustrated by what happened in Birmingham in 1974.[35] The local education authority in Birmingham adopted an agreed syllabus containing studies of humanism and communism in their own right as part of the course. There followed an outcry and so the council sought counsel's opinion. His view, which was endorsed by the Department of Education and Science, was that non-religious matters could only be included in a syllabus if 'they advanced the instruction of religion and related to religious instruction and were not taught for their own sake'.[36] The 1974 syllabus was then withdrawn and replaced with a new one which put the study of this non-religious matter in line with the advice that had been received. Even this modified version can be seen as an advance on previous syllabuses,[37] which seem to consist of three main types:

(1) a study of the Bible;
(2) more general considerations of Christianity with an emphasis on how it relates to the individual lives of the pupils;
(3) a general view of all the major religions.[38]

This progression marks the trend in which they are moving. For example in 1954 the Sunderland syllabus declared that the purpose of religious instruction should be to aid a school 'to do its positive best to guide children into church membership'. More recently syllabuses have tried to provide a general assessment of 'world religions', sometimes because of race relations pressure.[39] The modified Birmingham syllabus may be taken as a prime example of the newer type. Under it Christianity must always be studied, as must other major religions. Communism and humanism may be studied but only as 'minor' courses and with the object of creating 'a critical appreciation of distinctive features of religious faith'.[40] It has been strongly argued that any syllabus that devoted a major part of its time to non-religious philosophies would be outside the scope of 'religious instruction'.[41] The correct view seems to be that if such subjects are to be studied in their own right they should be included in such courses as 'general studies' or 'civics' but now in the time prescribed by law for religious instruction.

A teacher may not teach religious topics contrary to what has been laid down in the agreed syllabus. In *Watson* v *Hertfordshire County Council*[42] a teacher taught that the story of the creation contained in the book of Genesis was literally true, whereas the relevant syllabus charged that the story was to be taught as a collection of myths and legends. He was warned about this and, after refusing to sign a written undertaking that he would in future follow the agreed syllabus, was eventually dismissed from his post. An industrial tribunal held that in failing to abide by the legally drawn up syllabus of the county he was guilty of misconduct and that in the circumstances of the case it was reasonable to dismiss him.

'Religious instruction' is not further defined in the Act; there is no minimum of Christianity that should be taught nor is there any maximum amount of time that may be devoted to non-Christian religions. Despite these grey areas in the law many members of the House of Lords were recently prepared to subscribe to the following points, made in the important debate on religious education in 1977:[43]

(1) religious education was a valuable part of education and should continue to be taught in state schools;
(2) a central part of it was Christianity, as was implicit in the 1944 Education Act;
(3) too much stress should not be placed on the non-Christian religions since a very small proportion of the population followed them and indeed many of these other religions wished to discover something about Christianity — thus Christianity (with some comparisons to world religions) should be at the core, because it was so central to British culture.

In the debate Lord Blake[44] asked for: a Government circular to state that Christianity was the central part of religious education; an independent inquiry into religious education; and for moves to be made in order to produce both more and better teachers of religious education (earlier in that year the Government agreed that there was a serious shortage of such teachers).[45] The then Government,[46] whilst refusing Lord Blake's particular requests, endorsed the law as it was and stated that:

[Christianity] has been so entwined with the culture of this country as it has developed over the past century that it is necessary for pupils to understand the one so as to appreciate the other[47] for reasons of ethics, history and culture. Christianity has a major part to play in education, and not only in religious classroom teaching, but it cannot now, and probably never could, claim an exclusive proprietary right to those aspects of our civilisation.[48]

One reason for continued Parliamentary interest in this subject is the belief that many schools fail to provide religious instruction as they are required to do by law. Research by the Assistant Masters Association has shown this to be the case.[49] Thus in a survey where 895 schools provided information about conditions prevalent in 1975 it was found that whilst only three completely excluded religious education from school, over fifty per cent did not provide religious education for all their pupils (although in such schools it was either provided on an optional basis or just in some years). Furthermore only seventeen per cent of the schools closely followed what had been laid down in the agreed syllabus — a serious matter since the right to withdraw pupils from religious instruction can only be used sensibly if the parent is able to look at a public document that explains what it is that is taught as religious instruction in the school.

The daily act of worship

It is required[50] that the school day in every county or voluntary school shall commence with 'collective worship on the part of the pupils in attendance at the school', subject to the parent's right of being able to withdraw his child from it.[51] Although in county schools the worship must not be 'distinctive of any particular religious denomination',[52] voluntary schools often follow the form of worship set out in the trust deed of the school or continue to use the form of worship that was employed by them before they received state aid.[53] The 1944 Education Act gives no guidance as to the meaning of 'collective worship' and services now vary widely from the singing of traditional hymns in some schools to pop services and 'happenings' in others.[54] A survey conducted by the Assistant Masters' Association of 922 County and Voluntary schools revealed that in only one-fifth of them was an act of worship, consisting of the entire school, held every day.[55] A principal reason why the number seems so small relates to the changes in school size and organisation since 1944 — thus a school may now be split into small units, such as houses, which hold their own services, rather than the entire school all congregating together. It is legal for the single act of worship not to be held if 'the school premises are such as to make it impracticable to assemble them for that purpose'[56] (although the act of worship must take place, in county schools, on the school premises, save on special occasions)[57] — there might be no hall big enough or the school might be split over several buildings that are far apart. Where this is the case the school is expected to follow the spirit of the law as much as it is able[58] — the Assistant Masters' Survey discovered that one-half of the schools it examined could not physically assemble in any one place. As well as these legitimate reasons a few schools, without it seems any particular excuse, simply fail to obey the law.

In addition to the practical difficulties there have been other reasons why reforms have been called for:

(1) some feel that the general (albeit non-denominational) Christian character of these services may no longer be appropriate in a multi-religious Britain;[59]
(2) the fact that seventeen-year-old pupils must attend a service if they attend

a state school but need not if they are at a technical college has been seen as anomalous;[60]
(3) many teachers would like to see the law taken out completely from this area;[61]
(4) and the Church of England would like the law liberalised so as to allow schools far greater freedom in the running of their own affairs.[62]

The right to withdraw

A necessary guarantee to those parents who object to the 'Zoroastrianism', as Winston Churchill once called it,[63] of the agreed syllabus or to the act of collective worship is that the child may be wholly or partly excused from attending either religious instruction, or the act of worship, or both, at the request of his parent.[64] Furthermore, the parent may have the child sent to another place for religious instruction:

> during such periods as are reasonably necessary for the purpose of enabling him to receive religious instruction ... Provided that the pupil shall not be withdrawn unless the local education authority are satisfied that the arrangements are such as will not interfere with the attendance of the pupil at school on any day except at the beginning or end of the school session on that day.[65]

Alternatively, instruction in a particular faith may be given in a state school, on request, where withdrawal arrangements cannot conveniently be made 'unless [the local education authority] are satisfied that owing to any special circumstances it would be unreasonable so to do' and provided the local education authority does not have to pay for it.[66] Finally it may be noted that a parent does not commit any offence when he fails to send his child to school 'on any day exclusively set apart for religious observance by the religious body to which [the] parent belongs'.[67]

It is widely believed that a great many parents are ignorant of the right to withdrawal.[68] In any case the child might feel embarrassed if the school does not treat the request with sensitivity — thus it has been argued that when, in 1971, a school answered such a request by instructing the pupil to sit at the back of the classroom and not to take part in the religious instruction lessons, it was acting at least insensitively if not unlawfully.[69]

Some hold that a right of withdrawal no longer has a place in schools owing to altered teaching methods.[70] A new type of teaching involves taking broadly based headings such as 'humanities' and then teaching several disciplines as part of one large course. Some of the subjects might be so intermixed that it is not easy to extract the 'religious instruction' content from them. This modern style of teaching makes it impossible to guess at what might crop up in a lesson — it could be a discussion on politics or on church history. If it is possible to extract the religious elements from the course and the pupil is withdrawn, he will be at a disadvantage compared to his fellow pupils who have been able to follow the entire course. In any case a title such as 'humanities' may not make it apparent to the parent that there are religious elements in such a course. If religious education is only to be taught because it is of educational value perhaps a special right of withdrawal can be no more or less justified than would one in history or maths, where none at present exists.

Teachers

Provisions have been enacted to protect teachers who wish not to participate in the acts of worship or to give religious instruction. Section 30 of the Education Act 1944, states:

no person shall be disqualified by reason of his religious opinions, of his attending or omitting to attend religious worship, from being a teacher in a county school or in any voluntary school, or from being otherwise employed for the purposes of such a school; and no teacher in any school shall be required to give religious instruction or receive any less emolument or be deprived of or disqualified for, any promotion or other advantage or by reason of his religious opinions or of his attending or omitting to attend religious worship.

The ambit of this exemption is limited first by the statute, which does not extend its protection to outlaw discrimination in the recruitment of teachers in aided schools or to the recruitment of 'reserved teachers' in controlled and special agreement schools. It is also limited by the findings of the majority of the Court of Appeal in *Ahmad* v *Inner London Education Authority*.[71] In that case, a Muslim school teacher was employed to teach for five days a week in a county school. Every Friday, after the lunch break, he went to a mosque in order to pray. This meant that he was unable to teach for the first part of Friday afternoons. The local education authority were prepared to pay for him to work for four and a half days a week whilst he asserted that it would be unlawful religious discrimination, contrary to Section 30, if he was not to be paid for five whole days. The majority of the Court did not agree. Despite its literal meaning section 30 could not 'be construed as authorising a breach of contract by a teacher in absenting himself during school hours for the purpose of attending religious worship'.[72] One must look at the school's timetable and only if the teacher's absence did not conflict with his obligations under it would he be able to go to religious worship somewhere else in school hours.[73] In short the Court were not prepared to read the concept of 'indirect discrimination' into the section — thus the section does not prevent a school from adopting a practice that in fact adversely affects a teacher's religious observances provided that this does not extend to non-recruitment for 'religious opinions' (not, it may be noted, religious practices) or to him not benefiting from full pay and promotion prospects because of his opinions (but not, it must again be stressed, where a practice leads him to break his contract of employment) or because he refused to participate in religious worship and instruction. Furthermore, in the words of Lord Denning (speaking of the European Convention's article on religious freedom):

> Applied to our educational system, I think that Mr Ahmad's right to 'manifest his religion in practice and observance' must be subject to the rights of the education authorities under the contract and to the interests of the children whom he is paid to teach.

Scarman L.J., who dissented however, felt that more flexibility might have to be created in schools since religions such as Islam and Buddhism were now coming more and more to be represented in them. Section 30 now had to be construed:

> not against the background of the law and society of 1944 but in a multi-racial society which has accepted international obligations and enacted statutes designed to eliminate discrimination on grounds of race, religion [sic], colour or sex.

He was prepard to allow that a teacher could attend his own religious worship during school hours provided, '... he is not absent for longer than is reasonably necessary, nor so frequent or of such duration as to make it impossible for the teacher to offer full-time service'.[74] If it meant the employment of a few more teachers to take the place of those at prayer then '... when the cost is compared with the heavy expenditure already committed to the cause of non-discrimination in our society, expense would not in this context appear to be a sound reason for requiring a narrow meaning to be given to the words of the statute'. Whilst the sentiment in this may appeal to many it should be pointed out that Section 30 was enacted because of the special religious involvement in the running of state schools, as the wording of the section serves to underline. Had Scarman L.J.'s interpretation been accepted by the majority the school teacher who wanted to break off and pray for a while would be in a privileged position compared with other workers who wished to do the same,[75] thus meaning that teachers may legally pray at work while others cannot. Perhaps his views would be more attractive if they could apply to other workers (which given the generality of his reasoning could be their ultimate aim).

Despite the clear wording of the section there has been a feeling that there is occasional discrimination employed when making senior appointments. Senior teachers, such as Head and Deputy Head teachers, usually conduct the act of worship and it is sometimes felt that it would be a bad thing were a known atheist to conduct a service. As recently as 1964 a leading education journal[76] defended this practice on the ground that everyone must be taken to know about the position of religion in the state schools before setting out on a teaching career, and in 1977 a teachers' association advised:[77]

Having regard to the practice in the majority of schools that it is the Head or Deputy Head or a Senior member of the staff who conducts the assembly/act of worship for the whole or part of the school, those who aspire to such posts much consider their position very carefully and certainly make their views known (if the matter is not raised by the appointing committee) at the appropriate time.

The continued intermix of religion in semi-state educational institutions and the affect that this has on the teaching staff is further illustrated by the decision of the Court of Appeal in *Jones* v *Lee*.[78] A headmaster of a Roman Catholic voluntary school got divorced and remarried an assistant teacher, who worked at his school and who was also a divorcee. The school managers suspended him and contacted the local Roman Catholic bishop who appointed a tribunal of three to inquire into the matter. Whilst finding no fault in the headmaster's professional position, the tribunal stated:

we feel that the position of a head teacher of a Roman Catholic school makes a person a leader in the religious community and it is unthinkable that such a person could be permitted to retain that position while blatantly refusing to conform to the teachings of the Roman Catholic faith.[79]

The managers of the school resolved to apply this finding and the headmaster was dismissed. The Court of Appeal held that he had not been dismissed in accordance with his contract of employment as he had not been grantd the right of being heard before the managers dismissed him. Lord Denning M.R. and Roskill, L.J.[80] expressed the view that the managers had been wrong to delegate their authority to the ecclesiastical tribunal as it was for them to make the decision. As to the wider moral issue, Lord Denning[81] gave some support to the view that provided the managers followed the correct procedure they could dismiss in such circumstances. However, Roskill and Cumming-Bruce L.JJ. were careful to express no opinions at all upon this question.

Finally, it seems that because of the relatively small number of specialists in religious education their career and promotion prospects are not as good as are those of specialists in other fields.[82]

The clergy in schools

Before 1959 clergymen and ministers could not normally hold state school appointments save where there were exceptional circumstances, but since that date[83] they have been eligible for appointment in the same way as other qualified persons. As the provision of religious instruction is enforced by H.M. Inspectors of Schools alone,[84] clergymen have no right to come into schools in order to see whether the agreed syllabus is being followed or not. They may, however, be invited into school to assist with religious instruction when they are needed and this will be of especial importance when there are large numbers of non-Christian children attending the school. Thus the Moslem Education Trust has arranged with many schools for teachers of Islam to come onto school premises in order to instruct Muslim pupils in their faith.[85]

Race Relations Act 1976

It will be recalled that in *Mandla* v *Lee* (1983) the House of Lords determined that the Sikhs constituted a racial group for the purpose of the 1976 race legislation. Under section 17 of the 1976 Act, it is unlawful for either a local educational establishment or a private school

> to discriminate against a person —
> (*a*) in the terms on which it offers to admit him to the establishment as a pupil; or
> (*b*) by refusing or deliberately omitting to accept an application for his admission to the establishment as a pupil; or
> (*c*) where he is a pupil of the establishment —
>   (i) in the way it affords him access to any benefits, facilities or services, or by refusing or deliberately omitting to afford him access to them; or
>   (ii) by excluding him from the establishment or subjecting him to any other detriment.

Mandla v *Lee* makes clear that a school rule, even if based on religious grounds, would be unlawful if it prevented a Sikh wearing his turban at school. The state schools, given the 1944 Education Act provisions, will probably not be too worried about this result, but what of private schools established to advance a particular religion? In the House of Lords Lord Templeman stated that 'Discrimination cannot be justified by a genuine belief that the school would provide a better system of education'[86] and Lord Fraser said that discrimination could only be capable of being considered justifiable if (is seems from his judgement) the discrimination was not aimed against the manifestation of the ethnic origin (there — the turban).[87] Interestingly it was stated in the Court of Appeal that the father would not have wanted the son to have applied to go to the school had he known at the time of applying that they held compulsory Christian classes.[88] Would a rule insisting on such classes fall foul of the House of Lords' finding in *Mandla* v *Lee*? The answer probably lies with the justifiability test. Perhaps as this point it is best not to lose sight of the actual facts in that case. The school in *Mandla* v *Lee* was not catering exclusively for members of one religious sect, nor was the 'no turban' rule the result of applying a particular religious doctrine. Despite saying this the religious elements now recognised in 'ethnic origins' present serious difficulties — a school run for and by Sikhs would now seem to be caught,[89] as Sikh had been declared as covered by the term 'ethnic', which in turn, by virtue of section 3(1), constitutes racial grounds — thus to admit only Sikhs would seem to be discrimination on racial grounds.

Where the school is not a racially religious one (such as the Sikhs) — say, Roman Catholic — only then would such a rule not constitute direct discrimination, contrary to section 1(1)(a), but if it prevented Sikhs from being pupils it would constitute indirect discrimination subject to the justifiability principle. The difficulty is that being a Sikh is what is objected to (i.e. not being a Roman Catholic) and because of *Manda* v *Lee* that cannot, because of the wording of section 1(1)(b), be permissible. If these conclusions do flow from *Mandla* v *Lee* they present most serious implications for religious freedom in the sphere of education.

The future of religion as a compulsory element in schools

In 1981 the House of Commons Education, Science and Arts Committee presented a review of religion in school as part of their evaluation of secondary education.[90] They noted that the schools inspectorate had not found that the compulsory status of religious instruction had hampered change. The new ethnic minorities living in certain areas had generated fresh interest in the subject. An agreed syllabus which recognised the introduction of pupils to other world religions was met with approval, as was the justification for such instruction, that it 'impinges a moral judgment and practice'. The value of trained teachers was stressed, as was the need to modernise many of the agreed syllabuses. On the other hand there was a general feeling that the compulsory act of worship was unsatisfactory and could often be counter-productive. Thus the conclusion is that the value of religious education does not lie in the act of worship.

The existence of the special religious arrangements will mean that they continue to be of political interest. Religious schools naturally may seek to prefer pupils belonging to their own religions and this continues to be lawful under the existing law.[91] In 1982 the Conservative Government made clear[92] that it believed that it was right that, for example, Catholic schools should be able to choose Catholic pupils, something which it were prepared to defend 'on religious grounds and for the defence of freedom'.[93] It has also strongly supported the general advancement of religion in state schools: 'Let the young child from a Christian family learn the Christian faith, the life of Christ ... it is important that faith should be taught from conviction.'[94] A proposition that is justified because: 'all the surveys and all the evidence show that the vast majority of parents, whatever their religious practice, want their children taught their [sic] religion'.[95]

To this it may be replied that whereas there are honourable precedents in the past (e.g. Gladstone) for saying that compulsion and state involvement are justified when the views of the vast majority are that this religion is what is wanted, this is not true of modern society. An alternative is to have no religion in general, with some religious schools receiving state aid. Against this stand first, the travel factors sometimes involved for members of that religion, and secondly, mainly because of Northern Ireland, a strong opposition from some quarters (e.g. the National Union of Teachers) to the concept of retrenched denominational schools. The ethnic minorities have been mentioned several times in this chapter and one may perhaps close with them. The stronger Muslims see Islamic education as an overall concept and for them the problems do not just revolve round what may be termed the 'traditional' battlegrounds of acts of worship and a compulsory lesson a week but rather on the whole concept of education advanced in the average school. Thus 'accidental' Christian indoctrination, the dress of girls, mixed swimming and even school fund-raising can annoy the more zealous members of that religion,[96] whilst the inevitable exclusiveness that this attitude produces leads others to oppose the creation of separate schools for them within the state system.

Notes

1. The debate in recent years on the subject began with the publication of the Church of England's *The Fourth R*, 1970 (the 'Durham Report'). For a full list of published literature see M. Grimmitt, *What Can I Do in R.E.?*, 2nd edn, 1978, pp. 277–80. For the Scottish position see Francis Lyall, *Of Presbyters and Kings*, 1980, pp. 115–23. For Northern Ireland — Edgar Graham, 'Religion and education: the constitutional problem', *Northern Ireland Legal Quarterly*, XXXIII, 1982, pp. 29–43.

2. Education Act 1870, Section 7.

3. S. Koss, *Nonconformity in Modern British Politics*, 1975, at p. 39. See also pp. 48–9.

4. N. Middleton and S. Weitzman, *A Place for Everyone: A History of State Education from the End of the 18th Century to the 1970s*, 1976, p. 118.

5. Ibid.

6. Ibid.

7. Lord Butler, *The Art of Memory*, 1982, pp. 143–63.

8. See Middleton and Weizman, *Place for Everyone*, pp. 439–49, for a description of the religious settlement of the time.

9. Ibid., pp. 246–65. For final build-up to the passage of the 1944 Act see pp. 276–83 and 301–5.

10. For background details see J. Murphy, *Church, State and Schools in Britain 1800–1970*, 1971, Chapter 8.

11. In fact nearly all the state schools had already opted to include religious instruction in their curriculum, Murphy, *Church, State and Schools*, p. 115.

12. See Chapter 12.

13. Education Act 1944, Section 7. See H.L. Deb., 1977, vol. 379, col. 1698.

14. Education Act 1944, Section 76; and see also Section 33(4).

15. [1955] 1 Q.B. 408.

16. [1972] Ch. 12.

17. Education Act 1980, Section 6(3). Under 6(5) the provision also applies to applications concerning a child not in the area of the authority.

18. For example, see: E.R. Rolls, 'Changes in religious education', *New Community*, I, 1973, p. 241; M. Iqbal, 'Education and Islam in Britain', *New Community*, V, 1977, p. 397 and H. Kanitkar, 'A school for Hindus?', *New Community*, VII, 1979, p. 178.

19. Iqbal, 'Education and Islam', p. 397.

20. Under regulations made pursuant to Section 8(5) of the Education Act 1980.

21. See *The Times*, 21 June 1982.

22. *Kjeldsen, Busk Madsen and Pedersen* v *Denmark* 19 Y.B. 502, Eur. Court H.R., Series A, No. 24.
23. See Chapter 1, pp. 11–13.
24. J. Laffin, *The Dagger of Islam*, 1979, pp. 75–6.
25. Kanitkar, 'School for Hindus?', pp. 181–2.
26. Lord Butler, *The Art of the Possible*, 1973, pp. 100–1.
27. Education Act 1944, Sections 26 and 29 and Schedule 5.
28. H.L. Deb., 1977, vol. 379, col. 1701.
29. H.C. Deb., 1976, vol. 907, col. 1858.
30. Religious Education Council, *What Future for the Agreed Syllabus — Now?*, 1977.
31. Religious Education Council, *What Future for the Agreed Syllabus?*, 1975.
32. H.L. Deb., 1977, vol. 383, col. 866.
33. As the Assistant Masters' Association's *Religious Education*, 1977, shows.
34. Education Act 1944, Section 26.
35. See British Humanist Association, *Objective, Fair and Balanced*, 1975, pp. 2–8.
36. Minutes of the Education Committee of Birmingham District Council, 11 June 1974.
37. *What Future for the Agreed Syllabus — Now?*
38. H.L. Deb., 1977, vol. 383, co.. 863.
39. Thus in Rochdale, in 1980, following intervention by the local Council for Racial Equality, Islam was introduced as part of the course as eight per cent of the school population in that town are Muslim — *Daily Telegraph*, 26 and 28 August 1980.
40. (1976) H.C. Deb., 1976, vol. 907, cols 1861–2.
41. Ibid., col. 1849.
42. Unreported but see *Education*, 16 September 1977.
43. H.L. Deb., 1977, vol. 383, cols 702–874.
44. Ibid., cols 711–12.
45. Ibid., vol. 379, cols 1653–735.
46. Ibid., vol. 383, cols 858–74.
47. Ibid., col 864, *per* Lord Donaldson of Kingsbridge.
48. Ibid., col. 872.
49. *Religious Education*.
50. Education Act 1944, Section 25(1).
51. Ibid., Section 25(4).
52. Ibid., Section 26.
53. G.R. Barrell, *Teachers and the Law*, 5th edn, 1978, p. 245.
54. *Religious Education*.
55. Ibid.
56. Education Act 1944, Section 25(1).
57. Education Act 1946, Section 7.
58. H.C. Deb., 1976, vol. 907, col. 1863.
59. But in the 1977 House of Lords debate on the subject many peers stressed the importance of the Christian religion in British life. The Government felt that the daily non-denominational service was still of great value — H.L. Deb., 1977, vol. 383, cols 861 and 862.

60. H.C. Deb., 1976, vol. 907, col. 1806.
61. E.g. Professional Association of Teachers, *Religious Education in State Schools*, 1976.
62. *The Fourth R*, 1970.
63. Butler, *The Art of the Possible*, p. 100.
64. Education Act 1944, Section 25(4).
65. Ibid.
66. Ibid., Section 26.
67. Ibid., Section 39(2)(*b*).
68. See *Religious Education in State Schools*, p. 14.
69. Barrell, Teachers, p. 249.
70. I. H. Binie (ed.), *Religious Education in Integrated Studies*, 1972, pp. 86–9. For the content of these new courses, see pp. 105–10.
71. [1978] Q.B. 36. See also Chapter 1, pp. 12–13 and Chapter 11, p. 171.
72. At p. 44.
73. At p. 40.
74. At p. 50.
75. Thus see Chapter 11, pp. 169–72, and compare with such cases as *Esson v London Transport Executive* (1975) I.R.L.R. 48.
76. *The Times Educational Supplement*, 24 April 1964, quoted in Murphy, *Church, State and Schools*, p. 123.
77. *Religious Education*.
78. [1980] I.C.R. 310. The school was an aided one.
79. At p. 313.
80. At pp. 314 and 320.
81. Pp. 313–14.
82. Thus see H.L. Deb., 1977, vol. 379, cols 1653–735.
83. Schools Regulations 1959, S.I. 1959, No. 364.
84. Education Act 1944, Section 77(5).
85. *Sunday Telegraph*, 5 November 1978.
86. *Mandla v Lee* [1982] 2 W.L.R. 620, 632.
87. [1983] 2 W.L.R. 620, 629.
88. [1982] 3 W.L.R. 932, 943.
89. Save where the exception in Section 26 applies. Section 35 *may* lead a court to hold that a Sikh-only school is not unlawful — it states that it is not unlawful to afford 'persons of a particular racial group access to facilities or services to meet the special needs of persons of that group in regard to their education, training or welfare, or any ancillary benefits'. However, is the wish to have a religiously exclusive upbringing a special need particular to certain groups? It may in any case be hard to show that all that goes on at the hypothetical school fits in with this justification. Needless to say the section does not appear to have been aimed at such situations.
90. H.C. 1981–82 session, 116–1, *The Secondary School Curriculum and Examinations*, vol. I, xlviii–lii, and see also vol. II (Evidence), pp. 387–501, and vol. III, pp. 656–7.
91. Thus see Education Act 1980, Section 6(3)(*b*) subject to *Mandla v Lee*.
92. See H.C. Deb., 1982, vol. 20, cols 453–60.
93. Ibid., col. 460, *per* Dr Rhodes Boyson, Under-Secretary of State for Education and Science.

168 *Religion and the law*

94. H.C. Deb., 1982, vol. 21, col. 1135.
95. Ibid., col. 1136.
96. It may be noted that at the end of 1982 Bradford City Council launched a special programme of measures in its schools to cope with Asian religious customs. This included the right to wear special dress, to have halal meat at lunch time and information about withdrawal under the 1944 Education Act. At some schools in Bradford ninety per cent of the pupils are Asians. See *The Times*, 28 September 1982.

11 The workplace

He appears to have been a good worker and he has suffered as a result of his religious convictions.

[Industrial Tribunal decision]

In general

The orthodox position at common law has always been that 'a man has no right to be employed by any particular employer, and has no right to any particular employment'[1] — thus, Northern Ireland apart, there is no prohibition on religious discrimination as such in the recruitment of employees nor is there any legal prohibition on adopting trade practices which effectively bar a man from being able to take up a particular employment.[2] Once in employment, however, the position is somewhat different because of the protection provided by the law on unfair dismissal where, given that employment protection applies, it will be wrong to dismiss a protected employee on religious grounds unless that dismissal can be justified in the overall context of the particular work situation. In *Esson* v *United Transport Executive*,[3] Mr Esson, a bus conductor, was under a contractual duty to hold himself out for work on any day of the week. For a while he obeyed this provision in his contract but he then rejoined the Seventh Day Adventists and informed his garage manager that he would no longer, because of his religious beliefs, be able to work on Saturdays. His name was placed on a Saturday rota and he did not appear for work on that day. After repeat performances of this he was dismissed, a dismissal which the tribunal held to be fair since he was in breach of his contract and because his refusal to work on Saturdays had an unreasonable effect on the other bus drivers, who would have to work on more Saturdays than otherwise would have been the case. Sunday was the day causing difficulty in *Storey* v *Allied Breweries (U.K.)*,[4] where a rota system was changed with the result that a chambermaid was to be required, in the future, to work on that day. She wished to take old people to church on Sunday mornings and so did not agree to the change. The tribunal held that it was perfectly proper to dismiss her in such circumstances as these as her refusal to work on Sundays produced an unfair workload for the other chambermaids and, in any case, she had not been wholly deprived of the opportunity to worship as it was still open to her to attend church on Sunday evenings.

One particular problem that has arisen, especially with the Sikhs, is the potential clash between hygiene regulations and the wearing of beards for religious reasons. In *Singh* v *Lyons Maid Ltd*[5] a Sikh had worked in an ice-cream factory for six years and had been clean shaven for all of that time. He then decided to take his religion more seriously and so grew a beard which he intended to keep permanently. His employer maintained a strict rule that production workers should not wear beards and when it proved to be impossible to find him alternative work within the organisation he was dismissed. The firm was held to have acted reasonably and it was not considered relevant, by the tribunal which heard the case, to consider the possible effect that such a rule had on the Sikh community in general or to ask if similar firms enforced such a rule.

This approach has been followed in more recent cases although the position is somewhat complicated by the assumption that a rule that adversely affects a religious group that is strongly based in a particular race (such as the Sikhs) may also constitute indirect racial discrimination contrary to the Race Relations Act 1976.[6] In *Gill* v *The Walls Meat Co. Ltd*[7] a tribunal held that it was indirect racial discrimination to dismiss a Sikh for wearing a beard or a turban but that such an act could be justified (and thus be lawful) where the continued employment of the Sikh in those circumstances would constitute a breach of the Food Regulations 1970. A similar assumption was made by the Employment Appeal Tribunal sitting in Scotland when considering a rule against the recruitment of the bearded in *Singh* v *Rowntree Mackintosh Ltd*,[8] where such a rule was held to come within Section 1(1)(*b*) of the 1976 Race Relations Act in that:

he [i.e. the employer] applies to that other a requirement or condition which he applies or would apply equally to persons not of the same racial group as that other but — (i) which is such that the proportion of persons of the same racial group ... who can comply with it is considerably smaller than the proportion of persons not of that racial group who can comply with it.

Thus more Sikhs must wear beards than non-Sikhs.

Whereas the unfair dismissal provisions are capable of giving aid to a member of any religion the indirect racial discrimination provision will only protect a member of a racially based religion with the result that the English employer who will not recruit Roman Catholics acts lawfully at common law whilst the employer who refuses to employ Sikhs is in breach of the Race Relations Act.

This invidious result is confirmed by the importance placed on racially based religious factors by the House of Lords in *Mandla* v *Lee*,[9] but perhaps some additional points may now be advanced. Although religious belief frequently stems from 'colour, race, nationality or ethnic or national origins', this is not always so, and even where it does, the more zealous the adherent to the faith — that is, where the applicant is most likely to want time off or to grow a beard or whatever — the more likely it is that it is not true that the proportion of persons of the same racial group ... who can comply with it is *considerably smaller* (than those from other groups). For example, take Mr Ahmad[10] (without, of course, saying that in law the race relations legislation does apply to Muslims). He was the only Muslim teacher of the hundreds employed by the education authority who refused to work on the first part of Friday afternoon. Can a principle designed to protect the general (average) characteristics of an ethnic group apply to him? It would seem not; 'can comply' must be considered a very difficult question of fact in this area. The test adopted by the House of Lords in *Mandla* v *Lee*[11] was 'can in practice' or 'can consistently with the customs and cultural traditions of the racial group' comply, a test based on one applied in the field of sex discrimination.[12] With respect, it seems a pity that further consideration was not given to the matter. The differences between men and women are far easier matters for the courts to consider than the differences between the habits of religious groups. The only additional guidance came where Lord Fraser endorsed no-beard rules under public health principles and indicated that failure to cater for special needs may be justified on cost grounds.[13] Far clearer guidelines will need to be worked out in the future.

Discrimination on religious grounds can provide evidence of unreasonableness or improper motive so as to remove certain statutory immunities in the employment law area. Thus Lord Denning has said, in discussing the meaning of the phrase 'in contemplation or furtherance of a trade dispute' (which for many years now has been a vital question in determining whether important immunities from the ordinary civil law apply), '... if shop stewards, who object to a man's religious belief, say to an employer, "Dismiss this man or we will go out on strike," that is not a trade dispute. It is coercive interference with the man's freedom of religion and with the employer's business.'[14]

Northern Ireland[15]

Well known historic factors have made religious discrimination a grim reality in Northern Ireland for many years past. The Fair Employment (Northern Ireland) Act 1976 is the legislature's answer to it in the employment field — it aims to outlaw religious (and political) discrimination within that province. The scheme of the statute[16] is broadly similar to the United Kingdom's Race Relations and Sex Discrimination Acts. It sets up a special agency to enforce its provisions and it applies to most occupations (there are some exceptions to its operation — the clergy, employment within private households and school teachers). It is unlawful to discriminate with regard to recruitment or with regard to opportunities in the employment situation.[17] There is a scheme of conciliation with resort to law as the final sanction.[18] If the courts are involved they may award damages on the ground of religious discrimination.[19] Although it is a Northern Ireland statute it is capable of application to acts that have been committed in England, Wales or Scotland which affect a Northern Irish employment[20] — thus should a firm recruit applicants in England for a Northern Irish job and do so in a discriminatory manner or should a London board of directors decide not to promote a Roman Catholic employee in Northern Ireland, on religious grounds, the Act is breached.

The definition of discrimination is to be found in Section 16(2): 'a person discriminates against another person on the grounds of religious belief or political opinion if, on either of those grounds, he treats that other person less favourably in any circumstance than he treats or would treat any other person in those circumstances'.

To succeed the applicant must show:

(1) that he has received less favourable treatment than someone of a different religion; and
(2) that this happened because of religious influences or prejudices.[21]

The law does not seem to allow special treatment on religious grounds, e.g. extra time off in order to pray, rather it merely provides that all religions should be treated equally and so it is all right if an employer refuses the members of all religious groups time off to pray — he is only in breach of the Act if he allows some groups time off for this whilst refusing other groups the same opportunity.[22]

The difficult question of defining membership of a religion is cricumvented somewhat by providing that for the purposes of the Act it is sufficient to discriminate against a man because you think he is, say, a Presbyterian — there is no need for him to prove he was a member of that religion; it is enough if the employer acted under such a belief.[23]

The working and enforcement of this legislation is in the hands of the Northern Ireland Fair Employment Agency. It is set the task of promoting equality of opportunity within the province, and of eliminating discrimination on the grounds of religion or politics. To achieve these ends it has taken such measures as: issuing a Guide on Manpower Policy and Practice;[24] encouraging employers to sign a declaration of intent in those areas where employment has formally been 'regarded as the preserve of one section or other of the population';[25] and the mounting of research inquiries into employment trends.[26] A major function of the Agency is the investigation of individual complaints of religious discrimination.[27] The Agency noted in 1978 that many members of the public are considerably reluctant to complain.[28] The trouble caused by complaining may be seen as greater than any possible redress that could be obtained. As religious discrimination is felt to be so hard to prove a complaint may prove a worthless exercise. The Agency has discovered that complaints have tended not to come from areas that are strongly Catholic or strongly Protestant:

> Unfortunately the enactment of fair employment laws at such a late state in the development of industrial and community relations, has meant that the Agency has come into existence at a time when generations of actual discriminatory practice and unjustified suspicion have entrenched the patterns of labour mobility, job aspiration and skills acquisition. This has had the effect in some areas of creating two semi-discreet labour markets with a consequent identification of Protestant firms and Catholic firms; Protestant jobs and Catholic jobs. The pattern of applications for employment in many areas reveals the characteristics of what is now in effect voluntary religious segregation in seeking employment opportunities.[29]

The Agency, which is solely concerned with the *religious issues involved*,[30] publishes its findings in the incidents it has investigated. One case[31] concerned an estate manager who had left a borough council's service but then applied for his old post when it was upgraded.

He did not get the upgraded post and the Agency looked at the assessment sheets that had been made by the interviewing committee. These indicated that the applicant should have got the job. The explanation that the council gave did not satisfy the Agency and they concluded that the real reason why the applicant did not get the job was 'religious prejudice on the part of certain powerful Council members which had induced the Chief Recreational Officer to recommend the inferior candidate for the post advertised'. The Agency has found several cases of organised religious discrimination[32] but other incidents investigated by them have turned out not to involve religious prejudice. Indeed some complaints have been from those who had attempted to hang other reasons on a religious peg. Most of the cases so far investigated have not resulted in findings of religious discrimination, which perhaps reflects the difficulty in proving such discrimination. It may also reflect the fundamental problem that this prejudice is so engrained in parts of the province that only a few bother to complain at all.[33]

Finally it may be noted that the Act does not allow what has come to be known as 'positive' discrimination, that is specially favourable treatment for what is seen as the disadvantaged group. One council, mainly made up of Roman Catholics, preferred a Protestant rather than a Roman Catholic as Protestants constituted the minority group in that area. 'Benign' discrimination in favour of the minority or religious quotas is not, however, possible under the Act[34] and so this could not be allowed. Thus one must draw the line between the encouragement of non-discrimination in general and individual acts of favour of the minority.

Religious objection to the closed shop

In 1968 the Donovan Report on Industrial Relations[35] recognised that where trade union membership was a required condition of employment, protection should be given to those members of religious sects who objected to being 'unequally yoked with unbelievers'.[36] The Report discovered that usually trade unions tolerated such people (e.g. the Plymouth Brethren) but felt that they should be given a legal right of redress should they be dismissed for refusing to join a union in the closed-shop situation.[37] It was also felt that conscientious objectors should be under a duty to contribute the sum that they would have had to pay to the union to a charity instead.[38] Nationally the problem seemed small although there was the odd disturbing case — for example a member of the Salvation Army was dismissed from a Rolls-Royce factory for putting up notices on his machine that reproduced the right contained in the Universal Declaration of Human Rights of being free not to join a trade union.[39] Therefore the 1971 Industrial Relations Act created a right of being free not to join a trade union, coupled with a duty to contribute to a charity instead, if one did not wish to, if the employee 'objects on grounds of conscience both to being a member of a trade union and to paying contributions to a trade union in lieu of membership of it'.[40]

Although the word 'conscience' is capable of covering grounds other than those of religious objection, decisions under the section took a fairly restrictive view of the exemption. In 1973 one tribunal stated that 'Our general feeling is that religious grounds or matters of that kind may justifiably be put forward as grounds for refusing to belong to a trade union.'[41] Some while later the Industrial Relations Court adopted a similar approach: ' "grounds of conscience" necessarily points to and involves a belief or conviction based on religion in the broadest sense, as contrasted with personal feeling, however strongly held, or intellectual creed'.[42] Thus it was not enough merely to dislike the union concerned because of some personal, non-religious, motive.

When elected in 1974 the Labour Government determined to restrict conscientious objection to religious grounds. This narrowing of the exception was justified by the following reasons:

(1) if objection to membership of the closed shop is extended to those whose objection is based upon political grounds so many people might object that the concept of the closed shop could be rendered totally ineffective;[43]
(2) and if the exception is extended beyond religion, the religious objector would be in a worse position as their cases would get 'muddled up with political cases which will arouse a great deal of passion.'[44]

Not surprisingly the question was asked — why should religious objectors be placed in a better position than others? A forceful justification was supplied by Albert Booth, M.P.:

a special or peculiar nature attaches to religious convictions which requires that it should receive special treatment. People cannot always express their reasons for holding religious convictions in ways which will readily satisfy others. They cannot prove them as they would prove a mathematical formula. They cannot even express them by a process of logic that can be done with certain political or philosophical arguments so as at least to satisfy other people that there was a basis for holding the view. Very often the religious conviction is based upon a faith in something which to all others be intangible — a faith which can be tested only by those who possess it ... in the tradition of civilised societies a special place is afforded, as far as is possible, to the rights of people who wish to act on a belief which they alone wish to apply.[45]

With these ends in mind the 1974 Trade Union and Labour Relations Act provided that a dismissal would be regarded as fair if there was a recognised closed shop agreement and if the employee was dismissed for refusing to join the union, 'unless the employee genuinely objects on grounds of religious belief to being a member of any trade union whatsoever ... in which case the dismissal shall be regarded as unfair'.[46] The obligation to donate sums to charity was removed at this time. In one case[47] a father and son, who were Christadelphians, had been dismissed after they had failed to satisfy a panel, set up by British Railways, that their religion had written rules forbidding union membership. The tribunal did not approve of this 'doubting Thomas approach' which was considered an attempt to add additional words to the statute. The Christadelphians are a group that do not approve of union membership (one of the applicants in this case had made that clear to British Railways some twenty-six years beforehand) and that was sufficient — there was no need to produce a 'rule-book' in order to prove this. In *Goodbody* v *British Railways Board*[48] Mr Goodbody mainly worshipped in the Church of England although he was also 'in fellowship' with the Baptists, the Brethren and the Pentacostalists. British Railways said that they would only grant him exception on the grounds of his religion if he could furnish documentary evidence, from his Church, showing that he would be expelled from it should he join a union. Mr Goodbody told the tribunal that he had reached his conclusions from his own interpretation of scripture. The tribunal held that the test to be applied was subjective — that is, what did Mr Goodbody perceive his situation to be? In any case enough had shown to suggest that although the Brethren would not expell Mr Goodbody, his union membership would be 'a source of acute, deep-seated, and continuing disapproval and grave embarrassment' both to himself and to the Brethren.[49]

The most influential decision on the 1974 provision was *Saggers* v *British Railways Board*,[50] a case of general importance when construing a 'conscience clause'. A Jehovah's Witness (a creed that allows union membership) wrote to a union, 'I hereby wish to be excused from joining. My Christian convictions as they are, my conscience, does not permit my joining any union or political organisation.' The applicant had honestly arrived at this belief whilst attempting to develop his own faith. Arnold J., in giving the judgment of the Employment Appeals Tribunal, stated that these unique conclusions were not fatal to the applicant's success and said that the exemption was to be interpreted as follows:

(1) religious belief is something that is the accepted belief of the religious organisation to which the applicant belongs;
(2) the word 'belief' should be viewed subjectively;
(3) thus the applicant's belief can be different to the accepted belief in (1) if he has genuinely reached that conclusion;
(4) however the common belief of the religious group is a strong factor in determining whether he genuinely holds this personal belief.[51]

The case was then sent back to a tribunal so that these principles could be applied to the findings of fact. The tribunal held, by a majority, that Mr Saggers's objection was not based on his religious beliefs at all. The case again came before the Employment Appeals Tribunal[52] where it was argued that people should not be able to claim to belong to a religious sect and then tack on their own personal riders such as objection to trade unions.[53] Despite this objection the ruling in *Saggers (No. 1)* was held to apply and Mr Saggers's belief was accepted as a religious one. Whilst the sincerity of the belief still had to be tested as a question of fact *Saggers* produced the result that an applicant could say, 'I am a member of the Church of England and my unique interpretation of that faith is that I should not join a union' and possibly succeed, although had the word 'atheist' been substituted for 'Church of England' there could have been no possibility of success.[54] The subjective line adopted in *Saggers* was also unusual as it has been said that 'one would say that the identity of a religious community described as a Church must consist in the unity of its doctrines'.[55] When a belief becomes unique in the *Saggers* sense it ceases to be a belief in a religious doctrine at all. Donovan clearly had a particular religious doctrine in mind when the provision was suggested but *Saggers* postulates 'do it yourself' religion instead.

In 1979 a Conservative Government was elected and its policy, at the very least, was the extension of the exemptions to the closed shop. In 1980 the position was changed so that 'The dismissal of an employee ... shall be regarded as unfair if he genuinely objects on grounds of conscience or other deeply held personal conviction to being a member of any trade union whatsoever or of a particular trade union.'[56] Thus those with objections from their personal religious beliefs may now object to trade unions on wider grounds than before (although cases such as *Saggers* are of importance in determining whether the objection is 'genuine'). For example, suppose a particular union decides to endorse a policy of encouraging 'abortion on demand'. Any Roman Catholic could object to being a member of that particular trade union although neither he, nor his religion, are generally opposed to membership of trade unions. The 1980 provision also means that those whose objections are not on religious grounds may, as they could claim under the 1971 Industrial Relations Act, now claim conscientious objection to trade union membership.

Clergymen and ministers of religion

Employment protection legislation is dependent on the applicant being an employee in law and this question is resolved by the discovery of contractual obligations governing the service of the applicant. The more conventional view was that such obligations may be missing when the position of ministers of religion is examined. Thus in 1912[57] a Church of England curate was considered to be the holder of an ecclesiastical office governed by ecclesiastical authority rather than an employee under a contract of employment. This has also been considered to be the case with regard to Methodist ministers[58] and, more recently, with ministers of the Congregational Church.[59] In this last case the ministers at a Sheffield mission had to ask the Senior Chaplain's permission to take time off for holidays, and also received 'directives' from him. However, '... the manner in which they performed the duties assigned to them must, we feel, inevitably have been a matter for them and in any case they were to perform them in the way that a Minister of Religion called by God to devote himself to that Ministry would perform them'. Following this it seems that if a minister is under spiritual direction with regard to the carrying out of his duties he will not be considered an employee for employment protection purposes. It will be a question of fact with each different religion for they may be some 'ministers' who are so 'controlled' in their activities by a superior that they are employees in law. This seems to have been followed with clergymen of the Church of England[60] although *Barthorpe* v *Exeter Diocesan Board*[61] finds the Employment Appeal Tribunal somewhat more ready to find the employee situation than had the earlier decisions. They decided that although a stipendiary reader of the Church of England was an office-holder he could also, as a matter of fact, be an employee. Slyn J.'s judgment[62] contains a number of important points on this issue:

ordained clergyman can enter into contracts of employment (whether of service or for rendering service may have to be decided) which do not involve the holding of an office. Equally we consider that it does not follow, merely because there are some office holders [who will not be 'employees' for this purpose] in the Church of England, that everyone who plays a part in the ministry of the Church is necessarily an office holder who is not employed under a contract of service.

He also cast some doubt on the earlier *Church of England Curates* case.[63] Thus a contract of employment may coexist with an office. The amount of direction that the minister is under will be a crucial factor but even the newer trend acknowledges that some ministers and clergy are sufficiently independent so as not to be employees in law. Where this is so their protection in office will depend on the working of the Church of England disciplinary procedure,[64] if they are clergymen of that Church, or the particular rules of their Church, enforceable as part of the ordinary civil law of contract, if they are priests or ministers of another religion.

The appointment to office of ministers of religion will be outside the provisions of the Sex Discrimination Act, where 'qualification is limited to one sex so as to comply with the doctrines of the religion or avoid offending the religious susceptibilities of a significant number of [the relevant religion's] followers'.[65] Ministers who are in law employees and other employees of religions are similarly outside the ban on sex discrimination created by the Act.[66] It is sufficient to justify the discrimination (e.g. male-only priests) by showing that a significant number of the members of the religion will be offended by opening the post to members of the other sex thus avoiding the necessity of the court having to determine religious doctrines.

That religions should be placed in this special position is not a matter without controversy and, in addition, it has been argued[67] that the present position within the Church of England is not free from doubt. In 1975 the General Synod passed a resolution stating 'this Synod considers that there are no fundamental objections to the ordination of women to the priesthood', which, it has been argued, means that there can be no doctrinal objection to the ordination of women since any doctrinal objection must be regarded as 'fundamental'. With respect this seems to overlook the special nature of doctrines of the Church of England which have a more legalistic existence than doctrines in other Churches.[68] To allow that doctrine can be changed in this informal way would not be in line with the powers that Parliament has granted to (or depending on your point of view) recognised in those bodies.

Should the Church decide to change its doctrine in a way that could produce a new form of discrimination (for example, a local option scheme, leaving it open to a region to decide whether to have women priests or not) a special Act of Parliament might be needed.

Notes

1. *Allen* v *Flood* [1898] A.C. 1, at p. 173, *per* Lord Davey.
2. Although see Chapter 1, pp. 1–7, on 'racial–religious' discrimination.
3. [1975] I.R.L.R. 48.
4. (1976) 84 I.R.L.I.B. 9.
5. [1975] I.R.L.R. 328.
6. See note 2.
7. (1977) H.S.I.B. 12.
8. [1979] I.C.R. 554. See also: *Panesar* v *Nestlé Co. Ltd* [1980] I.C.R. 144 [Note] and cases cited in Chapter I, pp. 1–7.
9. See Chapter I, pp. 3–7.
10. *Ahmad* v *Inner London Education Authority* [1978] Q.B. 36.
11. [1983] 2 W.L.R. 620, 628–9.
12. *Price* v *Civil Service Commission* [1978] I.C.R. 27.
13. 'Again, it might be possible for the school to show that a rule insisting upon a fixed diet, which included some dish (for example, pork) which some racial groups could not conscientiously eat was justifiable if the school proved that the cost of providing special meals for the particular group would be prohibitive' — [1983] 2 W.L.R. 620, 629.
14. *British Broadcasting Corporation* v *Hearn* [1977] I.C.R. 685, at p. 692.
15. Note the legislation summed up between pp. 11–13 in *Standing Advisory Commission on Human Rights: The Protection of Human Rights by Law in Northern Ireland*, Cmnd, 7009, 1977.
16. R.R. Osborne, 'Fair employment in Northern Ireland', *New Community*, 1980, pp. 129–37.
17. Fair Employment (Northern Ireland) Act 1976, Sections 3 and 17.
18. Sections 24–6.
19. Section 31(1).
20. Section 57(8).
21. *Fourth Report of the Fair Employment Agency for Northern Ireland*, 1981, p. 33.
22. *Third Report of the Fair Employment Agency for Northern Ireland*, 1979, pp. 41–3.
23. Fair Employment (Northern Ireland) Act 1976, Section 57(2).
24. *Second Annual Report of the Fair Employment Agency for Northern Ireland*, 1977–78, pp. 5–6.
25. Ibid., p. 7. Since 1970 the Northern Ireland Government had required all those contracting with it to sign a Non-Discrimination Declaration.
26. *Second Annual Report*, pp. 7–16, and *Third Annual Report*, pp. 9–21.
27. The investigative procedure is set out in the *Second Annual Report*, p. 17.
28. *Second Annual Report*, p. 19.

29. *Third Annual Report*, pp. 23-4. The Agency believes that continuation of the system of segregated education will encourage this — *Second Annual Report*, pp. 21-2.
30. *Fourth Annual Report*, pp. 23-4.
31. *Third Annual Report*, pp. 37-8.
32. See *Third Annual Report*, pp. 52-4, for an example of a reorganisation of a job description in order to further a policy of not giving managerial jobs to Roman Catholics.
33. *Third Annual Report*, p. 58.
34. *Third Annual Report*, pp. 60-1.
35. *Royal Commission on Trade Unions and Employer's Associations, 1965-1968*, Cmnd. 3623, 1968.
36. 2 Corinthians, 6: 14.
37. Cmnd. 3623, paras 605 and 614.
38. Cmnd. 3623, para. 604.
39. H.C. Deb., 1971, vol. 810, cols 650-2.
40. Industrial Relations Act 1971, Section 9(1)(*b*).
41. *Drury* v *The Bakers Union* [1973]I.R.L.R. 171, at p. 172.
42. *Hynds* v *Spillers-French Baking Ltd and Scottish Union of Bakers and Allied Workers* [1974] I.R.L.R. 281, at p. 283, *per* Lord Thompson.
43. H.C. Deb s.c. 'F', 1974, vol. 4, col. 873.
44. Ibid., col. 878.
45. Ibid., cols 893-4.
46. Trade Union and Labour Relations Act 1974, Sched. I, para. 6(5). This was later re-enacted by Section 58(3) of the Employment Protection (Consolidation) Act 1978.
47. *Cave and Cave* v *British Railways Board* [1976] I.R.L.R. 400.
48. [1977] I.R.L.R. 84.
49. At p. 86.
50. [1978] 2 All E.R. 20.
51. At pp. 23-4.
52. *Saggers* v *British Railways Board (No. 2)* [1978] I.C.R. 1111.
53. At p. 1115.
54. See *Cave and Cave* v *British Railways Board* [1976] I.C.L.R. 400, at p. 402.
55. *General Assembly of Free Church of Scotland* v *Lord Overtoun* [1904] A.C. 515, at p. 612, *per* Earl of Halsbury L.C.
56. Employment Act 1980, Section 7(2). Under Section 3 of the Employment Act 1982 it is still possible to be fairly dismissed for non-union membership but only in rather limited circumstances. The dismissal is not fair, however, 'if the employee genuinely objects on grounds of conscience or other deeply held personal conviction to being a member of any trade union whatsoever or of a particular trade union' (Section 3(4)).
57. *Re National Insurance Act, 1911: In Re Employment of Church of England Curates* [1912] 2 Ch. 563.
58. *Re Employment of Ministers of the United Methodist Church* (1912) 28 T.L.R. 539.
59. *Parker* v *Orr* (1966) 1 I.T.R. 488.
60. *Houseman* v *Bishop of Ely*; *cf.* Norman W. Selwyn, *Law of Employment*, 2nd. edn, 1978, p. 20.

61. [1979] I.C.R. 900. See also *President of the Methodist Conference* v *Parfitt*, *The Times*, 18 November 1982, and St J.A. Robilliard, 'Diocesan liabilaity for negligence of a priest', *Law and Justice*, No. 72/3, 1982, pp. 54–9.

62. At p. 904.

63. Note 57.

64. See Chapter 5, pp. 95–7.

65. Sex Discrimination Act 1975, Section 19(2).

66. Section 19(1).

67. J.A. MacKenzie, 'Sex discrimination and the Church of England', *Poly Law Review*, IV, 1979, pp. 33–7.

68. Thus see Chapter 5.

12 Family matters

> My Lords, it is, as I think, a sad commentary on the attitude of some members of the Protestant and Roman Catholic faiths, that in so many of the reported cases over the last one hundred years the real contest has been as to religious upbringing of the infant and orders have been made with scant regard to the true welfare of the infant.
>
> [Lord Upjohn in *J* v *C* (1970)]

Historically family law disputes, especially those over the custody and religious upbringing of children, have been a major area where religious conflicts have had to be settled by law. This chapter examines that background and describes the current outlook of the courts and discovers that they attempt to apply the 'standards of their age', because statute law[1] only intervenes in the most general of terms. There then follows a brief description of some of the other problems encountered in the family law area.

Parental wishes at common law[2]

At one time the father had the right to select his (legitimate) child's religion, a situation that in the nineteenth century was seen as part of 'the principles of common sense and the principles of propriety'[3] as the father was the head of the household. If the father had died the court would pay 'great attention' to the instructions that he had left behind.[4] When the father had died the court purported to act in the best interests of the child and it would assume that the wishes left by the father were for the child's benefit.[5] This attitude sometimes meant that the courts placed far too much emphasis upon a dead father's wishes and too little upon any change of circumstances that may have taken place following his death. Where the father had died without exercising his right the mother could do so if she was the child's 'guardian by nurture' but had the father at anytime exercised his right she could find herself 'compelled to bring up her child in a religion which she abhors'.[6] If the child was illegitimate the mother exercised the right[7] although the views of the putative father could be taken into account. These hard, fast and arbitrary rules were at one time defended firmly: 'In every country where sectarian divisions exist it is essential that there should be a settled and intelligible rule as to the religion of wedlock; and, whether the rule be in the abstract right or wrong, it is better that there should be some rule than none at all.'[8]

Religious education, like other forms of education, was a power included in the bundle of rights known as custody.[9] While the law would not enforce religious education when the child himself protested,[10] it would zealously protect the parent's right when it was seen to be threatened by a third party. Thus in one nineteenth-century case[11] the sixteen-year-old daughter of a Protestant father had gone in secret to the Roman Catholics in order to be admitted to that faith. The response of the court was swift — an injunction was granted so as to prevent the priests from 'attempting to induce the girl to disobey her father'.

Although the parent could 'abandon' the right, the following was usually assumed:

'[The courts] cannot search the secrets of the heart or base their decision on the supposed intensity of the father's convictions. They have no spirit gauge, and must go by appearances. Many whose personal religion is lukewarm have a fervour of antipathy to other creeds. In the absence of evidence the other way the court attributes to the parent the wish that his offspring should be brought up in the Church of which he was a professing and ostensible member.[12]

However the parent's wishes would be disregarded if they could not in any sense be considered to have been held *bona fide*.[13]

The father would have abandoned the right where he had openly allowed the mother to bring the child up in a faith other than his own, but this was not true where the mother had done this in secret.[14] When this had happened the court would direct that in future the child should be reared in the religion of the father, even if it seemed that this could not be justified in the welfare of the child. The crucial factor of all times was the father's knowledge of and intention towards the child.[15]

The only grounds recognised at common law for interference with the father's right were either gross immorality or where the father wanted the child for some unlawful purpose.[16] In equity there was an early indication that the court would act where the father's activities would be grossly prejudicial to the child[17] but this line of thought did not develop.

The favouring of Christianity

In the nineteenth century a Christian upbringing was seen as a clear advantage whereas other types were regarded with suspicion. In Regency times Shelley[18] was deprived of his children by that most conservative of judges, Lord Eldon, for two reasons:

(1) some of Shelley's poems were blasphemous, that is he had committed a crime although he himself (unlike later publishers of his works) had not been prosecuted; and
(2) because he was considered to be immoral.

Both these factors sprang from Shelley's views on religion, as was made clear by Lord Cottenham in 1849,[19] when he explained that Shelley's children had been removed as a result of 'the impiety and irreligion of the father'. Extremist Christian cults were also viewed with suspicion, as *Thomas* v *Roberts*[20] shows. There a tiny Christian sect differed from orthodox views on both the rôle of prayer and on the position of the Sabbath. There was also, no doubt because of the outrageous views that they professed, suspicion that their community was immoral. Their religious opinions were denounced in strong terms by Knight-Bruce V.C. who described them as '... noxious to society, adverse to civilization, opposed to the usages of Christendom, contrary ... to the express command of the New Testament, and finally pernicious necessarily in the highest degree of any young person unhappy enough to be imbued with them'.[21] 'Overt ruin' would befall any child brought up in those beliefs.

Fifty years after *Shelley*'s case the courts were still hostile to atheists who wished to bring up children in their own beliefs. Judicial comments in *Re Besant*[22] were not encouraging: '[such views are] not only reprehensible but detestable, and likely to work utter ruin to the child';[23] 'the court cannot allow its ward to run the risk of being brought up, or growing up, in opposition to the views of mankind generally, as to what is moral, what is decent, what is womanly or proper'.[24] Annie Besant's defeat in this case[25] was perhaps one of the largest blows that the 'free thinkers' encountered in the second half of the nineteenth century.

The change to the child's welfare

After the twentieth century commenced the hard and fast rules of the nineteenth began to soften. By 1925 Viscount Cave was able to observe[26] that there had been a chain of unreported decisions that had placed more stress on the child's welfare rather than on the demands of the father. Although the father's wishes remained important they were not paramount — they had to be tested in the light of the overall circumstances of the case. Section 1 of the Guardianship of Infants Act 1925 gave statutory effect to this changed attitude by providing that where the custody or upbringing of any child was being considered in any proceeding before any court its welfare came first with the result that 'the court should pay serious heed to the religious wishes of the parents, but not to the extent of infringing the requirement of the paramount consideration being the welfare of the child'.[27]

In 1970 the House of Lords confirmed[28] that this was so in all possibilities, whether the dispute was between two parents or was between a parent and a stranger. When a child was given out for adoption it used to be possible for the parent to stipulate in what religion it must be raised[29] but this practice was not always thought to be one in the best interests of the child. So now, since 1975, a parent is not able to stipulate that his child should undergo an upbringing in a particular religion once adopted,[30] although where the child is placed with an adoption agency the agency must have regard to the parent's wishes 'so far as is practicable'.[31]

Judicial support of religious upbringing

Growing out of the general encouragement of Christian religious education in the past has come the assumption that a religious education is a good thing and should, if possible, be given judicial support. In 1975 Cairns L.J.,[32] in awarding the custody of two children to a clergyman father in preference to an adulterous mother, remarked that the moral upbringing that the father would be able to provide would be of great value to the children. In *Re K (Minors)*[33] the Court of Appeal awarded the custody of two children, aged five-and-a-half and two-and-a-half, to the mother rather than the clergyman father as it was not thought that the fact of his being a minister of religion should reverse what would otherwise, on all other family law principles, be the inevitable answer.[34] However the importance of the children having a religious upbringing was clearly underlined with Ormrod L.J. declaring that the court might take further action, 'If, as they get older there is any cause for anxiety about what may be called their spiritual welfare'.[35]

In the 1960s Willmer L.J. appeared as a supporter of a religious upbringing. In *Re C. (M.A.)*,[36] an adoption case, he declared that the opinions of a mother with regard to the religious upbringing of an eighteen-month-old child were to be taken into consideration but were not decisive and went on to stress his approval of the adopters by stating, '[they] have looked after him devotedly for seventeen months, and ... have the means to give him a good education and a good Christian upbringing'.[37] In two later cases[38] he was to place 'considerable importance' upon the religious education of young children that had already commenced.

Welfare and religion in disputes about children[39]

If the father had failed to exercise his common law right equity would look to the well-being of the child[40] and since 1925 this has been the first and paramount consideration. It will normally be in the welfare of the child to consider the parents' wishes about religion and even if it is not, such wishes, it has been argued,[41] should be honoured provided that this will not lead to the child's actual detriment. In considering whether particular types of religious upbringing are of benefit or not the following guidelines seem to emerge from the cases.

(1) *The court supports spiritual welfare:* Earlier decisions made great play of, 'the moral and religious welfare of the child ... as well as its physical well-being'[42] and this has continued to find echoes in the recent cases, especially where one of the parents is deeply religious. In the important decision of *Re K*, in 1977, Stamp L.J. declared, '... in considering the welfare of the children, one has to look also to their *moral and spiritual welfare*'.[43]

(2) *The presumption in favour of the status quo:* A factor on which a great deal of importance is placed is that the child has already commenced a religious upbringing. At one time to tamper with a child's mind in such a situation was thought likely to lead to its utter confusion with the possible horror of leaving it with no religion at all. These sentiments were colourfully expressed by Knight-Bruce V.-C., halfway through the nineteenth century:

the Protestant seed sown in his mind has taken such hold, that if we are to suppose it to contain tares, they cannot be gathered up without great danger of rooting up the wheat with them ... the child's tranquillity and health, his temporal happiness, and spiritual welfare also, are likely to suffer importantly from an endeavour at effacing his Protestant impressions.[44]

Closely akin to this was the thought that the child should enjoy peace of mind. Thus if a child was being brought up in one faith and, for example, its guardian was the member of another, there might be a general unsettlement of both the child's spiritual sphere and its physical environment.[45] Such a view was more appropriate to an age where religious differences were more keenly felt than they are at the present day and is not so likely to influence the courts now. Thus in 1962[46] the decision of a judge at first instance that a Jewish couple should not adopt a Protestant Christian child was reversed by the Court of Appeal as too much weight had been placed on the religious issue and too little on the other considerations affecting its welfare. Again, in 1963[47] Wilberforce J., in a case where a non-Catholic family of moderate views wished to raise a Catholic child, stressed[48] that given the make-up of the particular family in question he did not think that the child's faith would be undermined and he saw 'no more reason why a consciousness of religious difference should give rise to conflict then should a consciousness of racial difference'. The implication of his approach is clear — where, perhaps because the religious views involved are extreme, there is a likelyhood of an unsettling effect the older view will still be important but it will not be followed automatically today.

(3) *Social welfare:* The law does not encourage the production of social outcasts — a point of conflict with many of the minority sects that often have exclusiveness as a distinguishing mark. In *Re C*[49] displeasure was shown with a sect that would have produced a child so cut off from the rest of mankind that he would have been unable to share a table with non-believers. The fear of producing Ishmaelites influenced the Court of Appeal in 1974,[50] where a Jehovah's Witness mother, who seemed to be somewhat mentally disturbed, wished to raise her children apart from the rest of society and was also not going to allow them to enjoy Christmas. Mainly because of her mental state she was not awarded custody but it is important to note that when seeing them in future she was forbidden to take them to the Jehovah's Temple. This attitude can seem unfair towards sects like the Jehovah's Witnesses and in 1975 Scarman L.J. made an important statement that has affected the outcome of subsequent cases:

We live in a tolerant society. There is no reason at all why the mother should not espouse the beliefs and practice of Jehovah's Witnesses. There is nothing immoral or socially obnoxious in the beliefs and practice of that sect. There is a great risk, because we are dealing with an unpopular sect, in overplaying the dangers to the welfare of the children inherent in the possibility that they may follow their mother and become Jehovah's Witnesses.

The courts now tend to cope with this problem by allowing[51] Jehovah's Witness parents custody and access where they are prepared to give undertakings that they will not, for example, take their children with them when they go evangelising on the doorstep[52] or that they will allow them to enjoy Christmas, reasonable social facilities and have blood transfusions when necessary.[53] However, the courts will still take a hard attitude with those whose religion will not allow them to make such compromise — in 1981[54] a father, whose first marriage had broken down because of his preoccupation with the Jehovah's Witnesses, was denied even access to see the five-year-old daughter of the marriage until the court felt he would take 'a more rational and reasonable attitude over the child and the question of ... religion'. He could not see his daughter if it was likely that he would attempt to indoctrinate her.

A religion that is in a cultural minority within the country may feel that the welfare principle acts unjustly towards it. In *Haleem* v *Haleem*[55] the father was a strict Muslim and wished to raise his children in that faith whilst the mother did not possess a great deal of belief in any religion. The judge at first instance, inclining towards the view that some religion was better than no religion, awarded custody to the father. He was reversed mainly because children of the age of those in the case should normally go to the mother but also because the court felt that the mother, the non-Muslim, could provide a better social and cultural background for children growing up in this country. This solution to such problems has been criticised by Muslim commentators who feel that the courts should take the Islamic view more into consideration than they in fact do.[56]

(4) *Physical welfare:* The judges have never hesitated to take action when the physical safety and health of the child are likely to be in danger.[57] This is a consideration which has worked in recent times against Jehovah's Witnesses when they are likely to refuse their consent to blood transfusions for their children when they are necessary.[58]

(5) *The wishes of the child:* Some weight has in the past been placed on the wishes expressed by the child to the judge. These may be followed either because they provide evidence of what is in its welfare[59] or, it has been argued,[60] should, where the child has reached sufficient maturity, be seen and respected as his wishes in his own right.

'Christian' marriage and polygamy

The English law on marriage grew out of Christian definitions and ideals and it was not until 1836 that it was possible to contract a civil marriage at all. To this day persons domiciled in England and Wales are unable to enter a polygamous union anywhere in the world[61] and such a union celebrated in this country will not be recognised by our law wherever the parties to it might be domiciled.[62] Support for these rejections of polygamy has come from the eminent jurist Lord Devlin[63] on the grounds that our society grows from a Christian base and that the monogamous marriage is an essential element of that base. Its continued rejection is not today so much justified on the grounds of religion but because of the rôle that it fulfils in modern society. Monogamy is binding on Christians because they are Christians and 'a non-Christian is bound by it not because it is part of Christianity but because, rightly or wrongly, it has been adopted by the society in which he lives'. It is fair to point out that not all judges take this view of our society for at the same time that Lord Devlin was writing Simon P.[64] was prepared to recognise a marriage between two Sephardic Jews in Egypt (the husband being the maternal uncle of the wife) with the comment[65] that in deciding whether such a marriage was 'offensive to the conscience' of the English court 'it would be altogether too queasy a judicial conscience which would recoil from a marriage accepted by many peoples of deep religious conviction, lofty ethical standards and high civilisation'. Similar comments could be made about the institution of polygamy and Lord Devlin's views are open to question not only because fewer members of society are Christian but also because more members of our society recognise polygamy as a morally correct institution.[66] However, it should not be thought that the law does not now recognise polygamy. Unless it falls under one of the two important prohibitions mentioned above, polygamous unions are now recognised for many important purposes.[67]

The old attitude towards polygamy was made plain in *Hyde* v *Hyde and Woodmonsee* in 1866.[68] An Englishman had gone to live in Utah and married, in 1853, at Salt Lake City under the rule of the Mormon Church. After a little while he fell out with the Mormons and was eventually excommunicated by them. His wife, whom he had married whilst he was a Mormon, had been told that she was free to remarry and proceeded to marry one Woodmonsee. Hyde eventually returned to England and petitioned the English Divorce Court for a dissolution of the original marriage. Lord Penzance declared that an English court would not recognise a polygamous marriage in order to grant matrimonial relief,

> We have in England no law framed on the scale of polygamy or adjusted to its requirements. And it may well be doubted whether it would become the tribunals of this country to enforce the duties (even if we know them) which belong to a system so utterly at variance with the Christian conception of marriage, and so revolting to the ideas we entertain of the social position to be according to the weaker sex.[69]

Despite this there developed limited recognition of polygamy. Thus the children born in such unions are regarded as legitimate for such purposes as succession to property.[70] From about the end of the Second World War the courts were as restrictive as they could be with the rule in *Hyde*'s case[71] and thus in 1946[72] a polygamous Hindu marriage, which had been celebrated in India, was recognised to the extent that it acted as a bar to the contracting of a subsequent marriage in England. Where the marriage was 'potentially polygamous', that is to say it had been performed under a system permitting polygamy but where in fact the husband had married no subsequent wives, the English courts would recognise them for the purpose of granting matrimonial relief where they had been 'converted' into monogamous unions. This could happen by, for example, the parties converting their religion to one not allowing polygamy[73] or by the husband gaining a domicile of choice in England and thus losing his capacity to contract further polygamous marriages.[74] In the last two decades 'potentially polygamous' marriages have come to be recognised as valid for social security purposes where they have in fact at all times been monogamous.[75]

By 1970 the main disadvantage left (apart of course from the ban on those domiciled here contracting such marriages and also on the celebration of such unions in this country) was the inability of the courts to grant matrimonial relief (e.g. decrees of divorce and orders of judicial separation) to the party of what had been contracted as a valid, but polygamous, marriage[76] in another country. The Law Commission[77] recommended that the rule in *Hyde*'s case should be abolished and that social welfare provisions should extend to actually polygamous marriages as well.[78] The first change was supported on the ground that now Britain was multi-racial the *Hyde* rule 'does not facilitate the integration of immigrants into English society if they are to be denied the elementary rights which native born English people enjoy as of course'.[79] The recommendations on the recognition of these marriages were enacted,[80] although to some the change was seen as the undermining of monogamous (Christian) marriage. An alternative suggestion made at the time was that rather than treat polygamous marriages as 'marriages' at all they should be regarded as contracts, the terms of which were to be found in the religious laws and customs of the place where they were entered into.[81] There are others who feel that the present law does not sufficiently accommodate the religious minorities now in our midst. An immigrant may be domiciled in law in England (thus unable to contract a polygamous marriage) but still be very much attached to the social and religious bonds of his old culture. Such ties might be so strong that he returns to his former home to contract a marriage which, if it happens to be polygamous, will be void in English law. It has been argued[82] that some change in the law should be made in order to accommodate such citizens. It may also be observed that the integration of even recognised polygamous marriages into our legal system has not yet fully been achieved.[83]

Under the present law matrimonial relief may be granted to a party to an 'actual' or a 'potentially' polygamous marriage that has been entered into under a law permitting polygamy.[84] This power was first exercised in 1975 when the President of the Family Division granted divorces to two Nigerian women, on the same day, who were married to the same man.[85] New possibilities and indeed problems have been created for the courts which will now have to consider some forms of relationship (e.g. the Hanafi Fasidu union)[86] that will seem strange to them.

The improved position of polygamy does not affect the criminal law — bigamy[87] will be committed where a man enters into a polygamous union in another country, becomes domiciled in England,[88] and marries again without divorcing his first wife. This may lead to some hardship where the defendant's religious and moral code did not lead him to believe that he was doing wrong and it has been suggested[89] that there should be a special defence to bigamy where a person believed that English law allowed him to take more than one wife because of his religious beliefs.

Forms of marriage and religion[90]

The move away from ecclesiastical domination over matrimonial law has also been reflected in the law relating to the solemnisation of marriage. Under the Marriages Acts 1949–1970 marriages may either be solemnised according to the rites of the Church of England; or a superintendent registrar's certificate may be issued for solemnisation at a registered building[91] (which now include such places as Muslim mosques as well as older institutions such as the Nonconformist chapels and so on); or according to the usages of the Quakers or the Jews. Whilst these differences can be explained because of historic reasons the Law Commission[92] feels that in the interests of 'inter-religious' harmony all religious services should now come under the same legal footing[93] with a universal 'registered building concept'. Even where only a civil ceremony has been gone through, a religious service will be of importance where the religious beliefs of the parties lead them to believe that consummation of the marriage can only take place after a subsequent religious service — should one of the parties refuse to go through with such a service the marriage will be annulled on the ground of wilful refusal to consummate.[94]

Religious duress and marriage

Religious customs of non-Christian faiths have produced a problem with regard to the arranged marriage. In *Singh* v *Singh*[95] a marriage in West Bromwich had been arranged according to traditional Sikh custom. When the bride set eyes on her chosen husband she did not wish to go through with it but did so out of obedience to her parents' wishes and in line with her religious faith. These influences were not held to constitute duress sufficient in law to vitiate the marriage (to do that there must be a genuine and reasonably held fear of immediate danger to life, limb or liberty). Thus merely feeling obliged out of religious custom cannot constitute duress[96] and the facts in *Singh* v *Singh* did not seem to show a great deal of pressure in any case. Stronger pressure was evidenced in *Singh* v *Kaur*[97] where a man had gone through an arranged marriage in the belief that if he did not he and his family would be disgraced in the eyes of the Sikh community and that he would also have to give up his job. In refusing to vitiate the marriage on the grounds of duress the Court stressed that the test of duress would not be watered down when dealing with these religious arranged marriages.

Divorce

The operation of the English divorce law can cause difficulty for those whose religion causes them to reject that concept. In *Banik* v *Banik*[98] a Hindu, who had married in India, attempted to divorce his wife in England. She resisted on the grounds that she would suffer 'financial and other hardship' as the Hindu society in the part of India where she lived, would regard her as an outcast. Ormrod J. did not agree, feeling that it was 'just something which made her unhappy or distressed her, or which she regarded personally as immoral or contrary to the rules of her community', but it was not 'real hardship'. She appealed to the Court of Appeal which ordered a re-hearing before Hollings J. where she fared little better, as he rejected her evidence that she would become a social outcast. So the divorce went ahead. Likewise in *Parghi* v *Parghi*[99] Latey J. granted a divorce to a Hindu as he felt that educated Hindus now looked upon divorce with similar eyes to those of Westerners — the fact that *some* members of the society would object to divorce could easily be outweighed by the hardship incurred in not granting the divorce. Perhaps a rather more realistic attitude was taken by Cumming-Bruce L.J. in *Balraj* v *Balraj*,[100] who recognised that to assess the position of a divorced Hindu lady living with her daughter on the outskirts of Hyderbad 'calls for the exercise of perhaps greater insight than any English judge should be required to exercise'.

A somewhat different problem is where the religious practices of one of the spouses are themselves the reason for the divorce. Unlike the child upbringing cases this seems a rarer problem but in *Sheppard* v *Sheppard*,[101] in 1970, both spouses had originally been members of the Church of England. The husband had been converted to the Jehovah's Witnesses in 1964. He tried very hard to convince the remainder of his family that the celebration of Christmas was idolatrous and that blood transfusions were wrong. He forbade his daughter to join the Brownies, did not agree with wearing uniforms or with saluting the Union Jack. In allowing a divorce through the then ground of cruelty, it was held that he was under a duty to respect his wife's religious wishes (she being distinctly anti-Jehovah's Witness) and '[sic] he had no right to enforce or seek his views on anyone, including his children'.

Notes

1. The guideline being the 'welfare of the child', Guardianship of Minors Act 1971, Section 1.

2. P. H. Pettitt, *Parental Control and Guardianship*, in R. H. Graveson and F. R. Crane (eds), *A Century of Family Law*, 1957, pp. 75–7.
3. *Re Agar-Ellis* (1878) 10 Ch.D. 49, at p. 56, *per* Mallins V.C. See also *Re Besant* (1879) 11 Ch.D. 508, at p. 511.
4. *Talbot v Earl of Shrewsbury* (1840) 4 My. & Cr. 672, at p. 686.
5. *Hill v Hill* (1862) 31 L.J. (Ch.) 505, at p. 508.
6. *In Re McGrath (Infants)* [1893] 1 Ch. 143, at p. 148.
7. *Barnardo v McHugh* [1891] A.C. 388; *In Re Carroll (No. 2)* [1931] 1 K.B. 317.
8. *Per* Gibson J., *Re Grey* [1902] 2 I.R. 904, at p. 920.
9. *Condon v Vellum* (1887) 57 L.T. 154; J. C. Hall, 'The waning of parental rights', *Cambridge Law Journal*, XXXI, 1972B, p. 248 at p. 249. The power will be included in the term 'the parental rights and duties' — Section 85(1), Children Act 1975.
10. J. M. Eekelaar, 'What are parental rights?', *Law Quarterly Review*, LXXXIX, 1973, p. 210, at p. 221.
11. *Iredell v Iredell* (1885) 1 T.L.R. 260.
12. *Re Grey* [1902] 2 I.R. 684, at p. 699.
13. E.g. where money has changed hands — *R. v Barnardo* [1891] 1 Q.B. 194, at p. 205.
14. *Re Agar-Ellis* (1878) 10 Ch.D. 49.
15. *Knott v Cottee* (1847) 2 Ph. 192.
16. *Re Alicia Race* (1857) 26 L.J. (Q.B.) 169.
17. *Lyons v Blenkin* (1821) Jac. 245, at pp. 260 and 263.
18. *Shelley v Westbroke* (1817) Jac. 266.
19. *Warde v Warde* (1849) 2 Ph. 786, at p. 791.
20. (1850) 3 De G. & Sm. 758.
21. At p. 774.
22. (1879) 11 Ch.D. 508.
23. *Per* Jessel M.R., at first instance, at p. 514.
24. *Per* James L.J., in the Court of Appeal, at p. 521.
25. For an account of the opinions that she was condemned for holding see R. Manvell, *The Trial of Annie Besant and Charles Bradlaugh*, 1976.
26. *Ward v Laverty* [1925] A.C. 101, at p. 108.
27. *J v C* [1969] All E.R. 788, at p. 801, *per* Ungoed-Thomas J. See now the Guardianship Act 1973, Section 1(1), and the Children Act 1975, Section 13.
28. *J v C* [1970] A.C. 688.
29. See: A. M. Prichard, 'Conditions as to religion in adoption', *New Law Journal*, 1972, pp. 281–2; *Report of the Departmental Committee on the Adoption of Children*, Cmnd. 5107, 1972, paras 228–30; P. Harvey, 'Adoption and religious upbringing', *Quis Custodiet*, XL, 1973, pp. 103–6.
30. Children Act 1975, Sch. 4, Part III.
31. Children Act 1975, Section 13. In any case it is possible for the court to make its own order.
32. *B v B* (1975) 119 Sol.J. 610.
33. [1977] Fam. 179.
34. At p. 191, *per* Ormrod L.J.
35. At p. 191; but see Stamp L.J. at p. 188.

36. [1966] 1 All E.R. 838, at p. 856.
37. At p. 852.
38. *Re M (Infants)* [1967] 3 All E.R. 1071, at p. 1074, and *B (M)* v *B (R)* [1968] 3 All E.R. 170, at p. 172.
39. See A. Bradney, 'Religious questions in custody disputes', *Family Law*, IX, 1979, pp. 139-41, and R. Terrell, 'Religious considerations in custody and adoption', *Family Law*, IX, 1979, pp. 198-200. See also *Dipper* v *Dipper* [1980] 2 All E.R. 722, at p. 731 (Ormrod L.J.), and p. 733 (Cumming-Bruce L.J.).
40. *Stourton* v *Stourton* (1857) 8 De G.M. & G. 760, at p. 771.
41. Eekelaar, 'Parental rights', p. 217.
42. *R* v *Gyngall* [1893] 2 Q.B. 232, at p. 243 (Lord Esher M.R.).
43. [1977] Fam. 179, at p. 187.
44. *Stourton* v *Stourton* (1857) 8 De G.M. & G. 760, at p. 768.
45. See Farwell J. in *F* v *F* [1902] 1 Ch. 688, at p. 691.
46. *Re G (An Infant)* [1962] 2 All E.R. 173.
47. *Re E (An Infant)* [1963] 3 All E.R. 874. See also S. Seuffert, 'A question of religious upbringing', *Quis Custodiet?*, VII, 1965, pp. 40-1.
48. At p. 883.
49. *The Times*, 31 July 1964.
50. *T* v *T* [1974] 4 Family Law 190.
51. *Re T (Minors)*, unreported, 10 December 1975. *Cf. Hewison* v *Hewison* (1977) 7 Family Law 206.
52. *Re C* [1978] Fam. 105.
53. *Re H* (1980) 10 Family Law 248.
54. *Wright* v *Wright* (1981) 11 Family Law 78.
55. (1975) 5 Family Law 184.
56. S. M. Dash, *An Outline of Islamic Family Law*, (undated) p. 7.
57. E.g. *Thomas* v *Roberts* (1850) 3 De G. & Sm. 758, at p. 771, and *Re Alicia Race* (1857) 26 L.J. (Q.B.) 169, at p. 175.
58. *Buckley* v *Buckley* (1973) 3 Family Law 106.
59. *Re Newton* [1896] 1 Ch. 740, at p. 747.
60. Eekelaar, 'Parental rights', p. 223.
61. Matrimonial Causes Act 1973, Section 11(*d*).
62. *R* v *Bham* [1966] 1 Q.B. 159. See G. C. Cheshire and P. M. North, *Private International Law*, 10th edn, 1979, pp. 300-6.
63. *The Enforcement of Morals*, 1965, p. 9.
64. *Cheni* v *Cheni* [1965] p. 85.
65. At p. 99.
66. E.g. D. Pearl, 'Muslim marriages in English law', *Cambridge Law Journal*, XXX, 1972A, 120.
67. Cheshire and North, *Private International Law*, pp. 295-312, 348-50 and 353-5; J. H. C. Morris, *The Conflict of Laws*, 2nd edn, 1980, pp. 123-33, D. Pearl, *A Textbook on Muslim Law*, 1979, pp. 69-75. See also B. Wortley, *Polygamy in English Private International Law*, O'Sullivan Memorial Lecture, 1971; S. Poulter, '*Hyde* v *Hyde* — a reappraisal', *International and Comparative Law Quarterly*, XXV, 1976, p. 475; and A. J. E. Jaffey, 'The essential validity of marriages in the English conflict of laws', *Modern Law Review*, XL, 1978, p. 38.

68. L.R.I.P. & D. 130.
69. At p. 136.
70. *The Sinha Peerage Claim* [1946] 1 All E.R. 348N; *Hashmi* v *Hashmi* [1972] Fam. 36. This is not the case, however, for the right of the heir at law to succeed to entailed interests in land and also with regard to succession to a title of honour.
71. Poulter, '*Hyde* v *Hyde*', p. 491.
72. *Baindal* v *Baindal* [1946] P. 122. See also *Srini Vasan* v *Srini Vasan* [1946] P. 67.
73. *Parkasho* v *Singh* [1968] P. 233.
74. *Ali* v *Ali* [1968] P. 568.
75. Pearl, *Textbook*, pp. 187-95.
76. *Cf. Hussain* v *Hussain* [1982] 3 All E.R. 369.
77. *Report on Polygamous Marriages*, Law Com. No. 42, 1971.
78. Under Section 162(6) of the Social Security Act 1975, polygamous marriages will be recognised for social security purposes for any day on which they are in fact monogamous.
79. Morris, *Conflict of Laws*, 1st edn, 1971, p. 127.
80. See D. Lasok, 'The Matrimonial Proceedings (Polygamous Marriages) Act 1972', *Quis Custodiet?*, XXXVII, 1972, pp. 123-31.
81. Wortley, Polygamy. This idea had been acted on under the old law — *Shahnaz* v *Rizwan* [1965] 1 Q.B. 391.
82. Poulter, '*Hyde* v *Hyde*', p. 506. The general trend of thought seems to be in this direction — Jaffey, 'Essential validity', p. 40.
83. See *Nabi* v *Heaton, The Times*, 3 March 1981, where a tax allowance was not granted for a polygamous wife.
84. Matrimonial Causes Act 1973, Section 47(1).
85. *Daily Telegraph*, 18 July 1975.
86. Pearl, *Textbook*, p. 129.
87. *R* v *Sagoo* [1975] Q.B. 885.
88. Domicile in England may also result in the non-recognition of some types of religious divorces; *cf. Quazi* v *Quazi* [1980] A.C. 744.
89. M. Polonsky, 'Polygamous marriage: a bigamist's charter?', *Criminal Law Review*, 1971, p. 401 at p. 408.
90. *Solemnisation of Marriage in England and Wales*, Law Commission Working Paper No. 35, 1971, pp. 49-65.
91. It must be registered under the Places of Religious Worship Act 1855 and section 41 of the Marriage Act 1949. At least twenty householders must certify that it is their usual place of worship.
92. Law Com. Working Paper No. 35, p. 64.
93. As happens in Scotland — F. Lyall, *Of Presbyters and Kings*, 1980, pp. 132-3.
94. *Jodla* v *Jodla* [1960] 1 All E.R. 625 (Roman Catholic), *Kaur* v *Singh* [1972] 1 All E.R. 292 (Sikhs).
95. [1971] P. 226.
96. Megaw L.J. at p. 233.
97. (1981) 11 Family Law 152.
98. [1973] 1 W.L.R. 860.

99. *The Times*, 8 March 1973.
100. (1981) 11 Family Law 110.
101. *The Times*, 5 May 1970.

Appendix
Principle moves towards religious toleration in the nineteenth century [1]

A large amount of legislation passed between 1562 and 1678 aimed to enforce membership of the established Church whilst discouraging Protestant Nonconformists and Roman Catholics; thus:

(i) all Members of Parliament, holders of university degrees, schoolmasters etc. had to take an oath upholding the position of the King as the head of the English Church, and persons who did not adhere to this were liable to lose most of their civil rights;
(ii) all holders of municipal office had to receive the scarament of the Church of England;
(iii) the celebration and hearing of the mass was a crime;
(iv) unofficial religious meetings of more than five persons were illegal.

In 1688 the Toleration Act mitigated some of the severer parts of the code against Protestant Nonconformists (other than Unitarians) who shared certain basic doctrines with the Church of England. After this time such Nonconformists were in fact[2] able to take seats in Parliament. The Act did not apply to Catholics who, as well as being unable to hold any public office, were:

(1) liable to pay penalties for not attending their parish (Church of England) churches;
(2) only able to hold land in limited cases;
(3) unable to be teachers.

The saying of the mass remained illegal whilst those convicted as 'recusants' were unable to sue in any court of law or to take under any will and, in certain circumstances, could be deemed to be traitors. Priests were under a prohibition and, if they came from abroad, were liable to the death penalty. As only members of the Church of England (plus, to some extent 'Toleration Act' Nonconformists) could enjoy full civil rights, others (e.g. the Jews) were unable to exercise them whilst not being in the special position held by the Catholics. It took from (mainly) 1791 until 1888 to remove this code from the statute book, the major landmarks being as follows.

1791 Roman Catholic Relief Act — Catholics allowed to hold some public offices (but not to sit in Parliament). If they take a prescribed oath they are able to worship in their own places of worship. Catholics may become teachers. Catholic priests exempted from certain onerous public offices.

1812 Places of Religious Worship Act (continuing earlier legislation) - Nonconformist ministers may only preach and teach if they make a declaration before a justice of the peace (formally abolished in 1969). An offence to preach in any place (other than a private dwelling house) with the doors locked. An offence to preach or teach in any place without the consent of the occupier.

1813 — Unitarians permitted to enjoy the same privileges as those enjoyed by other Protestant Nonconformists.

1828 — Test and Corporation Acts formally repealed. Dissenters no longer required to make communion in the Church of England in order to hold certain public offices.

1828 — O'Connell is elected by a large majority to be the member for Clare but as a Roman Catholic may not take his seat. This leads to a crisis and to the passage of the Roman Catholic Relief Act 1829, by which Catholics are relieved from the taking of special oaths and may sit in Parliament. They may vote and own property. They may not it seems hold the posts of Regent, Lord Chancellor or Lord Lieutenant of Ireland or any position within the established Church. It is made an offence for any Catholic directly to interfere with the Church of England or for a Jesuit to enter Britain without the licence of a Secretary of State.

1832 Roman Catholic Charities Act — provides that property held by Roman Catholics for religious, educational or charitable purposes is to be considered in the same light as property so held by Protestant Nonconformists.

1833 — Joseph Pease, a Quaker, is allowed to affirm when taking his seat in the House of Commons rather than take the oath (Quakers had been able to do this in the law courts since 1749).

1833 and *1838* Quakers and Moravians Acts (extending earlier legislation) — generally allow members of these religions to affirm or to take a solemn declaration rather than an oath when they would otherwise be required to do so by law.

1836 Creation of Civil Marriages — Nonconformists may now hold their own marriages and no longer have to get married in the Church of England.

1844 Nonconformists Chapels Act — confirms title of Nonconformists over chapels and endowments which could have been open to some doubt due to changes in their doctrines.

1846 Religious Disabilities Act — last restrictions on Nonconformists formally removed. Jews to enjoy all the rights that Nonconformists enjoy with regard to education, charities and property. Former laws against Catholics (save the offences created in the Roman Catholic Relief Act 1829) removed.

1851 Ecclesiastical Titles Act (see now Ecclesiastical Titles Act 1871) — makes it an offence for any person to be called an archbishop, bishop or dean of an area that has a Church of England archbishop, bishop or dean. Ecclesiastical dignitaries of other religions may be named after areas that do not have Church of England titles.

1854 — it becomes possible to affirm in civil cases where the witness etc. believes that the taking of an oath is against his religious principles. This does not apply to atheists as their objections are not based upon religious belief.

1855 Liberty of Worship Act — makes it possible for congregations of more than twenty persons to meet in a private dwelling houses or (occasionally) in other uncertified buildings.

1855 Places of Worship Registration Act — lays down a system of registration for any religion. Advantages accrue from registration.

1858 Jews Relief Act — gives Jews the same civil rights (including that of sitting in Parliament) as was granted to the Catholics in 1829. It is an offence, however, for a Jew to advise the Crown, either directly or indirectly, on an appointment to any office of the Church of England.

1867 Test Abolition Act — Oaths of the Supremacy of the Crown in ecclesiastical matters abolished as a requirement of taking up certain public offices. Lord Chancellorship of Ireland opened to Catholics.

1868 and *1871* Promissory Oaths Acts — allow public office holders to take oaths, or affirm, without reference to their religious belief, or lack of it.

1869 Irish Church Act — disestablishes the Anglican Church in Ireland (a similar end is attained in Wales by the Welsh Church Act 1914).

1869 Endowed Schools Act — recognises the principle of religious toleration within state-aided schools.

1869 Evidence Further Amendment Act — allows affirmation rather than the taking of an oath in any court (before this there were difficulties with atheists giving evidence).

1870 Evidence Amendment Act — provides that any person having by law authority to administer oaths for the taking of evidence must allow affirmation instead should it be requested.

1871 University Tests Act — abolishes religious tests for admission to the Universities of Oxford, Cambridge and Durham.[3] Degrees (other than those in Divinity) and offices (other than those of Professor of Divinity) opened. No one is required to attend any lecture to wish he objects on religious grounds.

1880 — Nonconformists may now be buried in Church of England parish churchyards without the Church of England burial service.

1880 –5 — the atheist Bradlaugh[4] is four times elected to the House of Commons but is allowed neither to affirm nor to take the oath and incurs civil penalties for taking part in the proceedings of the House. In 1885, following a general election, he is allowed to take the oath by the Speaker and thus take his seat.

1888 Oaths Act — omissions in earlier Acts, with regard to jurors, justices of the peace, oath-taking in coroners' courts, those (who because of the wording used in those acts) who felt they could neither swear not affirm and difficulties with the oath of allegiance, dealt with.

1890 — following the passage of a motion through the House of Commons concerning Bradlaugh it seems clear that no person will again be excluded from the House of Commons simply because of his religious beliefs or lack of them.

After this date the final disability of note is the bar on Catholics becoming Lord Chancellor (of England) or Lord Lieutenant of Ireland. The question of whether the Lord Chancellorship was so closed was a matter of some doubt. In 1872 Sir John Coleridge[5] expressed the opinion that there was no such bar but the leading constitutional lawyer of the time, Sir William Anson, disagreed. In 1891 Gladstone introduced a Bill to remove the doubts but this failed to become law. Then, in 1900, the Lord Chief Justice, Lord Russell of Killowen, consulted Haldane, who ventured the opinion that the nineteenth-century legislation had removed the disability.[6] Sir John Simon (in effect) repeated this advice to Rufus Isaacs some years later.[7] Despite this (the ban on the Lord Lieutenancy of Ireland coming to an end in 1920 by virtue of Section 37(1) of the Government of Ireland Act 1920) the office was generally considered to be closed and an attempt to open it, by an amendment to what was to become the Catholic Relief Act 1926, failed. In 1943, however, Lord Simon (as Sir John had by that time become) stated that the position was still doubtful. In 1969 the then Prime Minister, Harold Wilson, agreed that the doubt remained but did not see any immediate need for legislation. The office was finally opened by the Lord Chancellor (Tenure of Office and Discharge of Ecclesiastical Functions) Act 1974. Even now the position is not fully free from doubt as the view has been put forward that there may be some difficulty in a non-Christian (e.g. a Jew or a Muslim) holding the office.[8]

Notes

1. See A. V. Dicey, *Law and Opinion in England during the Nineteenth Century*, 1905, pp. 342-50; F. W. Maitland, *The Constitutional History of England*, 1908, pp. 514-19; W. S. Holdsworth, 'The state and religious nonconformity: an historic retrospect', *Law Quarterly Review*, XXXVI, 1920, pp. 339-58; Sir Henry Slesser, 'The last religious disability', in *The Art of Judgement and Other Studies*, 1962, pp. 81-4; and M. Penty, 'The last penal relic', *Quis Custodiet?*, XXIX, 1970, pp. 181-97.
2. Blackstone, *Commentaries*, IV, p. 53.
3. See Dicey, *Law and Opinion*, pp. 477-81.
4. For details of this struggle see W. L. Arnstein, *The Bradlaugh Case: A Study in Late Victorian Opinion and Politics*, 1965, Chapters IV, VII, X, XI, XV, XXI, XXIII and XXV, and D. Tribe, *President Charles Bradlaugh M.P.*, 1971, pp. 191-237. See also: *Bradlaugh* v *Clarke* (1883) 8 App. Cas. 354 and *Bradlaugh* v *Gossett* (1884) 12 Q.B.D. 271.
5. W. S. Lilly and J. E. P. Willis, *A Manual of the Law Specially Affecting Catholics*, 1893, pp. 181-3.
6. *Quis Custodiet?*, XXX, 1971, pp. 2-5.
7. H. Montgomery Hyde, *Lord Reading. The Life of Rufus Isaacs, First Marquees of Reading*, 1967, p. 117.
8. See P. O'Higgins, *Cases and Materials on Civil Liberties*, 1980, p. 115.

Table of statutes

Sunday Fairs Act 1448   51
Appointment of Bishops Act 1533   91
Submission of the Clergy Act 1533, ss. 1 and 3   89
Suffragan Bishops Act 1534   101
Witchcraft Act 1542   128
Witchcraft Act 1563   128
Witchcraft Act 1580   128
Witchcraft Act 1604   128
Sunday Observance Act 1625   49
Sunday Observance Act 1677   47
Bill of Rights 1688
  s. 1   89
  s. 2   82
Toleration Act 1688   199
  s. 15   23
Blasphemy Act 1697   31
Act of Settlement 1700   89
  ss. 2 and 3   89
Witchcraft Act 1735   118
Profane Oaths Act 1745   44
Sunday Observance Act 1780
  s. 1   48
  s. 3   49
Roman Catholic Relief Act 1791   200
House of Commons (Clergy Disqualification) Act 1801   91
Places of Religious Worship Act 1812   200
Vagrancy Act 1824
  s. 4   118, 128
Roman Catholic Relief Act 1829   200, 201

  s. 9   102
  s. 18   90
  s. 34   124
Roman Catholic Charities Act 1832   200
Quaker Act 1833   200
Moravian Act 1838   200
Pluralities Act 1838   96
City of London Police Act 1839
  s. 35(12)   44
Metropolitan Police Act 1839
  s. 54(12)   44
Ecclesiastical Commissioners Act 1840   101
Nonconformist Chapels Act 1844   201
Religious Disabilities Act 1846   201
Town Police Clauses Act 1847
  s. 28   44
Ecclesiastical Titles Act 1851   201
Liberty of Worship Act 1855   201
Places of Worship Registration Act 1855   23, 62, 112, 197, 201
Jews Relief Act 1858   201
  s. 4   90
Ecclesiastical Courts Jurisdiction Act 1860
  s. 1   23
  s. 2   15–18
Offences Against the Person Act 1861
  s. 36   17
Parsonages Act 1865
  s. 4   102
Test Abolition Act 1867   201

Table of statutes

Poor Law Amendment Act 1868
   s. 37   121
Promissory Oaths Act 1868   201
Endowed Schools Act 1869   201
Evidence Further Amendment Act 1869   201
Irish Church Act 1869   201
Clerical Disabilities Act 1870   102
Education Act 1870
   s. 7   150
Evidence Amendment Act 1870   202
Promissory Oaths Act 1871   201
University Tests Act 1871   202
Public Worship Regulation Act 1874   95
Burial Law Amendment Act 1880   99
   s. 6   99
   s. 7   23, 99
Oaths Act 1888   202
   s. 1   123
Clergy Discipline Act 1892   24
Education Act 1902   150
Aliens Act 1905   104
   s. 1(3)   104
Accession Declaration Act 1910
   s. 1   89
Aliens Restriction Act 1914   104
Welsh Church Act 1914   70, 201
Military Service Act 1916
   s. 2(1)(d)   137
   Sch. 1, para. 4   137
Church of England Assembly (Powers) Act 1919
   s. 2   100
   s. 3   85
   s. 4   85
Guardianship of Minors Act 1925
   s. 1   186
Catholic Relief Act 1926   203
Methodist Church Union Act 1929   112
Sunday Entertainments Act 1932
   s. 3   55
   s. 5   48, 49
Children and Young Persons Act 1933
   s. 1(1)   129

Public Order Act 1936   7, 33
   s. 5   38, 39
   s. 5A   23
Tithe Act 1936   102
National Service (Armed Forces) Act 1939
   s. 5   137
   s. 5(12)   137
   s. 11(1)(e)   138
Education Act 1944   151, 156, 157, 168
   s. 7   152
   s. 25(1)   157, 166
   s. 25(4)   157, 158
   s. 26   157, 158, 166
   s. 29   166
   s. 30   159–60
   s. 33(4)   165
   s. 39(2)(b)   158
   s. 48(4)   144
   s. 76   152, 153
   s. 77(5)   162
   Sch. 5   166
Education Act 1946
   s. 7   157
National Service Act 1948
   Sch. I, para. 2   138
Marriage Act 1949
   s. 41   197
   s. 75(1)(d)   17
Shops Act 1950   52
   s. 22   53
   s. 47   51
   s. 51   51
   s. 53   52
   s. 74(1)   51
   Sch. 5   50
   Sch. 6   51
   Sch. 7   51
Fraudulent Mediums Act 1951   118, 119
   s. 1(1), 1(2) and 1(5)   118
Tithe Act 1951   102
Defamation Act 1952   10
Prison Act, 1952
   ss. 7(1) and 7(4)   133
   ss. 10(1) and (2)   140
   s. 10(3)   134

Table of statutes

s. 10(4) 134
s. 10(5) 134
Post Office Act 1953
  s. 11 11
Prevention of Crime Act 1953
  s. 1 129
Medical Act 1956
  s. 31 144
Obscene Publications Act 1959
  s. 1(3)(*b*) 32
  s. 2(4) 33
Factories Act 1960
  s. 109 53
Genocide Act 1961 39
Suicide Act 1961 142
Licensing Act 1964
  s. 66 47
Matrimonial Causes Act 1965
  s. 8 47
Race Relations Act 1965 7
Abortion Act 1967 146, 147
  s. 1(1) 148
  s. 1(2) 148
  s. 4 146
Criminal Law Act 1967 101
  s. 8 43
General Rate Act 1967
  s. 39(1) 70
  s. 40(1) 70
  s. 40(5) 71
  s. 40(9)(*a*) 70
  Sch. 1, para. 2 70
Race Relations Act 1968 4, 20
Theft Act 1968
  s. 15 119
Redundant Churches and other Religious Buildings Act 1969
  s. 1(1) 92
Sharing of Church Buildings Act 1969 88
Statute Law (Repeals) Act 1969 47, 49, 51
Income and Corporation Tax Act 1970
  s. 194 69
  ss. 250(4) and 265(2) 69
  s. 360 69
  s. 434 69

Guardianship of Minors Act 1971
  s. 1 183
Immigration Act 1971
  s. 13(5) 104–5
  s. 14(3) 114
  ss. 15(3) and 18(2) 114
Industrial Relations Act 1971 175, 178
  s. 9(1)(*b*) 175
European Communities Act 1972 12
Finance Act 1972 72
  s. 45(1) 72
  s. 45(3) 72
Local Government Act 1972
  s. 137 92
  s. 214 92
Matrimonial Proceedings (Polygamous Marriages) Act 1972 197
Sunday Cinema Act 1972 55
Sunday Theatre Act 1972 50
Guardianship Act, 1973
  s. 1(1) 195
Matrimonial Causes Act 1973
  s. 11(*d*) 190
  s. 47(1) 192
Powers of Criminal Courts Act 1973
  s. 15(3) 130
Finance Act 1974
  s. 49(2) 72
Lord Chancellor (Tenure of Office and Discharge of Ecclesiastical Functions) Act 1974 203
  s. 1 89
  s. 2 89
Slaughter-houses Act 1974
  s. 36(3) 124
Trade Unions and Labour Relations Act 1974 176
  Sch. I, para. 6(5) 176
Children Act 1975
  s. 13 186, 195
  s. 85(1) 195
  Sch. 4, Part III 186
Community Land Act 1975
  ss. 4(1)(*b*) and 25(5)–(7) 73

Finance Act 1975
  Sch. 6, para. 10 70
  Sch. 6, para. 12 70
  Sch. 6, para. 15 70
Nursing Homes Act 1975
  ss. 1, 2 and 18 144
Sex Discrimination Act 1975 172, 179
  s. 19(1) 179
  s. 19(2) 179
Social Security Act 1975
  s. 162(6) 197
Development Land Tax Act 1976
  s. 24 73
  s. 25 73
Motor-Cycle Crash-Helmets (Religious Exemption) Act 1976 124
Race Relations Act 1976 3, 33, 125, 171, 172
  s. 1(1)(*a*) 163
  s. 1(1)(*b*) 3-7, 116, 163, 170
  s. 3(1) 163
  s. 5(2)(*d*) 83
  s. 17 162-3
  s. 25 116
  s. 26 116, 167
  s. 34(1)(*a*) 83
  s. 35 116, 167
  s. 70 7, 9
Criminal Law Act 1977
  s. 31 and Sch. 6 144
Finance Act 1977
  Sch. 6 82
Employment Protection (Consolidation) Act 1978
  s. 58(3) 181
Oaths Act, 1978
  s. 1 123
  s. 5 123
Capital Gains Act 1979
  s. 145 69
  s. 146 69
Nurses, Midwives, and Health Visitors Act 1979
  s. 14 144
  s. 17 144
Education Act 1980
  s. 6 152
  s. 6(3)(*b*) 164
  s. 6(3) and 6(5) 165
  s. 8(5) 165
Employment Act 1980
  s. 7(2) 177
Indecent Displays (Control) Act 1981 44
United Reform Church Act 1981 112
  ss. 5(1), 6, 7, 15, 21, 27 and 28 112
Employment Act 1982
  s. 3(4) 181

Statutes (Northern Ireland)

Government of Ireland Act 1920
  s. 5 20
  s. 37(1) 202
The Prevention of Incitement to Hatred Act (Northern Ireland) 1970
  s. 1 7
  s. 2 7
Housing Executive Act (Northern Ireland) 1971 20
Northern Ireland Constitution Act 1973
  Part III 20
Fair Employment (Northern Ireland) Act 1976 20, 172
  s. 3 172
  s. 16(2) 172
  s. 17 172
  ss. 24-26 172
  s. 31(1) 172
  s. 57(2) 173
  s. 57(8) 172

Table of statutory instruments

Shops Regulations (S.R. & O. 1937, No. 271) 52
Shops (Regulations for Jewish Tribunals) Regulations (S.R. & O. 1937, No. 1038) 52
Schools Regulations (S.I. 1959, No. 364) 162
Prison Rules (S.I. 1964, No. 388)
   Rule 10(2) 133
   Rule 11(2) and (3) 134
   Rule 12 133
   Rule 12(3) 134
   Rule 13(1) 134
   Rule 13(2) 134
   Rule 15 135, 136
   Rule 16 136
Shops Regulations (S.I. 1979, No. 1294) 53

Table of Church of England measures

Parsonage Measure 1938   72
Church Commissioners Measure 1947
   ss. 2 and 18(2)   102
Parsonage Measure 1947   72
Ecclesiastical Jurisdiction Measure 1963   95, 96
   s. 49   97
   s. 59   93
   s. 82   97
Ecclesiastical Jurisdiction Measure (No. 1) 1964
   s. 81   93
Faculty Jurisdiction Measure (No. 3) 1964
   s. 11   93
Vestures of Ministers Measure 1964   100
Prayer Book (Alternative and Other Services) Measure 1965   100
Synodical Government Measure 1969
   s. 1(3)   89
   Sch. 2, para. 7   85
   Sch. 2, para. 8   85
Church of England (Worship and Doctrine) Measure 1974   87, 88, 100
Ecclesiastical Officers (Age Limit) Measure 1975   101
Church of England (Miscellaneous Provisions) Measure 1976
   s. 6(1)   103
Incumbents (Variation of Benefice) Measure 1977   103
Church of England (Miscellaneous Provisions) Measure 1978
   s. 1   85
Ecclesiastical Jurisdiction (Legal Aid) Rules 1966   93
Church Representation Rules 1969   87
Vacancy in See Regulations 1977   90

Table of international covenants

United Nations Declaration of
Human Rights 1948
Art. 18   13, 175
European Convention on Human
Rights and Fundamental
Freedom 1953   11–13, 175
Art. 6   11
Art. 8   11
Art. 9   11, 12–13, 35, 75, 147, 153, 160
Art. 10   11
Art. 11   11
Art. 12   11
Art. 14   11, 22
First Protocol, Art. 2   23
Proclamation of Tehran 1968   23
Helsinki Final Act 1975

Art. VII   23
United Nations International
Covenant on Civil and Political
Rights 1976
Art. 2(1)   23
Art. 4(1)   23
Art. 18   14
Art. 20(2)   14, 21
Art. 24(1)   23
Art. 26   23
Art. 27   23
United Nations International
Covenant on Economic, Social
and Cultural Rights 1976
Art. 2(2)   23
Art. 13(1)   23
Art. 13(3)   23

Table of cases

United Kingdom

Abrahams v *Cavey* [1968] 1 Q.B. 479
   15-16, 18, 33
Ahmad v *Inner London Education
   Authority* [1978] Q.B. 36   12-13,
   159-61, 171
Ali v *Ali* [1968] P. 568   191
Allcard v *Skinner* (1887) 36 Ch.D.
   145   75-6, 76-7
Allen v *Flood* [1898] A.C. 1   169
Arbon v *Anderson* [1943] K.B. 252
   141
   Asher v *Calcroft* (1887) 18 Q.B.D.
   607   16
Attorney-General v *British Broadcasting
   Corporation* [1981] A.C. 303   81
Attorney-General v *Howard Church
   Trustees* [1975] 2 W.L.R. 961
   79
Attorney-General v *Mulholland;
   Attorney-General* v *Foster* [1963]
   2 Q.B. 477   122
Attorney-General v *Pearson* (1817) 3
   Mer. 353   60
Attorney-General v *Pemsel* [1891] A.C.
   531   59
Attorney-General for Canada v *Cain*
   [1906] A.C. 542   114

B v *B* (1975) 119 Sol.J. 610   186
Baindal v *Baindal* [1946] P. 122
   191
Baker v *O'Gorman* [1971] 1 Ch. 215
   112
Balraj v *Balraj* (1981) 11 Family

Law 110   194
Banik v *Banik* [1973] 1 W.L.R. 860
   194
Barbanell v *Naylor* [1936] 2 All E.R.
   66   118
Barking and Dagenham L.B.C. v
   Essexplan Ltd, The Times, 20
   November 1982   57
Barnado v *McHugh* [1891] A.C. 388
   184
Barnes v *Jarvis* [1953] 1 All E.R.
   1061   49
Barralet v *Attorney-General* [1980]
   3 All E.R. 918   61-3
Barthorpe v *Exeter Diocesan Board*
   [1979] I.C.R. 900   178
Beatty v *Gillbanks* (1882) 9 Q.B.D.
   308   23
Becker v *Home Office* [1972] 2 Q.B.
   407   141
Betta Cars Ltd v *Ilford Corporation*
   (1959) 124 J.P. 19   51
Bexley Congregational Church Treasurer
   v *Bexley London Borough Council*
   [1972] 2 Q.B. 222   81
Binns v *Wardale* [1946] 1 K.B. 451
   50
Bland v *Archdeacon of Cheltenham*
   [1972] Fam. 157   95, 98
Blathwayt v *Baron Cowley* [1976]
   A.C. 397   74
B(M) v *B(R)* [1968] 3 All E.R. 170
   187
Bourne v *Keane* [1919] A.C. 815   63

Bowman v *Secular Society* [1917] A.C.
406   30, 31, 37, 63, 65
Bradlaugh v *Clark* (1883) 8 App.
Cas. 354   203
Bradlaugh v *Gossett* (1884) 12
Q.B.D. 271   203
Bratt v *Auty* (1917) 26 Cox C.C. 67
139
British Broadcasting Corporation v
Hearn [1977] I.C.R. 685   172
British Steel Corporation v *Granada Television Ltd* [1981] A.C. 1096
129
Broad v *Pitt* (1828) 3 C. & P. 518
129
Broxtowe Borough Council v *Birch (and others)* [1983] 1 All E.R. 641   81
Buckley v *Buckley* (1973) 3 Family Law 106   189

Cave and Cave v *British Railways Board* [1976] I.R.L.R. 400
176, 181
Cheni v *Cheni* [1965] P. 85   190
Chichester District Council v *Flockglen Ltd* (1978) 122 S.J. 61   57
Church of Scientology v *Johnson-Smith* [1972] 1 Q.B. 522   10
Church of Scientology of California v *Customs and Excise Commissioners* [1981] 1 All E.R. 1035   72
Clayton v *Ramsden* [1943] A.C. 320
73-5
Cole v *Police Constable 443A* [1937]
1 K.B. 316   98
Condon v *Vellum* (1887) 57 L.T. 154
184
Cope v *Barber* (1872) L.R. 7 C.P.
393   17
Cully v *Harrison* [1956] 2 Q.B. 71
48-9
Cumings v *Birkenhead Corporation* [1972] Ch. 12   152
Commissioner of Valuation v *Trustees of the Redemption Order* [1971]
N.I.L.R. 114   80

Dennis v *Hutchinson* [1922] 1 K.B.
693   51
Dipper v *Dipper* [1980] 2 All E.R.
722   196
Director of Public Prosecutions v *Smith* [1961] A.C. 290   43
Dodd v *Venner* (1922) 27 Cox C.C.
297   130
Drury v *The Bakers Union* [1973]
I.R.L.R. 171   175

Ealing London Borough Council v
Race Relations Board [1972] A.C.
342   1-2, 20, 45
Eldorado Ice Cream Co. Ltd v *Clark, Knighton and Keating* [1938]
1 K.B. 715   51
Esson v *London Transport Executive* [1975] I.R.L.R. 48   167, 169
Ex parte Blackmore (1830) 1 B. & Ad.
123   99
Ex parte Church of Scientology of California, The Times, 20
February 1978   115
Ex parte The Bishop of Norwich [1932]
2 K.B. 402   93

F v *F* [1902] Ch. 688   188
Fennell et al v *Ridler* (1826) 5 B. &
C. 406   54
M. & F. Frawley Ltd v *The Ve-Ri Best Co. Ltd* [1953] 1 Q.B. 318   51
Free Church of Scotland v *Lord Overtoun* [1904] A.C. 515   60, 111, 139,
177

Gaiman v *National Association for Mental Health* [1971] Ch. 317
115
Gill v *The Walls Meat Co. Ltd* (1977)
H.S.I.B. 12   170
Gilmour v *Coates* [1949] A.C. 426
61, 64-5, 80, 81
Girt v *Fillingham* [1901] P. 176   16
Glasgow City Corporation v *Johnstone and Others* [1965] A.C. 609   81
Goldsmith v *Pressdram Ltd* [1977]
1 Q.B. 83   11, 44
Goodbody v *British Railways Board* [1977] I.R.L.R. 84   176

Gorham v Bishop of Exeter (1850) Brod. & F. 64   95
Green v Berlinger [1936] 1 All E.R. 199   49
Green v Kursaal (Southend-on-Sea) Estates Ltd [1937] 1 All E.R. 732   55
Greenwood v Whelan [1967] 1 Q.B. 396   51
Gregory v Fern [1953] 2 All E.R. 559   55

Haleem v Haleem (1975) 5 Family Law 184   189
Hashmi v Hashmi [1972] Fam. 36   191
Hawkes v Moxey (1917) 25 Cox C.C. 689   139
Henning v Church of Jesus Christ of Latter-Day Saints [1964] A.C. 420   70–1, 116
Hewison v Hewison (1977) 7 Family Law 206   196
Hill v Hill (1862) 31 L.J.(Ch.) 505   183
Homes and Others v Attorney-General, The Times, 17 February 1981   60, 80
Housman v Bishop of Ely (unreported)   179
Hudson v Marshall (1976) 75 L.G.R. 13   56
Hunter v Mann [1974] 1 Q.B. 767   129
Hussain v Hussain [1982] 3 All E.R. 369   197
Hyde v Hyde and Woodmonsee (1866) L.R.I.P. & D. 130   190–1, 192
Hynds v Spiller-French Baking Ltd and Scottish Union of Bakers and Allied Workers (1974) I.R.L.R. 281   175

Ilford Corporation v Bettaclean (Seven Kings) Ltd [1965] 2 Q.B. 222   51
Immigration Appeal No. TH/1326/74, 12 September 1974   109
In the Estate of Harden, The Times, 20 June 1957   83
Iredell v Iredell (1885) 1 T.L.R. 260   184

J v C (H.C.) [1969] 1 All E.R. 788   186
(H.L.) [1970] A.C. 688   183, 186
Jarmain v Wetherall (1977) 75 L.G.R. 537   51
Jodla v Jodla [1960] 1 All E.R. 625   197
Jones v Catterall (1902) 18 T.L.R. 367   16
Jones v Lee [1980] I.C.R. 310   161–2

Kaur v Singh [1972] 1 All E.R. 292   197
Keren Kayemeth Le Jisroel v Commissioners of Inland Revenue (1931) 17 T.C. 27   79
Kick v Donne (1917) 33 T.L.R. 325   139
Kingstone and Richmond Area Health Authority v Kaur [1981] I.C.R. 631   19
Kipps v Lane (1917) 116 L.T. 95   141
Kitchen v Evening Standard Co. Ltd [1936] 1 All E.R. 48   49
Knott v Cottee (1847) 2 Ph. 192   184
Kruse v Johnson [1898] 2 Q.B. 91   130

Lawrence v Smith (1822) Jac. 471   27
Leeds Kashrut Commission and Beth Din Administrative Committee v Customs and Excise Comrs [1977] B.T.R. 555   82
Leigh v Gladstone (1909) 26 T.L.R. 139   147
Lyon v Home (1868) L.R. 6 Eq. 655   76, 83
Lyons v Blenkin (1821) Jac. 245   185

Maby v *Warwick Corporation* [1971] 2 Q.B. 242   51
Mackonochie v *Lord Penzance* (1881) 6 App.Cas. 424   92–3
Malik v *British Home Stores* (1980) (unreported)   19
Mandla (Sewa Singh) v *Dowell Lee* (C.A.) [1982] 3 W.L.R. 932   3–4
Mandla (Sewa Singh) v *Dowell Lee* (H.L.) [1983] 2 W.L.R. 620   4–7, 21, 83, 116, 162–3, 171
Marshall v *Graham Bell* [1907] 2 K.B. 112   84
Matthews v *King* [1934] 1 K.B. 505   16
McCausland v *Young* [1949] N.I.L.R. 49   74
McTaggart v *McTaggart* [1949] P. 94   129
Modbury Parochial Church Council v *Customs and Excise Comrs* [1980] B.T.R. 828   82
Mole v *Mole* [1951] P. 21   129
Monaco Garage Ltd v *Watford Borough Council* [1967] 1 W.L.R. 1069   51
Morgan v *Director of Public Prosecutions* [1976] A.C. 182   127
Morley v *Loughman* [1893] 1 Ch. 736   76
Morris v *Associated Newspapers Ltd* (1932) (unreported)   120
Murray v *Benbow* 4 St. Tr. N.S. 1409   42

Nabi v *Heaton, The Times*, 3 March 1981   197
Naylor's Case (1656) 5 St. Tr. 825   41
Neville Estates v *Madden* [1962] Ch. 832   60
Newberry v *Cohen's Smoked Salmon Ltd* (1956) 54 L.G.R. 343   56
Newell v *Gillingham Corporation* [1941] 1 All E.R. 552   137
Nock v *Malins* (1917) 26 Cox C.C. 38   141

Norton v *Relly* (1767) 2 Ed. 286   83
O'Hanlon v *Logue* [1906] 1 I.R. 247   78
O'Neil v *Murphy and Others* [1936] N.I.L.R. 16   76
Orme v *Associated Newspapers Group Ltd, The Times*, 4 February 1981   10
Ostreicher v *Secretary of State for the Environment* [1978] 3 All E.R. 82   12
Oxford Group v *Inland Revenue Commissioners* [1949] 2 All E.R. 537   65, 80

Pais v *Pais* [1971] P. 119   129
Palmer v *Snow* [1900] 1 Q.B. 725   55
Panesar v *Nestlé Ltd* [1980] I.C.R. 144 (Note)   19
Pankhurst v *Thompson*; Pankhurst v *Souter* (1886) III T.L.R. 199   42
Parghi v *Parghi, The Times*, 8 March 1973   194
Parkasho v *Singh* [1968] P. 233   191
Parker v *Orr* [1966] I.R.L.R. 488   179
Parochial Church Council of All Saints, Wellington v *Customs and Excise Comrs* [1979] B.T.R. 955   82
Parochial Church Council of St Luke's, Great Crosby v *Customs and Excise Comrs* [1978] V.A.T.T.R. 218, [1982] B.T.R. 990   72
Parochial Church Council of the Church of St James v *Customs and Excise Comrs* [1974] V.A.T.T.R. 245   72
Penny v *Hanson* (1887) 18 Q.B.D. 478   118
Phillips v *De la Warr* (1960) (unreported)   120
President of the Methodist Conference v *Parfitt, The Times*, 18 November 1982   182
Price v *Civil Service Commission* [1978] I.C.R. 27   180

Table of cases

Quazi v *Quazi* [1980] A.C. 744   197

Randell v *D. Turner (Garages) Ltd* [1947] 1 W.L.R. 1052   51
Re Agar-Ellis (1878) 10 Ch.D. 49   183, 184
Re Barnes [1930] 2 Ch. 80   64
Re Besant (1879) 11 Ch.D. 508   185, 195
Re Budlong and Kember (1980) 2 C.M.L.R. 125   107
Re C, The Times, 31 July 1964   188
Re C [1978] Fam. 105   189
Re C (M.A.) [1966] 1 All E.R. 838   187
Re Carroll (No. 2) [1931] 1 K.B. 317   195
Re E (An Infant) [1963] 3 All E.R. 874   188
Re Employment of Ministers of the United Methodist Church (1912) 28 T.L.R. 539   178
Re G (An Infant) [1962] 2 All E.R. 173   188
Re Grant's Will Trusts [1979] 3 All E.R. 359   65
Re Grey [1902] 2 I.R. 684   184
Re H (1980) 10 Family Law 248   189
Re K (Minors) [1977] Fam. 179   186 – 7
Re Lea (1887) 34 Ch.D. 528   64
Re Lysaght, Hill v *Royal College of Surgeons* [1966] 1 Ch. 191   19
Re M (Infants) [1967] 3 All E.R. 1071   187
Re MacManaway [1951] A.C. 161   91
Re McGrath (Infants) [1893] 1 Ch. 143   184
Re N (Infants) [1967] 1 All E.R. 161   55
Re National Insurance Act 1911, In Re Employment of Church of England Curates [1912] 2 Ch. 563   178, 179
Re Newton [1896] 1 Ch. 740   190

Re Pinion [1965] Ch. 85   78
Re Alicia Race (1857) 26 L.J. (Q.B.) 169   184, 196
Re St Andrews, Heddington [1978] Fam. 121   93
Re St Columb. Londonderry (1863) 8 L.T. 861   98
Re St Mary's Barnes [1982] 1 All E.R. 456   102
Re St Mary The Virgin, Ilmington [1962] P. 147   94
Re St Peter, Roydon [1969] 2 All E.R. 1233   103
Re St Savourgate Chapel, York (1898) (unreported)   79
Re St Thomas's, Lymington [1980] 2 All E.R. 84   94
Re Schoales [1930] 2 Ch. 75   64
Re T (Minors) (1975) (unreported)   188 – 9
Re Watson [1973] 3 All E.R. 678   60, 65, 78
R v *Aldred* (1909) 22 Cox C.C. 1   21
R v *Annet* (1762) 1 Black W. 395   26
R v *Aylesbury Crown Court, ex p. Chahal* [1976] R.T.R. 489   124
R v *Barnado* [1891] 1 Q.B. 194   195
R v *Bham* [1966] 1 Q.B. 159   190
R v *Blaue* [1975] 3 All E.R. 446   125
R v *Boulter* (1908) 72 J.P. 188   29
R v *Bourne* [1939] 1 K.B. 687   129, 143, 145, 146, 148
R v *Bradlaugh* (1883) 15 Cox C.C. 217   28 – 9
R v *Burns* (1886) 16 Cox C.C. 355   21
R v *Carlile* (1819) 3 B. & Ald. 161   26, 43
R v *Carlile* (1821) 1 St. Tr. N.S. 1034   26 – 7, 41
R v *Caunt, The Times*, 17 November 1947   9
R v *Clark* [1962] 1 All E.R. 428   130

Table of cases

R v *Cleworth* (1864) 4 B. & S. 927 55
R v *Dammaree and Purchase* (1709) 15 St.Tr. 521 8
R v *Downes* (1875) 1 Q.B.D. 25 121, 129
R v *Duncan* [1944] 1 K.B. 713 118
R v *Else*, R v *Kemp* [1964] 2 Q.B. 341 17
R v *Farrant* [1973] Crim. L.R. 240 16
R v *Foote and Ramsey* (1883) 15 Cox C.C. 231 29, 37
R v *Gathercole* (1837) 2 Lewin 237 10, 22, 44
R v *Governor of Brixton Prison, ex p. Soblen* [1963] 2 Q.B. 243 114
R v *Gott* (1922) 16 Cr. App. Rep. 87 31, 35
R v *Griffin* (1853) 6 Cox C.C. 219 129
R v *Gyngall* [1893] 2 Q.B. 232 187
R v *Hereford Licensing JJ., ex p. Newton* [1940] 4 All E.R. 479 55
R v *Hetherington* (1841) 4 St. Tr. N.S. 563 27, 34, 41
R v *Hines* 13 Cox C.C. 114n 128
R v *Holyoake* (1842) 4 St. Tr. N.S. 1381 28
R v *John (Graham)* [1974] 2 All E.R. 561 125-6
R v *Johnson* (1686) 11 St. Tr. 1339 8
R v *Keach* (1665) 6 St. Tr. 701 41
R v *Kennedy* (1902) 20 Cox C.C. 230 124-5
R v *Leaman Street Police Inspector, ex p. Venicoff* [1920] 3 K.B. 72 105
R v *Leese, The Times*, 19 and 22 September 1936 9
R v *Lemon and 'Gay News' Ltd* (1977) (unreported) 33-4, 130 (C.A.) [1978] 3 All E.R. 175 34
(Sub. nom. *Whitehouse v Lemon and 'Gay News' Ltd*) (H.L.) [1979]

A.C. 617 34-5
R v *London Committee of Deputies of British Jews, ex p. Helmscourt Ltd, The Times*, 16 July 1981 57
R v *Martin* [1981] Crim.L.R. 109 128
R v *Miller* [1954] 2 Q.B. 282 116
R v *Morby* (1882) 15 Cox C.C. 35 121
R v *Moxon* (1841) 4 St. Tr. N.S. 693 42
R v *Osborn* (1732) 2 Barn 138 and 166 9
R v *Petcherini* (1855) 7 Cox C.C. 79 43
R v *Pooley* (1857) 8 St. Tr. N.S. 1089 28, 42
R v *Registrar-General, ex p. Segerdal* [1970] 2 Q.B. 697 24, 33, 62, 107, 109, 133
R v *Relf* (1979) 1 Cr. App. Rep. (S.) 111 142
R v *Sagoo* [1975] Q.B. 885 197
R v *Secretary of State, ex p. Hosenball* [1977] 3 All E.R. 452 110
R v *Sedley* (1663) 17 St. Tr. 155 25
R v *Senior* [1899] 1 Q.B. 283 121, 143
R v *Sharpe* (1857) 7 Cox C.C. 214 121
R v *Sheppard* [1981] A.C. 394 121, 129
R v *Southwell* (1842) (unreported) 28
R v *Stewart* (1911) (unreported) 30
R v *Stone* [1977] Q.B. 354 143
R v *Taylor* (1676) Vent. 293 25
R v *The London County Council, ex p. The Entertainment Production Association Ltd* [1931] 2 K.B. 215 48
R v *Tyler and Price* (1838) 8 Car. & P. 616 126
R v *Wagstaffe* (1868) 10 Cox C.C. 530 121, 126, 143
R v *Wenham* (1712) (unreported) 117-8
R v *Williams* (1797) 26 St. Tr. 653 41

R v *Williams* (1822) 2 Modern State Trials 231   8
R v *Woolson* (1729) Fitz. 64   26, 42
Roche v *Sherrington* [1982] 2 All E.R. 426   77–8
Roe v *Harrogate JJ.* (1966) 64 L.G.R. 465   55
Rolloswin Investments Ltd v *Chromolit Porgugal Cutelarias e Produtos Metalicos SARL* [1970] 2 All E.R. 673   47
Rule v *Charity Commissioners for England and Wales* (1979) (unreported)   67–8

Saggers v *British Railways Board* [1978] 2 All E.R. 20   176–7
Saggers v *British Railways Board (No. 2)* [1978] I.C.R. 1111   177
Schmidt v *Secretary of State for Home Affairs* [1969] 2 Ch. 149   105, 107, 107–8
Shahnaz v *Rizwan* [1965] 1 Q.B. 391   197
Shelley v *Westbroke* (1817) Jac. 266   185
Sheppard v *Sheppard, The Times,* 5 May 1970   194
Shore v *Wilson* (1842) 9 Cl. & Fin. 354   82
Simmonds v *Elliot* (1917) 26 Cox C.C. 54   138
Singh v *Kaur* (1981) 11 Family Law 152   193
Singh v *Lyons Maid Ltd* [1975] I.R.L.R. 328   170
Singh v *Rowntree Mackintosh* [1979] I.C.R. 554   19, 170
Singh v *Singh* [1971] P. 226   197
Sinha Peerage Claim [1946] 1 All E.R. 348 N.   191
Srini Vasan v *Srini Vasan* [1946] P. 67   197
Stafford Borough Council v *Elkenford* [1977] 2 All E.R. 519   51–2
Stone v *Boreham* [1959] 1 Q.B. 1   51
Stonehouse v *Masson* (1921) 27 Cox C.C. 23   118

Storey v *Allied Breweries (U.K.)* (1976) 84 I.R.L.I.B. 9   170
Stourton v *Stourton* (1857) 8 De G.M. & G. 760   187, 188

T v *T* (1974) 4 Family Law 190   188
Talbot v *Earl of Shrewsbury* (1840) 4 My. & Cr. 672   183
Taske's Case (1618) Hob. 236   41
Taylor v *Timpson* (1888) 20 Q.B.D. 671   98
Thanet District Council v *Ninedrive Ltd* [1978] 1 All E.R. 703   52–3, 57
Thomas v *Roberts* (1850) 3 De G. & Sm. 758   185, 196
Thornton v *Howe* (1862) 31 Beav. 14   59–60, 65
Trinity Methodist Church, Rayton (Building Committee) v *Customs and Excise Comrs* [1979] B.T.R. 936   72

Vallancey v *Fletcher* [1897] 1 Q.B. 265   23
Van Duyn v *Home Office* [1975] 3 All E.R. 190   108

Walsh v *Lord Advocate* [1956] 3 All E.R. 129   23, 138
Ward v *Laverty* [1925] A.C. 101   186
Warde v *Warde* (1849) 2 Ph. 786   185
Waterman v *Wallasey Corporation, Hesketh* v *Same* [1954] 1 W.L.R. 771   51
Watson v *Hertfordshire County Council* (1977) (unreported)   155
Watt v *Kesteven County Council* [1955] 1 Q.B. 408   152
White v *Meade* (1840) 2 Ir. Eq. 420   76
Willesden Urban District Council v *Morgan* [1915] 1 K.B. 349   51
Wise v *Dunning* [1902] 1 K.B. 167   23

Withers v *Director of Public Prosecutions* [1975] A.C. 842   21
Wolverhampton Borough Council v *B&Q (Retail) Ltd, The Times*, 27 April 1983   58
Worth v *Terrington* (1845) 13 M. & W. 781   15
Wright v *Wright* (1981) 11 Family Law 78   189

Other countries etc.

Canada
Boucher v *R* [1951] 2 D.L.R. 369   9–10

New Zealand
King Ansell v *Police* [1979] 2 N.Z.L.R. 531   20

Republic of Ireland
In Re McKenna [1947] I.R. 277   74

United States of America
Beauharnais v *People of the State of Illinois* 343 U.S. 250 (1952)   22, 45
Cruz v *Beto* 405 U.S. 319 (1972)   136
John F. Kennedy Memorial Hospital v *Heston* 58 N.J. 576 (1971)   142
McGowan v *Maryland* 366 U.S. 420 (1961)   54
People v *Woody* 394 P 2d 813 (1964)   129
Reynolds v *United States* 98 U.S. 145 (1878)   121, 142
Torcasso v *Watkins* 367 U.S. 488 (1961)   79
United States v *Ballard* 322 U.S. 78 (1944)   119–20
United States v *Seeger* 380 U.S. 163 (1965)   62
Welsh v *United States* 398 U.S. 333 (1970)   79

Court of the European Economic Community
Vivien Prais v *Council of the European Communities* [1976] E.C.R. 1589   12

European Court of Human Rights
Kjeldsen, Bust-Madsen and Pedersen v *Denmark* 19 Y.B. 502, Eur. Court H.R., Series A, No. 24   153

European Commission of Human Rights
Dec. Ad. Com.
1068/61   13
1735/63   13
229/64   13
2988/66   13
3498/68   108
4517/70   13

Index

Abortion, 47, 123, 143, 145–7
  conscientious objection to, 145, 146–7
Act of worship, schools, 157–8, 161, 164
Affirmation, 123–4, 200–2 passim
Agreed syllabus, 153–7, 158, 164
Apollo, 123
Armed forces, 137–40
Assistant Masters Association, 156, 157

Baptism, 85, 98
Beards, worn for religious purposes, 6, 135, 170, 171
Besant, Annie, 185
Bible, 28, 155
Bills of Rights, 11
Bishops, appointment of Church of England, 90–1
  retirement of Church of England, 101
Birth control, 39
Black magic, 16, 119
Black Muslims, 83, 133
Blasphemy, 25–44, 185
Blood transfusions, 143
Bradlaugh, Charles, 28, 202
Brainwashing, 66, 113
Buddhism, 62, 134, 160
Burial, 99, 202
Byron, Lord, 27

Capital gains tax, 69
Capital transfer tax, 70
Catholics, 2, 5, 10, 17, 64, 71, 74, 83, 89, 89–90, 94, 123, 133, 134, 143, 145, 147, 151, 171, 172, 173, 174, 178, 183, 184, 188, 197, 199–203 passim
  schools of, 152, 161–2, 163
Chaplains, prison, 133–5
  armed services, 140
Charities, 59–65
Charity Commissioners, 22, 66–8
Children of God, 110
Christadelphians, 176
Christianity, protected by law of blasphemy, 25–8, 31, 38
  position in religious education, 150–9 passim
  as favoured upbringing, 185
  and marriage, 190–2, 199–203 passim
Church Commissioners, 92
Church in Wales, 70
Church of England, 8, 17, 24, 64, 70, 71, 84–103, 133, 134, 150, 151, 154, 158, 193, 194, 199–203 passim
  canons, 88–9
  constitutional position, 84–103
  relations with the state, 84–92
Church of Scotland, 136
Churchill, Sir Winston, 150, 158
Clergymen, attacks on, 17
  licensing function, 27–8
  exclusion from House of Commons, 91, 92
  discipline of Church of England, 95, 97

in schools, 162, 172
employment, 178-80
Closed shop, conscientious objection to, 174-8
Coke, Sir Edward, 117
Communism, 154-5
Community service orders, 130
Confessional secrets, 122
Congregationalists, 178
Conscientious objection, to military service, 13, 62, 137-40
Advisory Committee, 140
Contempt of Court, 12, 122-3
Crash helmets, 122, 123, 124, 130
Criminal libel, 11
Crown, as Supreme Governor of the Church of England, 89, 101
Custody, of children, 184

'Daily Mail', 10-11
Darwin, Charles, 'Origin of Species', 28
Defamatory libel, 10-11
De-programming, 113-4
Development land tax, 73
Diets, 135, 180
Diminished responsibility, 130
Divine Commands, 127
Donovan report, 174, 177

Ecclesiastical Committee, of Parliament, 85, 86
Ecclesiastical Courts, Church of England, 92-7
Ecumenism, 154
Education, 23, 150-68
comprehensive, 153
'Education After The War', 151
Ethiopian Orthodox Church, 133
Ethnic groups, 3-6, 163, 164, 171
European Commission on Human Rights, 11
European Court of Human Rights, 11
European Economic Community, 12
Exclusive Brethren, 60, 67-8, 71, 76, 80

Exorcism, 66, 127

Faculties, Church of England, 93-5
Fair Employment Agency, Northern Ireland, 173-4
Flying saucer, 112
Fortune telling, 118
Fraud, 119-20
'Freethinker', 28-9

'Gay News', 32-5
General Synod, Church of England, 85, 86
Genesis, 155
Gladstone, W. E., 164

Hale, Sir Matthew, 25, 117
High Church, 16, 18
Hindus, 2, 132, 191, 194
Holt, Sir John, 117
Holy Prophet, 40
Home Secretary, admissions to the country, 104-11
Humanism, 61-3, 68, 154-5, 185

Income tax, 69

Jehovah's Witnesses, 9-10, 13, 125, 134, 138, 142, 143, 176-7, 188-9, 194
Jesuits, 124
Jesus Christ, 32
Jews, 5, 9, 12, 20, 23, 29, 39, 52-3, 65, 73-5, 123, 124, 134, 135, 136, 140, 188, 190, 193, 199-203 passim
John the Baptist, 32
Jury service, 123

Labour Party, 65
Lane Committee, Abortion Act 1967, 147
Law Commission, 9, 17-19, 22, 37-41, 65, 191-2, 193
Lawrence, D. H., 'The Man Who Died', 31
'Life of Brian', 45

Local Education Authorities,
    religious education, 152–3, 154,
    158, 162
Lord Chancellorship, 89, 202–3

Manslaughter, 121, 127, 129, 143
Mary Magdalene, 32
Marriage, 99, 190–3, 200–1
Mass, 63–4
Measures, Church of England, 85,
    87, 100, 101
Medical treatment, refusal of on
    religious grounds, 120–2
Mental illness, 126–7, 143
Methodists, 15, 112, 122, 133, 134,
    171
Mill, J.S., 'On Liberty', 28, 38
Ministers of Religion, 69, 70, 105,
    110, 137–9, 144
    employment of, 178–80
Missionaries, 105, 110, 111
Mistake, in Criminal law, 127
Mormons, 70–1, 134, 139, 140,
    191
Moral Rearmament (Oxford
    Group), 65, 105–6
Moses, 27
Muslims, 2, 5, 18, 37, 54, 56, 123,
    124, 132, 134, 136, 153,
    159–61, 162, 164, 166, 168,
    189, 193, 203

National Health Service, 143–4,
    147
National Union of Teachers, 164
Native American Church, 120
Nonconformists, 8, 150, 151, 193,
    199–203 passim
Non-disclosure, insurance, 144–5
Northern Ireland, 7–8, 89, 124,
    141, 164, 169
    fair employment in, 172–4
Nursing Homes, 144

Oaths, 123–4, 199–203 passim
O'Connor, Daniel, 200
Old Testament, 27, 29
Opus Dei, 77–8

Paine, Tom, 'Age of Reason', 26
Palestine, 9, 65
Parents, rights over child's religion,
    151, 152–3, 183–9
'Passover Plot', 33
Peculiar People, 120–1
Plymouth Brethren, 174, 176
Polygamy, 190–2, 197
Possession, by demons, 126–7
Prayer Book, 87–8, 99
Presbyterians, 173
Prime Minister, and appointment
    of Church of England
    bishops, 90–1
Prisons, 132–7
Profanity, 31, 36
Public services, disturbances in,
    15–17
    public's right to attend, 70–1,
    81, 98

Quakers, 134, 193, 200

Racial discrimination, 1–7, 162–3,
    170–1
Racial hatred, 7, 9, 20, 23
Radionics, 120
Ramadan, 18, 40, 136
Rastafarians, 123, 133, 141
Rates, 70–1
Religious discrimination, 1–7, 11,
    138, 145–6, 147, 159–61, 169,
    171–2, 172–4
Religious hatred, 7–8, 9, 23,
    39–40
Ritual slaughter, 124, 130

St. Stephen, 27
Salvation Army, 64, 134, 175
School teachers, 150, 151, 159–62,
    172
Schools, county, 151, 157
    independent, 3–7, 151, 153,
    162–3
    inspectors, 162, 163–4
    voluntary, 151, 157
Scientology, 1, 10, 22, 59, 72, 79,
    106–10, 133

Scotland, 172
Sedition, 8–10, 106, 117
Seventh Day Adventists, 52, 134, 169
Sex education, 153
Shelley, P.B., 27, 42, 185
Sickness benefit, 145
Sikhs, 2, 3–6, 19, 39, 78, 83, 114, 116, 123, 124, 132, 135, 136, 162–3, 170, 171, 193, 197
Socialists, 27
Spiritualist mediums, 76, 83, 118–9, 120
Stamp duty, 73
Stiffkey, Rector of, 93
Suicide, 142
Sunday, employment, 47, 53
  entertainments, 48–50
  observance, 46–58, 135
  trading, 50–3

Taoism, 62

Tests, religious, 150, 199
Tithes, 65, 92
Trollope, Anthony, 'The Warden', 42
Turbans, 3–4, 135, 163, 170

Undue influence, 75–8
Unfair dismissal, 169–71
Unification Church ('Moonies'), 5, 10–11, 66, 110–11, 113–4
Unitarians, 199, 200
United Nations, 13–4

Value Added Tax, 68, 71–3

Wales, Sunday opening, 47, 172
Westminster Abbey, 98
Whitehouse, Mary, 31–2, 35
Withdrawal, of children from religious activities in school, 150, 156–7, 158–9
Women, as priests, 179–80